# SOCIAL PROBLEMS
# IN AFRICA

# SOCIAL PROBLEMS IN AFRICA

## New Visions

EDITED BY
## Apollo Rwomire

Westport, Connecticut
London

**Library of Congress Cataloging-in-Publication Data**

Social problems in Africa : new visions / edited by Apollo Rwomire.
    p.  cm.
    Includes bibliographical references and index.
    ISBN 0–275–96343–8 (alk. paper)
    1. Social problems—Africa.   2. Africa—Social conditions—1960–  I. Rwomire,
Apollo, 1945–
    HN777.S63   2001
    361.1'096—dc21       00–032376

British Library Cataloguing in Publication Data is available.

Library of Congress Catalog Card Number: 00–032376
ISBN: 0–275–96343–8

First published in 2001

Praeger Publishers, 88 Post Road West, Westport, CT 06881
An imprint of Greenwood Publishing Group, Inc.
www.praeger.com

Printed in the United States of America

The paper used in this book complies with the
Permanent Paper Standard issued by the National
Information Standards Organization (Z39.48–1984).

10 9 8 7 6 5 4 3 2

# Contents

# Preface

This book is about social problems, one of the most popular and exciting courses offered at many universities across the world. Drawing on substantial knowledge and the firsthand experiences of a diverse team of respected scholars in the field, this book offers extensive coverage of the major social problems facing sub-Saharan Africa. It covers the characteristics, magnitude, determinants, and consequences of social problems. It examines the institutional and structural factors which generate social problems, namely, situations or conditions that various observers have described, among other things, as "inappropriate," "perplexing," "undesirable," "threatening," "intolerable," or "deleterious." It also investigates the nature, dynamics, effectiveness, and repercussions of strategies aimed at mitigating such problems.

## THE RATIONALE FOR *SOCIAL PROBLEMS IN AFRICA*

In recent years there has been a rapid growth in the number of documents on social problems. Surprisingly, however, there is an acute dearth of detailed, multidisciplinary, comparative, and accessible literature in this area. As of now, virtually no book systematically and comprehensively analyzes and integrates ideas and information on Africa's social problems and related policies. The apparent paucity of the relevant literature can be partially explained in terms of the lack of adequate and accurate data. It can also be attributed to the widespread tendency among Africans to adopt foreign (especially Western) theories, models, and paradigms that are contained, for instance, in American or British texts. Indeed, most textbooks being used in African universities have been written by Western scholars. Needless to say, these books tend to be inordinately Eurocentric (more precisely, Americentric) and may be of little relevance and have limited application to Africa.

During the last few years, a number of African scholars have produced a variety of research materials relating to social problems. However, this work is generally scattered in various parts of the continent. Besides, the literature tends to be country-specific, narrow in scope, and still hopelessly dominated by Western approaches. Thus, the idea for this book originated in the growing realization that the relevant literature, in terms of quality and coverage, has left important gaps that need to be filled. The book represents a timely response to the inadequacies and flaws of the existing literature. The existence of this book confirms that there is sufficient talent and ability among African scholars that can be harnessed to produce robust, thought-provoking, up-to-date, authoritative, lively, accessible, and useful texts illuminating a wide range of theoretical, paradigmatic, and programmatic issues and aspects of social problems and policies in Africa.

This book adopts an eclectic and holistic approach, basically because social problems and policies constitute amorphous, complex, and controversial rather than well-defined and agreed-upon phenomena. In order to capture the complexity and intractability of these phenomena, a large frame of reference becomes an essential prerequisite. Accordingly, the many facets of social problems are examined from several disciplinary perspectives including, for example, criminology, economics, education, history, law, management, political science, public health, public policy, social work, and sociology.

## AIMS AND SCOPE OF THE BOOK

The major goals and objectives of the book include the following:

- To encourage theoretical, empirical, and comparative research and publications in all aspects of social problems and policies in Africa.
- To deepen understanding and stimulate interest among researchers, academics, policy makers, and practitioners who are concerned with social problems and policies.
- To provide opportunities for discussion and critique of taken-for-granted beliefs and assumptions about social problems.
- To examine the contemporary forms, trends, and patterns of social problems in Africa.
- To explore the philosophical, theoretical, and ideological foundations and functions of social policy in Africa.
- To provide a medium for critically examining the formulation, implementation, and evaluation of social policies and programs.

• To promote thorough investigation and analysis of the principal problems and challenges confronting social policy makers in Africa.

## THE AUDIENCE FOR THIS BOOK

This timely and informative book constitutes a valuable contribution to the literature of social problems and will unquestionably appeal to multiple audiences. It will be of interest and use to undergraduate and postgraduate students, academics, and researchers in the social sciences, especially in Africa's universities and colleges. It is also anticipated that this book will be widely used by policy makers, practitioners, and informed citizens.

## ORGANIZATION OF THE BOOK

This book is organized into four parts that in turn comprise 12 chapters. The two-chapter, introductory Part I sets the scene by providing a broad conceptual framework for analyzing social problems. It examines the meaning, nature, and manifestations of social problems largely from a sociological perspective. To a considerable extent, the two chapters are complementary. In Chapter 1, based on a markedly diverse literature, the editor provides a working definition of *social problem* and presents a variety of perspectives as well as assumptions surrounding this controversial concept.

In Chapter 2, David Macdonald extends and illustrates the concepts and ideas introduced in Chapter 1. He provides a detailed conceptual and contextual background for understanding social problems in Africa. By using a systematic framework, Macdonald demonstrates how the sociological imagination can help in understanding and analyzing the nature of social problems in the African context. Although such a framework is applicable globally, emphasis is placed on the social structures, processes, and relationships unique to Africa informing the nature of its social problems. The relevant areas included in such a framework are the historical and comparative dimension (in particular Africa's colonial past and current effects of globalization), claims-making activities, and the processes by which social problems are defined. Also included is the reliability of available information on the nature and extent of social problems; the problematic nature of different types of explanation; and strategies of intervention for solving social problems.

Part II focuses on the social, cultural, and political dimensions of social problems. The issues dealt with include language and political power, cultural incongruity and norm violation in the organizational setting, and human rights violations.

In Chapter 3, Euphrase Kezilahabi argues that foreign languages, through the development of a "high" culture with books, journals, and newspapers, limit the flow of information. This has made the public unable to interpret events that control their destiny. Foreign languages interfere directly in the thinking process of Africans, thus making it difficult for them to recover their long-repressed desires and give them a proper bearing. They have suffocated creative thinking and turned people into slaves as "speaking subjects." Kezilahabi also maintains that foreign languages have an economic backing and are therefore hegemonic. He highlights certain language issues that should be resolved in order to promote freedom, democracy, and economic and technological development.

In Chapter 4, Anthonia Adindu and Norma Romm direct our attention to the notion of cultural incongruity that is associated with the discrepancy between satisfaction of personal and family obligations on the one hand and fulfillment of occupational roles and responsibilities on the other. They contend that in the African context cultural values and norms tend to push people toward violation of organizational norms, thus creating moral dilemmas and social costs for those involved. They propose a conception of cultural incongruity as a way of redefining social problems in changing Africa. They highlight the web of incongruities that may become perpetuated unless efforts are made to counter problematic issues through information sharing and public discussion.

In Chapter 5, Dauda Abubakar observes that three decades after political independence most African states continue to operate under authoritarian military regimes, one-party autocracies, or personalist rule, characterized, among other things, by intolerance to any form of opposition. This political tendency has resulted in the failure to establish meaningful democracy, protect human rights, and promote viable social and economic development. Abubakar explores the sociopolitical forces that create oppressive regimes and widespread violation of human rights in Africa. He uses the Nigerian experience to demonstrate the character, dynamics, and consequences of bad governance, with emphasis on military rule.

The selections in Part III deal with the twin problems of poverty and inequality, focusing on the meaning, extent, causes, and consequences of economic disadvantage and marginality. Special attention is paid to the structural and institutional factors that generate poverty, especially where vulnerable groups such as women are concerned.

In Chapter 6, Kyama K. Kabadaki looks at how gender-based inequalities and poverty affect the quality of life for women in sub-Saharan Africa. Utilizing the literature and data obtained from women in a rural district in Uganda, she explores various correlates and impacts of poverty, including malnutrition, poor health, premature death, inadequate clothing, substandard housing, stress, depression, child abuse, spouse abuse, and rural-urban migration. She identifies a number of reasons why rural African women remain trapped in poverty, such as traditional beliefs, attitudes, ideologies, and practices that contribute to gender inequality, low educational levels, the changing structure of rural societies, and limited gains from agriculture.

In Chapter 7, Felix E. Onah grapples with issues involved in defining and measuring poverty with a view to facilitating policy initiatives toward poverty alleviation in Nigeria. After reviewing the indices of poverty, the author estimates poverty lines for the rural and urban sectors, using the cost-of-basic-needs approach and allowing for differences in urban and rural prices but not for differences in taste. The author finds that in terms of all indices, poverty increased over time among urban dwellers between 1975 and 1984. When urban and rural sectors are compared, poverty appeared to be greater and more severe in the urban areas despite greater inequality in the rural sector. A plausible explanation for the former phenomenon could be that the harsh economic conditions in the early 1980s pushed many more people into poverty in the urban areas while at the same time narrowing their expenditure gaps. With regard to the comparison between rural and urban poverty, the economic stabilization measures applied from 1982 to 1985 probably succeeded in altering the terms of trade between the rural and urban sectors in favor of the former. As a consequence, the adverse economic conditions pushed proportionately fewer people below the poverty line in the rural areas, even though the degree of inequality was greater there.

In Chapter 8, Oludele A. Akinboade analyzes the factors that have contributed to the unprecedented rural-urban migration in contemporary Africa, with particular attention to Botswana. In his study, Akinboade examines the interrelationships among urbanization, migration, and economic growth. The main focus is on the factors affecting the exponential growth of Gaborone, Botswana's capital. Akinboade specifies a number of models relating to age, sectoral income differential, government employment, and gender-related migration. Drawing on a set of quantitative data, the study demonstrates a positive relationship between migration and central government employment as a proportion of total formal employment. The difference between agricultural and average nonagricultural income, especially for male migrants, is similarly explained. The analysis also shows that with time, male and female migration to Gaborone is likely to increase. Further evidence shows that, although migration raises the average incomes of those left behind in agriculture, it increases government recurrent expenditures on security, law and order, urban infrastructure, and the health sector.

Part IV explores various facets of violence in Africa. It examines the situational, intergroup, and interpersonal variables that contribute to a vicious cycle of violence as manifested in conflict, aggression, wars, and crime that have ravaged the continent in the last three decades. During these years, violence has been employed, among other things, to settle ethnic and territorial grievances, overthrow autocratic regimes, or acquire scarce resources. Consequently, millions of people have been killed, displaced, or have lost their property.

In chapter 9, Tibamanya mwene Mushanga examines the social and political bases of violence and the consequent degradation of the quality of life. He highlights factors that have generated and perpetuated violence, including colonialism, ethnic and racial discrimination, political sectarianism, religious fundamentalism, economic and political inequalities, values and ideologies that encourage violence, and easy access to guns and other weapons. Several country-specific case studies are provided to illustrate the scale, dynamics, and ramifications of collective and interpersonal violence in sub-Saharan Africa.

In Chapter 10, Emmanuel U.M. Igbo discusses the pervasive and disturbing incidence of robbery with deadly violence in post–civil war Nigeria against the backdrop of the country's military cultures of violence and commandeering, easy availability of firearms, and economic hardship in the midst of the "oil boom." He argues that the political response in the form of the "death penalty" and long prison sentences appears to have exacerbated the problem instead of abating it. To reduce the propensity toward armed robbery, he suggests a reduction in inequality and social injustice as part of the policy changes in the country. He also suggests "decapitalization" as a way of reducing armed robbery at least in the Nigerian context.

In Chapter 11, Rodreck Mupedziswa presents a thorough analysis of the plight of refugees and other displaced people in Africa. In mid-1998, of the world's total refugee population of about 20 million, Africa's share was estimated at more than 30 percent. Some of the causes of the refugee crisis identified and analyzed in this contribution include ethnic conflict, political upheavals, religious fundamentalism, population pressures, environmental degradation, and the resultant threat of famine. Mupedziswa then details the formidable challenges facing the refugees as well as the countries of asylum. He also outlines some intervention strategies that states and international organizations can adopt to deal with one of Africa's greatest challenges.

In Chapter 12, Daniel D. Ntanda Nsereko, focusing on Southern Africa, discusses the phenomenon of crime which, based on official records, victimization surveys, and self-reports, is assuming unprecedented and alarming proportions. For many reasons, crime debases the quality of human life. From the psychological point of view, it instills fear in the minds of its victims, both potential and actual. It also inflicts physical and economic damage to people and national economies. As a result of crime, property is lost or damaged; manpower is lost; and governments have to defray tremendous resources to repair the damage caused or to combat it. Nsereko notes that the incidence of crime tends to be dictated by the social conditions extant in any given society. Change in these conditions may constitute its cause, catalyst, or solution. Accordingly, he discusses major social changes that have taken place in the region and their impact on the incidence of crime. The changes examined embrace independence or majority rule, rural-urban migration, and the disintegration of the traditional family. He also examines specific forms of criminality that constitute a major threat to the social fabric in the subregion, notably organized crime and drug trafficking. These crimes, he notes, transcend national boundaries and affect all the nations of the regions alike. Finally, attention is paid to the role of the law, both national and international, and other forms of cooperation necessary to combat rampant crime.

## ACKNOWLEDGMENTS

I am deeply indebted to the contributors for their tremendous response. It was a great pleasure working with such a knowledgeable and dedicated "team" of scholars.

I would like to thank the Research and Publication Committee of the Faculty of Social Sciences, University of Botswana, for a grant toward the cost of processing the draft manuscript for publication.

I am also grateful to the many reviewers who generously and conscientiously offered valuable comments and suggestions that helped to improve this book. I gratefully acknowledge their outstanding attention to detail, timely feedback, and technical assistance.

Oludele Akinboade (Nigeria)

Arnon Bar-On (Israel)

John Bigala (Uganda)

Dorothy Brandon (United States)

Eugene Campbell (Sierra Leone)

Kenneth Good (Australia)

Anthony Hopkin (United Kingdom)

Mfandaidza Hove (Zimbabwe)

Euphrase Kezilahabi (Tanzania)

David Macdonald (United Kingdom)

Felix Mnthali (Malawi)

Mohamed Mukras (Kenya)

Mike Neocosmos (United Kingdom)

Daniel Nsereko (Uganda)

John Oni (Nigeria)
Kwaku Osei-Hwedie (Ghana)
Michael Picardie (South Africa)
Joan Powell (Jamaica)
Logong Raditlhokwa (Botswana)
Keshav Sharma (India)
Sheldon Weeks (United States)

# Part I

# Introduction

Part I
Introduction

Chapter 1

# The Nature of Social Problems

## Apollo Rwomire

Although the term *social problem* is widely and frequently used, there is no consensus as to what condition or behavior constitutes a social problem. Social problems consist of phenomena that are difficult to define concisely and clearly. This is largely because socially problematic conditions and behaviors are shrouded in value judgments and cultural relativity, as well as political contention. The problems in question tend to arouse passionate and compassionate feelings. Furthermore, social problems are not only culture-specific, but they also vary from time to time. Because various societies are differently affected by social problems, their perceptions and definitions of these problems will vary. In fact, a problem for the lower class could be a golden opportunity for the middle class. This introductory chapter provides a comprehensive overview of the major sociological approaches to understanding social problems. The chapter includes a definition and conceptualization of social problems. It covers the criteria traditionally used to categorize certain conditions and behavior as undesirable. Given the multiple and divergent perspectives on social problems, an attempt is made to deal with the following questions: What are social problems? What distinguishes these problems from other problems? What are the causes and consequences of these problems?

### WHAT IS A SOCIAL PROBLEM?

Social problems come in many shapes and sizes. A sample of some of the apparently critical problems is shown in Table 1.1. This catalogue is not exhaustive, and the social problems contained within it are not mu-

**Table 1.1**
**Types of Social Problems**

| | |
|---|---|
| abortion | inequality |
| AIDS | juvenile delinquency |
| alcoholism | loneliness |
| bereavement | mental illness |
| bigotry | murder |
| capital punishment | police brutality |
| child abuse | population pressure |
| corruption | poverty |
| crime | prostitution |
| cultural degradation | queuing |
| dictatorship | racial discrimination |
| disability | spouse abuse |
| divorce | stress |
| drug abuse | suicide |
| environmental degradation | unemployment |
| ethnic conflict | unplanned parenthood |
| family instability | urbanization |
| gambling | vandalism |
| genocide | violence |
| human rights violation | war |
| incest | xenophobia |

tually exclusive. However, it represents the major social ills, some of which are discussed in the following chapters.

According to Rose (1964: 662), a social problem is "a situation affecting a significant number of people that is believed by them and/or by a significant number of others in the society to be a source of difficulty or unhappiness, and one that is capable of amelioration." Likewise, George Theodorson and Achilles Theodorson (1969: 392) define a social problem as "any undesirable condition or situation that is judged by an influential number of persons within a community to be intolerable and to require group action toward constructive reform." By and large, these definitions are widely accepted by most sociologists who have dominated the study of social problems. These include Dressler (1969), Dentler (1973), McKee and Robertson (1975), Palen (1979), Rubington and Weinberg (1981), Zastrow and Bowker (1984), Julian and Kornblum (1986), Montero and McDowell (1986), Maris (1988), Henshell (1990), Curran and Renzetti (1996), Eitzen and Zinn (1994), and Coleman and Cressey (1999).

The definitions contain assumptions, or premises, about the nature, sources, dynamics, consequences, and policy implications of social problems in general. The basic assumptions include the following:

### Social Problems Are Undesirable and Harmful

Social problems are conditions or behaviors that are perceived as undesirable, dangerous, or costly, especially in relation to human health and social welfare. They represent what some people consider to be "wrong," "improper," "unjust," "oppressive," or "offensive."

### Social Problems Have Social Roots

The problems under consideration are "social" insofar as they involve human social interaction and interrelationships. To be sure, problems like intergroup prejudice and discrimination (in Sudan), political instability (in Nigeria), corruption (in Kenya), war (in Sierra Leone), genocide (in Rwanda), and crime (in South Africa) stem largely from the structure or functioning of the society. Such conditions are clearly distinguishable from natural disasters or certain epidemics that humans are still unable to control. Social problems arise whenever social institutions fail to provide amenities or services such as food, employment, health care, education, or law and order to a substantial segment of the population. They are intimately linked to inadequate, inappropriate, risky, or unfair institutional structures and operations.

### Social Problems Have Objective and Subjective Dimensions

Social problems can be viewed as objective conditions as well as subjective perceptions. According to the "objectivist" school, not only do social problems threaten or imperil human life and well-being but their existence, magnitude, causes, and consequences can be directly observed or felt. The bigger or more widespread the threat or damage, the more serious the problem. Indeed, those affected do not have to be concerned or even conscious of the so-called problem (Goode, 1997: 56).

On the other hand, the "subjectivists" or "constructionists" contend that social problems are ultimately matters of collective definition or theoretical construction. Unlike the objectivists who focus on the real, concrete aspects of social problems, the constructionists concentrate on the process by which certain conditions and behaviors come to be perceived as problematic. Pawluch (1996) points out that social phenomena currently regarded as problematic were previously either unnamed or unrecognized (e.g., child abuse, date rape, and environmental degradation). Likewise, certain forms of sexual behavior, for example, homosexuality and extramarital sex, which were generally considered abnormal in the past, are nowadays viewed with less disapproval.

The constructionists further argue that lack of consensus, especially in heterogeneous societies, makes it virtually impossible for people, particularly those with vested interests, to agree on the existence and causes of social problems. Furthermore, scarcity of resources means that disagreements are bound to arise over proposed remedial measures. It is clear then that most definitions and perceptions of social problems are shrouded in value judgments and controversy. Social values and attitudes, which are related to people's social backgrounds and experiences, influence not only the choice and definition of social problems but also the recommended solutions.

The values and controversies surrounding social problems fundamentally revolve around the apparent chasm between social ideals and social reality. As Merton and Nisbet (1971) have put it, a social problem represents a discrepancy between what is and what ought to be. Hence, it follows that social problems arise when shared goals or expectations are threatened. For example, while observance of laws is expected in all societies, many people engage in criminal activities. Most people want to own land, houses, shops, cars, and other properties, and are willing to use legitimate means to this end. However, certain individuals or groups do not subscribe to this ideal and therefore resort to criminal activities such as corruption, fraud, or armed robbery to acquire property. As shown throughout this book, factors such as social background and experience influence people's values, attitudes, and behavior in relation to social problems. This applies to social scientists, political leaders, the mass media, business operators, and other influential social actors.

Although the constructionist perspective sounds interesting, at least theoretically, defining social problems solely on the basis of public recognition poses some difficulties. For one thing, one group's opportunity or solution may be another's disadvantage or problem. The rulers who perpetrated selective genocide in Germany in 1939 and in Rwanda in 1994 believed that ethnic cleansing was a solution to their racial problems. However, the Jews, Hutus, and Tutsis who perished or were injured in the genocidal wars certainly thought otherwise. Because of ignorance, misconceptions, opportunism, erroneous values, or sheer wickedness, public perceptions and definitions can be a disputable basis for determining the existence, severity, and consequences of social problems and their solution.

## THE PERCEPTION OF SOCIAL PROBLEMS

A social problem arises when a significant number of people, or a number of significant people, perceive a condition as problematic. Social problems are conditions that are socially recognized and shared. However deplorable or disgusting a situation may be, it will not be defined as a social problem unless and until it is recognized as such by a large number of people or by a number of influential people within a given society.

Mills (1959) made a useful distinction between personal problems and social problems or personal troubles and public issues, respectively. Personal problems are undesirable conditions or behaviors that largely affect, or are largely attributed to, a few isolated individuals, such as drug addicts or battered women. Social problems, however, affect, or are thought to affect, a significant number of people. But how many people constitute a significant number? This question is virtually impossible to answer, for there is no consensus regarding the actual numbers or percentages of the people that must be affected.

Dressler (1969) has suggested that "a significant number" means a majority, or an overwhelming consensus of the people affected by, or concerned about, an undesirable condition. Although the numerical criterion is crucial in terms of defining a social problem, it is not sufficient. To be sure, majority opinion may be erroneous, misguided, inaudible, ambiguous, or inconsequential. To begin with, more often than not, many social conditions tend to be defined as problematic by small groups of people as well as individuals including political leaders, representatives of the mass media, the clergy, civil rights campaigners, chiefs, and union leaders. These people are deemed to be more "significant" than others in that the rich, experts, politicians, church ministers, men, and adults have more power and influence than the poor, the disadvantaged, the believers, women, and children. The former use their organizational capacity and political and economic power to shape the beliefs and perceptions of the vulnerable groups in relation to the causes and consequences of social problems. Accordingly, people's beliefs and attitudes toward certain conditions considered to be problematic are likely to be influenced by their social position in society, in terms of class, ethnicity, age, education, income, occupation, and religion.

Ultimately, those who possess more power determine not only how problems are defined but also what responses can be considered, adopted, and implemented. According to Neubeck and Neubeck (1997), powerful groups are in a strategic position to determine whether personal or private problems will become public issues; to promote their self-interested version of the sources or causes of the problems; and to determine how problems will be defined. They also play a crucial role in determining what measures to take in rectifying problematic conditions. To buttress this point, Smelser (1996: 285) asserts that "in the last analysis, a social problem is a matter of persuasion and a matter of politics. To get a social problem on the agenda, visible and powerful people have to persuade those who officially name social problems that a situation exists and that it has a harmful incidence in society."

### Collective Action Is Needed to Solve Social Problems

However abhorrent, shocking, or painful a condition may be to some people, it will not be recognized as a social problem unless people believe there is the capacity to change or improve the condition. Thus, problems such as natural disasters, which humans cannot avoid or control, are not regarded as social problems. However, we can use our collective intelligence, creativity, foresight, and responsibility to correct or prevent troublesome social conditions that are fundamentally attributable to human action or inaction.

Furthermore, social problems should be conceptualized as a collective responsibility in that no single person (e.g., Idi Amin, Mobutu Sese Seko, P.W. Botha, Emperor Bokassa, or any of Africa's bizarre and despotic rulers) can be held responsible for the existence of a social problem. Similarly, mitigation of social problems requires collective action; government or the whole community must be involved. Individuals operating alone cannot solve the problems such as those covered in this book. Even a head of state, an archbishop, or a millionaire is practically powerless to protect himself, his wife, or his children from all the impacts of social problems such as auto accidents, crime, and corruption.

## SOCIAL PROBLEMS ARE INTERTWINED WITH SOCIAL CHANGE

Social problems are closely interrelated with social change, which refers to alterations in social structures, institutions, roles, and relationships. Social change is inevitable and universal, even though the rate at which it occurs varies from society to society. According to Wilmot (1985), social change involves slow, gradual alterations in the social organization of society or its constituent parts over time. This statement suggests that social change tends to be evolutionary rather than revolutionary. Indeed, social problems do not erupt suddenly; they originate in protracted and extensive social, economic, cultural, and technological changes that occur over decades or centuries. Nonetheless, many people tend to associate social change with instability and uncertainty, especially where extraordinary technological innovations (such as the computer) and cataclysmic events, such as wars and political revolutions, are involved. Whereas traditional societies experience relatively slow and little change, modern societies have witnessed rapid and profound changes. Some observers have remarked that the changes we are witnessing are not really new, but what seems to be novel about contemporary problems is their magnitude, enormity, and complexity. Some features of the modern world are unprecedented, notably, the possibility for mass destruction; the effects of the mass media; and the impact of globalization. Yet it may be inferred that, unlike our ancestors, we are now more concerned about and more willing to recognize problems and seek ways and means to tackle them.

Social change can be a source of, or a solution to, social problems. The industrial revolution—characterized, in part, by population concentration and urbanization, division of labor, and modifications in occupational organization—created and/or exacerbated many social problems. The accumulation of technological innovations and social innovations, for example, is often blamed for depletion of natural resources, environmental degradation, overcrowded and obnoxious urban conditions, miscellaneous diseases, poverty, unemployment, crime, drug abuse, anomie, suicide, and family disorganization. Paradoxically, however, social change also engenders solutions to problems. In fact, a variety of scientific, technological, and social advances have fundamentally contributed to increased food supplies, improved economic opportunities, declining death rates, changes in women's roles, and greater equality. Although these developments constitute solutions to problems, they also create new ones. Clearly, the relationship between social change and social problems is not only interactive but reciprocal as well.

**Causes of Social Problems**

Cause is an elusive concept, especially when applied to social problems (Cuber, 1963). The so-called causes may be the effects of other causes. Moreover, social problems do not exist in "air-tight" or "self-contained" compartments; that is, they are highly interrelated and interdependent. The rising divorce rate, for example, is in various ways correlated to the liberation of women from traditional roles, changing attitudes toward marriage, women's participation in the labor force, domestic violence, declining functions of the family, and changes in laws pertaining to divorce. Divorce also intersects with differences in the partners' age, ethnic group membership and religious affiliation, level of educational attainment, occupational membership, and socioeconomic class. Needless to say, divorce itself generates other problems such as stress, loneliness, child abuse, poor health, and suicide. It is wise to remember, therefore, the interrelated causes of social problems when remedial or preventive programs are undertaken.

It is also noteworthy that social problems have multiple causes. For instance, the high crime rate in countries like South Africa and Nigeria can be explained in terms of social disorganization, inadequate families, child abuse, poverty, economic inequality, rapid social change, inappropriate parenting styles, cumbersome bureaucratic structures, and inadequate legislation to deter and combat crime.

In light of the foregoing, it is clear that almost every social problem is somewhat connected with one or more causes (and consequences) that may be social, psychological, economic, legal, or political. Consequently, it becomes difficult to establish cause-effect relations among social problems and to identify factors that are both necessary and sufficient to produce specific problems.

Based on this analysis, it should be clear that social problems are complex, multidimensional, and controversial as well. To qualify as a social problem, a condition or behavior should meet certain criteria. It must be social in origin; it must be perceived as such by a large group of people or by a number of influential people; and it must be amenable to solution. Social problems are also closely interconnected with social change.

Based on many years of academic and practical experience, the contributors to this premier book provide substantial and comprehensive accounts of certain areas of research into what we consider to be pressing social problems in sub-Saharan Africa. Collectively, we present a presumably accurate review of our current knowledge on social problems. This book comprises a wide range of material collected using a combination of methodologies, including observation, documentary analysis, historical analyses, survey research, evaluation research, and quantitative data analysis. A number of contributors attempt to break new ground, whereas others cover familiar territory. Numerous examples are provided throughout the book to illustrate the relevant concepts, ideas, and experiences.

## REFERENCES

Coleman, J.W. and Cressey, D.R. (1999). *Social Problems*. New York: Longman.
Cuber, J.F. (1963). *Sociology: A Synopsis and Principles*. New York: Meredith Publishing Co.
Curran, D.J. and Renzetti, C.M. (1996). *Social Problems: Society in Crisis*. Boston: Allyn and Bacon.
Dentler, R.A. (1973). *Major Social Problems*. Chicago: Rand McNally and Co.
Dressler, D. (1969). *Sociology: The Study of Human Interaction*. New York: Alfred A. Knopf.
Eitzen, D.S. (1989). *Society's Problems: Sources and Consequences*. Boston: Allyn and Bacon.
Eitzen, D.S. and Zinn, M.B. (1994). *Social Problems*. Boston: Allyn and Bacon.
Goode, E. (1997). *Deviant Behaviour*. Upper Saddle River, NJ: Prentice-Hall.
Henshel, R.L. (1990). *Thinking about Social Problems*. San Diego: Harcourt Brace Jovanovich.
Henslin, J.M. (1996). *Social Problems*. Upper Saddle River, NJ: Prentice-Hall.

Julian, J. and Kornblum, W. (1986). *Social Problems*. Englewood Cliffs, NJ: Prentice-Hall.

Lauer, R.H. (1986). *Social Problems and the Quality of Life*. Dubuque, IA: William C. Brown Publishers.

Maris, R.W. (1988). *Social Problems*. Belmont, CA: Wadsworth.

McKee, M. and Robertson, I. (1975). *Social Problems*. New York: Random House.

Merton, R.K. and Nisbet, R. (1971). *Contemporary Social Problems*. New York: Harcourt Brace Jovanovich.

Mills, C.W. (1959). *The Sociological Imagination*. New York: Oxford University Press.

Montero, D. and McDowell, J. (1986). *Social Problems: A Critical Approach*. New York: John Wiley.

Neubeck, K.J. and Neubeck, M.A. (1997). *Social Problems: A Critical Approach*. New York: McGraw-Hill.

Palen, J.J. (1979). *Social Problems*. New York: McGraw-Hill.

Pawluch, D. (1996). "Social Problems." In A. Kuper and J. Kuper (eds.), *The Social Science Encyclopedia*. London: Routledge.

Rose, A.M. (1964). "Social Problem." In *A Dictionary of the Social Sciences*. London: Tavistock Publications.

Rubington, E. and Weinberg, M.S. (1981). *The Study of Social Problems*. New York: Oxford University Press.

Smelser, N.J. (1996). "Social Sciences and Social Problems." *International Sociology* 11(3): 275–290.

Theodorson, G.A. and Theodorson, A.G. (1969). *A Modern Dictionary of Sociology*. New York: Barnes and Noble Books.

Wilmot, P.F. (1985). *Sociology: A New Introduction*. London: Collins.

Zastrow, C. and Bowker, L. (1984). *Social Problems*. Chicago: Nelson-Hall.

Chapter 2

# Understanding Social Problems in Africa

## David Macdonald

### INTRODUCTION

One of the difficulties in trying to understand "social problems" and analyze them is that such forms of human behavior are complex and need to be considered along each of their constituent dimensions, for example, anthropological, cultural, economic, historical, moral, political, and social. Indeed, to understand any social problem, it is necessary not only to analyze these dimensions and how they relate to each other, but also to draw on a wide range of other relevant information and data, including those generated by sources such as journalism and literature. In the African context, for example, some of the most descriptive and insightful writing on the nature of social problems comes in literary form (Achebe, 1958, 1966; Akare, 1981; Biko, 1978; Ngugi, 1981; Soyinka, 1997).

Primarily, however, social problems need to be analyzed in the context of the social structures, processes, and relationships within which they develop, and this is the domain of sociology. Although all social problems involve individuals, their form and extent are influenced mainly by the social milieu in which they occur. It is essential, therefore, as Mills (1959) points out, to recognize the fundamental link between "private troubles" and "public issues," that is, the fate of individuals and the social forces that surround them (Robertson, 1980).

Having said this, we should acknowledge that "sociology" itself is a vast, heterogeneous, and often conflicting set of theories, paradigms, and methodologies. What should be regarded as common to all enterprises of a sociological nature, however, is what Mills (1959) calls "the sociological imagination," summarized by Giddens (1992: 20) as "being able to 'think ourselves away' from the familiar routines of our daily lives in order to look at them anew." Mills (1959: 211) himself suggests that the sociological imagination consists of "the capacity to shift from one perspective to another, and in the process to build up an adequate view of a total society and its components." One of the principal features of the sociological imagination is that it concerns "our possibilities for the future"; thus, it is not an apolitical or value-free endeavor (Gouldner, 1975). In other words, analysts of social problems will arrive clutching their own ideological agendas and vested interests which need to be openly declared.

Although several textbooks are available on sociology within the African context (Bloom and Ottong, 1987; Odetola and Ademola, 1983; Odetola et al., 1993), they do not deal substantively with social problems. Indeed, sociology, as part of Western "bourgeois" social science, has been dismissed as irrelevant to Africa's problems and as little more than an "apologetic ideology" for capitalist values, such as materialism, individualism, and acquisitive aggression (Onimode, 1988). Within the context of its northern roots, particularly the United States, Bauman (1990: 25) also argues that "sociology put itself at the service of the construction and maintenance of social order." Sociology, he observed, was deployed for such purposes as defusing and preventing antagonism and conflicts in factories and mines, helping the promotion of new commercial products, and increasing the effectiveness of social welfare provision. Becker and Horowitz (1972) further assert that many social scientists conduct research that promotes the interests of the powerful at the expense of the powerless. Notwithstanding the questionable tasks of some individual sociologists, however, it is the sociological imagination that is most essential for an analyzing and understanding social problems in Africa. To that end, what follows is a systematic and generalized framework for just such an enterprise.

Although parts of this framework may be more relevant to or carry different inflections and interpretations in the African context, it is basically a universal framework for understanding and analyzing social problems globally. To separate out large sections of the world, particularly Africa, as homogeneous sociopolitical blocks is to imply that they are somehow "different." For Africa this has often meant the stereotypical and repressive images, perpetuated by Northern media, that still culminate in labels such as "the dark continent" and all that this implies (Ankomah, 1993). In fact, Patton (1990) has argued that Africa, and particularly sub-Saharan Africa, is more culturally, linguistically, religiously, and socially diverse than either North America or Europe.

Generally, and in basic human terms, Africa is with little doubt a continent in crisis. Given the methodological problems involved in collating the extensive comparative data used to construct the United Nations' comprehensive annual Human Development Report (UNDP, 1996a), it still accurately paints an extremely depressing picture of Africa. The Report's "Profile of Human Development," including such basic human needs as health services, safe water, and sanitation, shows that of the world's 174 nation-states, 37 of the 50 that ranked lowest are African, as are 9 out of the bottom 10. Between 1990 and 1995, for example, less than 50 percent of the population of each of 16 African countries had access to safe water. In 1993 the life expectancy of people living in 21 African countries was less than 50 years, and in sub-Saharan Africa nearly 170 million people, nearly a third of the region's population, did not get enough to eat, with about 23 million children malnourished (UNDP, 1996a: 42). Even the basic need for secure shelter was not afforded to the 6 million refugees who in 1994 fled to escape conflict and civil strife throughout the region: "such conflict has shattered years of progress in human development in countries such as Rwanda, Somalia, Mozambique and Angola" (UNDP, 1996a: 4).

Although the extreme severity and scale of many of Africa's social problems should not be minimized or underestimated, these problems need to be put into perspective against the major social problems that also face the so-called developed societies of the North, such as Europe's recent genocidal ethnic war in Yugoslavia and terrorist attacks and the state's response in Northern Ireland, England, France, and Germany. Similarly, in the case of the United States, one should remember that official apartheid only ended in the Southern states in the 1960s and that in the early 1990s a black American male was four times more likely to be in prison than a black South African male. In the same period, the life expectancy of a black man living in Harlem in New York was lower than that of his counterpart in Bangladesh (*The Guardian Weekly*, 1992–1993: 1), and the indigenous population of modern Australia, the Aborigines, was relatively worse off than the indigenous peoples within African societies (Reid and Trompf, 1991).

We should also remember, as Fuglesang (1982: 227) aptly points out, that

Africa offers unique examples of social behaviour from which Western society has much to learn. Our sociologists have gone astray. They analyse man's behaviour in Western society as if only one social model is thinkable and desirable. Africa demonstrates a variety of social models, some of which provide viable options for a restructuring of Western society in a more humane direction.

Such a statement counters the commonly held myth of "development" that the only good and desirable social development is synonymous with that form of economic growth which constitutes a linear process of social change ending in the model of Western consumer society (Fuglesang,

1982: 22). Such a distortion leads to the value judgments implicit in terms like "undeveloped," "underdeveloped," and "Third World" with their patronizing connotations of inferiority, subordination, and secondary status.

## HISTORICAL AND COMPARATIVE DIMENSIONS

> Until the lions have their historian, tales of hunting will always glorify the hunter.
>
> —African proverb

Perhaps the most important first step toward an understanding of any social problem is to situate it within its historical context. This provides a dynamic scenario, a moving picture, rather than the ahistorical one-dimensional "snapshot" provided by the current presenting features of the problem. In the context of Africa, for example, it is impossible to understand contemporary social problems without understanding the colonial legacy experienced and inherited to a greater or lesser extent by all countries in the region. Obvious legacies such as the imposition of foreign legal systems and other social institutions used to coerce and subjugate native peoples (Shaidi, 1992), the exploitation of racial groups as cheap labor, and the demarcation of national boundaries that ignored indigenous tribal and economic structures still bear tragic consequences. The ethnic war in the Democratic Republic of Congo, involving not only the Tutsi and Hutu ethnic groups, but also armies from neighboring countries, is only the latest example of these consequences.

Indeed, as Cabral (1969) cogently points out, European colonialism and imperialism in Africa constituted the end of a particular African history. According to Cabral, the imperialists and colonialists compelled the Africans to adopt European history at the expense of African history. This has led to the necessary reinterpretation of colonialist histories of Africa in the post-independence period, particularly in post-apartheid South Africa. "When a people have been robbed of the knowledge of their past struggles they become passive . . . the suppression of working class history, and of the history of conflict, has been a powerful tool in keeping poor people, ethnic minorities, and women, confused, deluded and quiet" (Campbell, 1987: 7). Illiffe (1987: 1) also suggests that what is needed is a comparative social history that "treats people on a basis of equality rather than subjugation." While he agrees that "old imperial history" was dominated by the elitism of a very small white minority that often degenerated into racialism, he notes that the post-independence national histories that replaced it are themselves "marred by their parochialism."

While acknowledging the major impact of colonialism in the region, one should not lapse into historicism whereby social problems are perceived as being determined solely by historical circumstances, thus negating freedom of action and human beings' capacity to change their circumstances, albeit within the limits and parameters of a particular historical, cultural, and social context. Moreover, although there has been a conceptual shift in thinking away from the "colonial" to the "postcolonial," the day-to-day experience of many Africans, in particular those who are most marginalized and powerless because of their race, ethnicity, gender, and economic position, still remains one of living within the dominant and exploitative structures typified by the colonial world (Purdy, 1996).

The household power relationships between "masters" and "servants" throughout Southern Africa during the colonial period, for example, was underpinned by race as the dominant factor. These relationships have now been replaced by social class and the notion of "employers" and "employees," which, however, still maintains the continuing exploitation of both men and women as "domestic servants." As Pape (1993: 404) says of Zimbabwe (where during the 1980s, after independence, many black urban households became employers of domestic workers): "much of the inequity of the colonial period reasserted itself, this time with class instead of race as its driving force. By 1989 a 22 year old black woman domestic worker could report that she had been sacked by her 19 year old black employer for failing to address the employer as 'madam'." Busia (1989: 11) further suggests that the name "domestic servant" in an African context is a misnomer and that "the duties they perform without any corresponding rights, makes them slaves in all but name." It needs to be acknowledged, of course, that domestic servitude and serfdom existed in Africa well before the advent of colonialism.

If the historical dimension gives depth to an understanding of social problems, then the comparative dimension gives breadth. Comparisons need to be made on global, regional, and national levels. To understand social problems in most contemporary African societies, for example, it is essential to look at the role of Northern countries and institutions such as the International Monetary Fund (IMF), the World Bank, and its private sector division, the International Finance Corporation (IFC), as well as their economic reforms.[1] Commentators have noted that the introduction of structural adjustment programs (SAPs) has actually increased the level of social problems such as poverty and unemployment in several African countries (Hope, 1997b; Jackson, 1990).

Laakso and Olukoshi (1996: 21) provide a penetrating analysis of the feelings of alienation engendered by SAPs which, they suggest, have "either triggered or deepened Africa's existing socio-political crisis." In particular, they show how SAPs have led to cutbacks in social and welfare services, declining school enrollment and attendance, and a lack of formal economic opportunities, which, in turn, have produced a dramatic increase in informal employment. People, in other words, have increasingly been left to fend for themselves and doubt has been cast on the ability of the "retrenched state" to regulate "this kind of economy."

A comparative view of solutions for social problems can provide African societies with invaluable information and models for what should be done (and should not be done) in the elusive search for workable answers. Further examples in the next section illustrate the need for such a comparative approach.

## DEFINING SOCIAL PROBLEMS

Tintner (1989) notes that the areas of human behavior defined as social problems are the main areas of a human being's life: health, welfare, relationships, freedom, public order, and the environment. He then goes on to describe over 100 such social problems, including areas like accidents in the home, TV viewing as an addiction, exam results, anti-gay discrimination, toxic waste, and traffic jams, as well as the more easily definable and socially recognized poverty, crime, and mental illness. This approach illustrates the problems inherent in defining exactly what is a social problem and determining which are the most serious problems so defined.

Basically, a social condition may be defined as a social problem in two different ways: objectively and subjectively. The objective definition recognizes that a social problem exists "as soon as a significant number of individuals are adversely affected by a phenomenon related to social factors, even if no one recognises it" (Henshel, 1990: 8). This has also been pointed out by Merton and Nisbet (1971) who make the distinction between a manifest social problem, which is recognized as such, and a latent social problem, which is real but unnoticed and not defined as problematic. This distinction is a particularly important one to make in the African context where social conditions that have historically been perceived as normative are now being redefined as problematic in the context of the post-independence modernization process.

One example is that of female circumcision, which is practiced as a culturally normal tradition in several African societies but is now being redefined as a barbarous, dangerous, and repressive act used to control women. This example highlights a fundamental issue contained in the subjective definition of social problems. Here it is not the behavior itself or the social conditions that are inherently problematic, but the *perception* of these events that define the problem. Known as the "public awareness conception" of social problems, it is defined by Blumer (1971: 248) as follows: "social problems are fundamentally products of a process of collective definition instead of existing independently as a set of objective social arrangements." In other words, an individual or group often defines a social condition as problematic in terms of his or her own ideology and perceived self-interest. The initial definition, therefore, is often a highly political event, such as the demands by the African National Congress (ANC) in apartheid South Africa that the denial of the black population's voting rights be recognized as a social problem.

Many different groups are likely to engage in such "claims-making activities" with regard to social problems, for example, the victims or the sufferers themselves, lobbying groups who practice "victim advocacy" such as social workers, human rights groups and other NGOs, and official groups such as the mass media, organized labor, and the government which are usually more strategically located in the power structure than these other claims makers. In particular, the ruling elite is dominant in this hierarchy of power and thus is more likely to have its claims heard and legitimized.

One dimension of this definitional process is the role of "moral entrepreneurs" who try to develop and promote legislation protecting what they consider to be a threatened morality. Religious groups, psychiatrists, and the mass media are the more obvious examples of those who proselytize about "problem" areas such as prostitution, homosexuality, and drug taking. Indeed, the role of the mass media in defining what is and what is not "acceptable" as a social problem, especially to governments, is a central feature of issues surrounding press freedom and censorship. Frederikse (1982) shows very clearly how the white colonialist–dominated media in pre-independence Zimbabwe tried to suppress any information that countered the Smith regime's announcement that in declaring a Unilateral Declaration of Independence (UDI) they had "struck a blow for the preservation of justice, civilization and Christianity and in the spirit of this belief we have this day assumed our sovereign independence."

The process whereby social conditions become defined as a social problem, then, is complex and problematic in itself. Although we might normally accept a definition of crime, for example, based on a specific society's legal code, this conceptualization has been challenged by some sociologists (Schwendinger and Schwendinger, 1970). Such a legalistic, state definition of crime, they argue, needs to be reconsidered within a context of universal social justice, ethics, public wrong, and "antisocial" behavior. It can then be claimed that any institutional behavior that denies human rights and that allows or engenders imperialism, racism, sexism, and poverty should be defined as criminal. The collapse of the state in the former Zaire, partly due to rampant corruption (especially under the dictatorship of Mobutu Sese Seko with the connivance of Western powers), is only the most obvious example of the effects of criminal leaders and corrupt state regimes plundering national coffers and impoverishing an African country.

Generally, in "developing" societies, one issue in redefining and recognizing social conditions as social problems is that this process is now likely to be carried out within an international human rights discourse and related policy documentation, declarations, and covenants. As Tungwarara (1995) points out, however, the governments of many African societies regard these developments, and indeed the UN itself, with suspicion. They argue that the very idea of individual human rights is eurocentric and may be foreign to African societies where traditionally economic, political, cultural, and judicial rights were more likely to be held by communities and not by individuals. Shivji (1989) also maintains that the main human rights discourse in and on Africa, "however well intentioned," has objectively been a part of the ideologies of domination. He emphasizes that human rights need to be considered within the wider context of the struggles of the African people and that the central human rights are the "right to self-determination" and the "right to organize."

While we have considered some of the problems inherent in defining social problems, a related issue is that of how social problems should be ranked in terms of their level of seriousness. One such paradigm is to classify social problems on the basis of their hypothesized influences. As Figure 2.1 shows, primary problems like war and racism are the most serious and lead to secondary problems, which themselves can lead to tertiary problems. The figure illustrates the important point that social problems may be causally interrelated; it helps us conceptualize the "big" problems that need to be solved to prevent other problems from occurring.

War has been one of the most serious and severe social problems experienced in Africa during the past 40 years, although, paradoxically, it can also be considered a part of the solution to some social problems. Sogge (1992: 25) provides a graphic account of "the legacy of war" in Angola, where between 1975 and 1991 it is estimated that nearly one million people died, including approximately 90 percent noncombatants: "many more people died of preventable illness and hunger than died as a result of armed action."

One immediate example of the consequence of war in Africa is the destructive capacity of landmines, often indiscriminately used over large areas of land. "Their capacity to maim and kill arbitrarily long after wars have ended leads to unacceptable levels of human suffering . . . the medical care, physical and social rehabilitation of these people (injured civilians) is a challenge and a burden to their respective societies" (SAPEM, 1996: 3). The severe damage caused by landmines is reflected in the ratio of amputees to the total population in countries such as Angola (1:470), Mozambique (1:1,682), Northern Somalia (1:650) and Uganda (1:1,100). By contrast, a society like the United States which is unaffected by land-

Figure 2.1
Classification of Social Problems on the Basis of Their Hypothesized
Influences

| Primary | Secondary | Tertiary |
|---------|-----------|----------|
| | segregation ⟶ | alienation |
| Racism ⟶ | discrimination | underemployment<br>unemployment<br>theft |
| | conflict | fear<br>violence |
| | death | bereavement<br>widowhood<br>orphanhood |
| War ⟶ | physical/mental<br>injuries | occupational handicaps<br>dependency<br>traumatic stress disorder |
| | waste of<br>resources | shortage of consumer goods<br>increased cost of living |

mines has a ratio of 1:22,000 amputees to its total population (*The Sunday Independent*, 1997: 11).

Apart from killing and maiming innocent people, landmines are also responsible for leaving land unusable for purposes such as building and food production. In Angola, for example, it is estimated that 33 percent of the country's land "is virtually unusable due to landmines," and that even in Zimbabwe, where the war of liberation ended in 1979, one million acres of land are totally unusable (*SAPEM*, 1996: 11).

## THE NATURE AND EXTENT OF SOCIAL PROBLEMS

Part of the definition of any social problem, and a necessary prerequisite for the analysis, interpretation, and explanation of the problem, is the nature and extent of that problem. What is the problem exactly? How do we measure it? How much of it actually exists? These can be difficult questions to answer, particularly in the context of African and other developing societies where scarce resources, political instability, and poor technology militate against the collection of reliable and valid data. Official statistics, for example, even if they exist, can be misleading and open to manipulation, and need to be supplemented by other sources of information such as media reports, research reports, and victims accounts.

The classic example used to illustrate this point is official police statistics on the nature and prevalence of crime. Even if we accept a legalistic definition of crime (that it is behavior that contravenes the penal code/law), only a small percentage of officially defined crimes, known as "the crime rate," ends up being reported to, and recorded by, the police. Crimes of sexual violence against women, for example, are not likely to be reported to the police to the same extent as other types of crime and will therefore not end up in official crime statistics. Women may fear reprisals from the perpetrator, feel ashamed, or have no confidence or trust in the police. Moreover, there is likely to be no special unit or trained staff within the criminal justice system to deal sympathetically with such a victim.

An international comparative crime victimization study carried out by the United Nations Interregional Crime and Justice Research Institute (UNICRI, 1993) shows that corruption, defined here as the taking of bribes by minor government officials in return for a service, was the second most frequently reported crime victimization experience in developing countries in 1991, especially in Northern and sub-Saharan Africa. In answer to the following question, for example, 41 percent of respondents in Kampala and 32 percent of respondents in Cairo answered, "yes": "In some areas there is a problem of corruption among government officials. During 1991 has any government official, for instance a customs officer, police officer or inspector in your country, asked you to pay a bribe for their service?" In the same study, 70 percent of respondents in Kampala, 30 percent in Dar-es-Salaam, and 24 percent in Johannesburg answered "yes" to the following question: "Last year, 1991, were you the victim of consumer fraud? I mean, has someone when selling something to you or delivering a service cheated on you in terms of the quality or quantity of the goods/services?" This leads UNICRI (1995: 20) to suggest that among the types of crime covered by their survey, "consumer fraud and corruption stand out as the most frequent in all the regions of the developing world and in most of the cities within the specific region."

As pointed out elsewhere (Macdonald, 1997), the substantial empirical evidence contained in this research clearly challenges commonly held stereotypes about the nature of crime found in official accounts and reports. It refutes the popular myth that "crime" is predominantly predatory street crime like burglary, theft, and assault, carried out by the lower classes and marginalized groups within society. The research also confirms commonly held impressions and perceptions that official corruption is indeed endemic in several African countries and a distinct barrier to socioeconomic development.

Another example of the difficulties in determining the nature and extent of social problems in Africa (and other regions of the world) is that of AIDS. For example, although AIDS is purely a biological disorder and medical condition, it needs to be recognized that "the social component here is of overwhelming importance" (Henshel, 1990: 6). The main cause of AIDS in Africa, the transmission of HIV through sexual intercourse, can only be understood by examining culturally conditioned patterns of social (in this case sexual) behavior. In several countries over the last decade, authorities have seemed reluctant to accept the existence of HIV and AIDS and, instead, have scapegoated foreigners and outsiders with its arrival and threatened spread. The tendency to downplay the importance of AIDS may have been the result of lack of accurate information or denial or suppression of the facts for economic or other reasons (Macdonald, 1996a). Agadzi (1990) states that as the AIDS epidemic has progressed, many African countries may have deliberately held back information for fear of being singled out and stigmatized, or even losing valuable revenue from the lucrative tourist trade or the reluctance of international business to invest in their country.

Although there can be little doubt about the significant increase in the cumulative number of persons infected with HIV in Africa, estimated at 1.5 million in 1985, rising to 19.2 million in 1996, and constituting 63 percent of the worldwide total (Hope, 1997b: 73), official statistics from individual countries that make up these totals vary considerably in terms of reliability and validity. Barnett and Blaikie (1992: 16) suggest that generalizations in some African countries are made from nonrepresentative samples and that the reporting of AIDS cases can underestimate actual numbers because of factors such as "mis-diagnosis, reporting fatigue by returning health units, incomplete or missing returns especially from outlying and under-staffed centres, and, most significant of all, people with AIDS not reporting to any returning health care facility."

## IN SEARCH OF EXPLANATIONS

Too often the perceived cause of a social problem is attributed to an abstraction like "society" or "capitalism." This is, as Lauer (1986) points out, the fallacy of "misplaced concreteness." To what extent can society "make" or "cause" or "do" anything? This process of reification, of making what is abstract into something concrete, can divert attention from the complexities of trying to identify and unravel the web of interrelated causal factors, including the crucial role played by individual power-holders and social groups, that leads to any "explanation" for a social problem.

This is not to deny the social causes of problems, which are central to any sociological approach to social problems. What needs to be identified, however, are the social processes whereby people behave in accord with certain social arrangements and power structures and within a particular cultural system. It is necessary to distinguish between this type of "systemic attribution" and "personal attribution," or what is termed a "blame the victim" approach, which emphasizes psychological or biological abnormalities and pathologizes individuals, or even groups, as being largely responsible for their own problems.[2] Within the context of the pre-industrial North, for example, mental disorder was frequently perceived as divine punishment for earthly sins or as an indication of the subhumanity of those affected (Henshel, 1990: 20). Within the African context, mental disorders, as well as a range of other "misfortunes" such as unemployment, poverty, or marital problems, may further be seen as being caused by witchcraft or other supernatural means. Hoogvelt (1978: 117) suggests that such beliefs are likely to be increasingly used to explain personal misfortunes and failures and "to help the individual cope in a hazardous and unpredictable world" brought about by the rapid social transformations of colonialism and Westernization.

With social problems like suicide and mental disorders, which can easily be perceived as "personal troubles," the attribution of systemic factors is often seen as irrelevant. Berger (1965), however, provides a provocative social analysis regarding the increase in mental disorders in modern industrialized societies, and thus increasingly those African societies undergoing a process of "modernization." He suggests that such societies permit "the differentiation between public and private institutional spheres," resulting in an individual's identity being dichotomized into a public and a private self.[3] In other words, "the psychological concomitant of the structural patterns of industrial society is the widely recognised phenomenon of identity crisis" (Berger, 1965: 36). This "privatization of identity" is, then, a main contributing factor to psychological difficulties, alienation, and the development of mental disorders. The segregation between the economic sphere and the family, coupled with the eventual erosion of the family and the community, as well as the lack of firm social controls in the private sphere are seen as the main contributing factors.

On a more general level, sociologists have identified several theoretical perspectives to explain the development of a wide range of social problems. Rubington and Weinberg (1989) suggest that the six main perspectives found in Western sociology are social pathology, social disorganization, value conflict, deviant behavior, labeling, and the critical perspective. Although it is not possible to examine all these perspectives in depth or to evaluate their specific usefulness (or not) for understanding social problems in Africa, they are all derived from common sets of assumptions and ideas based on either a conflict or a functionalist perspective of human behavior. Although this distinction is a crude one, it can serve to illustrate the need for an eclectic approach and the avoidance of theoretical dogmatism when it comes to understanding and explaining social problems.

Functionalism, with its emphasis on value consensus, social order, and stability, is rightly criticized for being too conservative and resistant to social change. Nevertheless, it can provide valuable insights for understanding social problems. Merton (1968), for example, distinguishes between the manifest functions of a social institution—that is, those that are obvious and intended—and the latent functions—those that are generally unrecognized and unintended. For example, although one of the anticipated consequences of prison systems is the deterrence and punishment of criminal offenders, an unanticipated consequence of prisons is that they provide criminals with an opportunity to learn new criminal techniques and make new criminal connections that may *increase* the likelihood that they will offend again upon release. The latent function of prison, in other words, is that they are "schools of crime" and actually cause crime rather than prevent it.

Crime itself, along with other forms of deviant and censured behavior, can be conceptualized as performing positive functions for society and contributing to its maintenance and well-being. For example, by demarcating for people the difference between "right" and "wrong," they help to maintain the moral boundaries of a community, and by uniting the community against the criminal, or other "outsiders," they contribute to social cohesion. By adopting the Durkheimian notion that some forms of crime can be regarded as an "anticipation of the morality of the future," Haralambos and Heald (1991: 586) suggest that terrorists or freedom fighters may represent a future established order, as in the examples of Nelson Mandela and Robert Mugabe who were both wanted "criminals" and "terrorists," yet later became the legitimate leaders of their countries.

Gans (1971) has shown that even a social problem as negative in its consequences as poverty has uses for a society, particularly the ruling elite. Here he is not referring to the type of "conjectural poverty" that is temporary and can happen to ordinary self-sufficient people thrown into crisis by famine, drought, or wars and that has been all too frequent an experience for many Africans. Rather, he is referring to the type of structural poverty experienced in relatively rich and stable capitalist African states where the existence of poverty ensures that a low-wage labor pool is available to do the dirty, dangerous, undignified, menial, and underpaid jobs. By working for low wages, the poor subsidize a variety of economic activities that benefit the more affluent. For example, by paying a higher proportion of their income in sales tax, they subsidize state and local governmental services also enjoyed by the elite, and by purchasing substandard or out-of-date goods that others do not want, thus prolonging their economic usefulness, they increase profits for the merchant class. These functions signify that some social groups will have a vested interest in "profiting from poverty" and may work against its eradication.

Underlying any functionalist analysis is the premise that society consists of a structure of interrelated parts, such as institutions, statuses, norms, and roles, and that each has a function in maintaining the stability of society. When a part of the social system becomes dysfunctional (as with the unintended consequences of prison), then the result is social disorganization that leads to social problems. Although this approach is overly static, undeniably one of the main causes of social disorganization and dislocation is rapid social change and this has been a particular characteristic of African societies over the past 100 years. Such change has not only occurred under the cataclysmic changes wrought by colonialism but also the contemporary changes created by increasing modernization, urbanization, and industrialization.

In the case of crime as a social problem, however, commentators have pointed out the limitations of this type of approach. Cohen (1986: 418) criticizes the apolitical nature of functionalism, for

in this theory the Third World is simply seen as passing through the stages completed by the West in the early phases of industrialisation; crime is a result of rapid social change, the by-product of over-rapid modernisation, and can be explained in terms of "universal processes" that cross cultural lines (such as anomie, urban drift or social disorganisation).

In the specific case of South Africa, Davis and Slabbert (1985: 7) argue that the functionalist or "consensus" approach to crime was adopted precisely because for Afrikaner academics it was "firmly embedded within the dominant ideology of the South African State" and for others it provided what was perceived as a pragmatic approach to the crime problem that kept within the limits, and limitations, of government policy. As they further point out, this approach omitted any analysis of crime "in relation to the changing nature of the South African State, which in responding to political and economic developments has sought to institutionalise and thereby limit the scope of political challenges to its existence." In the Western context, functionalism was superseded in the 1960s by more critical theories in the study of crime precisely because it failed to provide "a rigorous theoretical analysis of the relationship between law, political economy and the state under advanced capitalism" (Sim et al., 1987: 1).

This illustrates the main criticism of the functionalist approach—that its inherent conservatism fails to acknowledge that the main sources of social change, and therefore social problems, in society are the conflicts, struggles, disagreements, contradictions, and competitions between different groups over values and scarce resources such as power, wealth, and status. Conflict in this context, of course, does not necessarily imply violence, although it can include it. A conflict perspective essentially assumes that many social problems are created and perpetuated by the action of interest groups working for their own advantage, often at the expense of others. Unequal access to, and distribution of, power and wealth inevitably leads to the social inequalities that manifest themselves in such social problems as sexism, racism, unemployment, poverty, and inequities in the provision of health care, education, housing, and social welfare.

In the case of Africa, the main "interest group" responsible for creating many social problems has been the state itself. Indeed, the state is central to any analysis of social problems in Africa, particularly with regard to the abuse of power, for example, the tendency of ruling military juntas or political parties to restrict political discourse and discussion, and the lack of probity, ethical behavior, and accountability of those in public office. "The consequences of these weaknesses is a state without legitimacy, whose largesse benefits only a few" (Dag Hammarskjöld Foundation, 1992: 20). The legacy of the apartheid state in South Africa, for example, means that the new ANC-led government has to deal with an enormous problem of poverty and its concomitants. A recent study revealed that more than 70 percent of South Africans earn less than R301 per month (approximately U.S.$80). Of these 31 million poor people, 95 percent were black (Republic of South Africa, 1995).

Apart from the obvious exploitation of the population under apartheid and "state kleptocracies" such as Kenya, Nigeria, and Gabon, however, serious socioeconomic inequalities also exist in more liberal and democratic African states that have adopted the new global philosophy of privatization and entrepreneurship. In the case of Botswana, often cited as "the model for capitalist development in Africa," there has been extremely unequal development since independence in 1966. Over the last 20 years, mainly because of the discovery of large diamond deposits, this country has become one of the world's fastest growing economies with, until recently, an annual GDP growth of 14.3 percent, a per capita GNP of U.S.$2,580 in 1991, and current foreign reserves of over 4 billion U.S. dollars in a population of only 1.4 million people (Government of Botswana, 1993). At the same time, it now has one of the highest degrees of inequality of income distribution among all countries of the world for which figures are available, with 43 percent of the total population between 1980 and 1991 living in absolute poverty (UNDP, 1994). In a country where cattle ownership is still the main indicator of wealth and status, 70 percent of the people have no cattle, and in 1990 one-third of all cattle farms, approximately 18,000, held only an average of 6 beasts while 35 commercial farms averaged over 4,100 head each (Young, 1995).

Certainly, there has been no lack of analysis of such inequalities in Africa using a conflict perspective, as verified by the works of writers and activists such as Amin (1976), Cabral (1969), Fanon (1967), and Memmi (1965). Although none of these writers focuses on social problems per se, they have analyzed various colonial and postcolonial capitalist systems that they perceived lay at the root of many of their country's social problems. Perhaps the following sentiments expressed by Samora Machel, leader of the Front for the Liberation of Mozambique (FRELIMO) and one of the architects of the struggle against Portuguese colonial rule in Mozambique, best echo those of the many other African thinkers and political activists who have utilized the conflict perspective:

In the colonial period the enterprises were organised and operated with the sole aim of serving the interests of capitalism. All our strength, dedication, energy and sweat merely went to the interests of capitalism. But now we say power belongs to us. The colonial government, with its repressive laws, its administrators, its native police, was an instrument that capitalism used for the greater exploitation of Mozambican workers. (Munslow, 1985: 114)

Any conflict perspective on contemporary Africa, however, must move beyond generalities and analyze the modalities and dynamics of capitalism within a context of globalization and the "new socioeconomic world order," and how this is manifested in specific locations, countries, and subregions within the continent. This is no easy task. The complexity of this process is best expressed by Iliffe, a historian with a sociological imagination, who stresses that both colonialism and capitalism came in many shapes and forms and did not simply replace the old order "but blended with it, sometimes revitalised it, and produced novel and distinctively African syntheses. Capitalism, urbanisation, Christianity, Islam, political organisations, ethnicity and family relationships all took particular forms when Africans reshaped them to meet their needs and traditions" (Iliffe, 1995: 212).

Any analysis of this continuing "reshaping" process, and how it contributes to social problems, needs to move beyond the parameters of "traditional" Marxism and incorporate the ideas of feminist theory and such thinkers as Foucault (1980) and Gramsci (1971). The suppression and domination of half the African continent, that is, women under patriarchal systems, for example, is not only a social problem in itself but, according to feminist theory, leads to other problems such as disempowerment, underemployment, domestic violence, and rape. On the other hand, Foucault illustrates how power in a modern society is increasingly linked to the production, control, and utilization of knowledge (including social scientific knowledge), while Gramsci challenges Marx's notion of the centrality of the class struggle within the discourse of conflict theory. In particular, he takes the more flexible view that conflict is not the sole prerogative of social class, but also takes place between a wide range of groups, parties, individuals, and ideologies. Thus, as countries and regions like Southern Africa democratize and stabilize, the use of force and coercion to control populations is likely to be replaced by control over their ideas and beliefs. Hegemony, in Gramsci's words, is then achieved by persuading the population to accept the political and moral values of the ruling class, including their definition of what constitutes and causes social problems.

Finally, in searching for explanations for social problems, it is left to a historian like Iliffe to remind us of the need for an eclectic interdisciplinary approach. His exemplary study of the African poor (1987) shows that any explanation for poverty needs to include historical, cultural, social, and economic factors, and not be viewed through the myopic lens of the compartmentalization of knowledge practiced by many academic theoreticians and political leaders.

## STRATEGIES OF INTERVENTION

An essential part of the definition of a social problem is that "a social condition must be considered capable of solution through collective action" (Robertson, 1980: 6). Although some individuals may be able to ameliorate the effects of such problems as poverty, unemployment, crime, and mental disorders through their own efforts, these conditions will persist until they are effectively confronted by concerted collective social action. In this sense, "collective social action" can refer to any measures taken by people acting together, which can incorporate such diverse forms as strikes, lobbying, national campaigns, new legislation, street demonstrations, and revolutionary activity.

Logically, any form of collective action that strives to solve a social problem must be based on a comprehensive understanding of the defining process; the extent and nature of the problem; and, most importantly, the causes of the problem. Frequently, however, those who are most likely to be engaged in initiating, developing, and resourcing problem-solving strategies, especially national governments and state agencies, are least likely to take a rational and objective approach. They may be the ones most likely to be guilty of "politically enforced neglect," reinterpreting history for their own benefit, holding nontransparent hidden agendas, and, in general, taking collective action that is based primarily on political expediency and self-interest.[4] These forces are often the last ones likely to utilize the sociological imagination!

Within an increasingly globalized free market context, where even public services such as health and education are becoming privatized and affordable only to wealthy elites, "politically enforced neglect" becomes of paramount concern. Even the responsibility for providing the basic human right to security and safety of the person and property is being handed over by the state to the commercial sector. In Southern Africa, for example, policing is becoming increasingly privatized in the hands of a few security firms who offer protection—at a price—to those who can afford to pay for it. The poor are left to protect themselves as best they can, often with only an underresourced, poorly trained, and corrupt police force at their service.

This privatization of security and social control even exists at the state level, with 30 countries in Africa having now established "links" with Executive Outcomes, "a private Pan-African peace-keeping force of a kind which the international community has long-promised but failed to deliver" (*The Mail and Guardian*, 1996–1997). Originally South Africa–based, Executive Outcomes, which has been described as "the world's first corporate army," offers training and advice to armies; installation of telephone and communication systems; construction and repair of strategic installations such as bridges, harbors, pipelines, and roads; air transport; mine clearance; medical support; protection and guarding of mines, oil-fields, and airports; and "involvement in military conflicts." Media reports suggest that this company, like others of its kind, is largely a neocolonial mercenary group whose soldiers are preoccupied with maximizing their business interests, especially those of non-African multinational corporations desperate for a slice of the commercial action in the new "scramble for Africa."

In particular, African governments are guilty of what can be referred to as "plagiarism at the highest level," in which "solutions" to social problems are merely copies of those intervention strategies used by Western nations where they have already often proved to be less than successful. At the same time, African governments may be held to economic and political ransom by the dictates of the IMF, the World Bank, the UN, and other international pressure groups to conform to new global standards and regulatory practices. Macdonald (1996b: 139), for example, shows how the adoption of new legislation by several African countries, based on northern paradigms and dealing with perceived "drug problems," particularly that of cannabis,

may not be attuned to the cultural complexities and socioeconomic realities of African societies and may even be counterproductive. The introduction of Kenya's recent draconian drug legislation, declaring that all dealers in cannabis will face a minimum of ten years imprisonment, led Justice Samuel Oguk, the head of the criminal division of Nairobi's High Court, to suggest that the new law would soon fill up the prisons because "it does not distinguish *bhang* (can-

Figure 2.2
Classification of Strategies of Intervention

| Essentially Preventive | Essentially Restorative |
|---|---|
| Deterrence | Retribution |
| Incapacitation | Restitution |
| Rémoval of Opportunity | Expiation |
| Amelioration of Conditions | Moral Regeneration |
| Prevention | Relief |
| Reduced Intervention | |
| Rehabilitation | |
| Social Reorganization | |

*Source*: Henshel, 1990: 107.

nabis) smoking from other drugs and yet this is a way of life in the sprawling suburbs of Kibera or Mathare," Nairobi's major slum areas.

On a more general level, Henshel (1990) claims that a limited number of basic strategies have been used throughout history to respond to social problems, and each strategy, either explicitly or implicitly, has been based on a theory of the problem's cause and on a theory of human nature.

Henshel's classification of these strategies (Figure 2.2) clearly illustrates the wide and diverse range of perceived solutions, or "strategies of intervention" that have been used, and are indeed still being used, to try and deal with social problems. Historically, reactions to social problems were essentially punitive, whereby individuals and groups were "blamed" for their own problems and treated accordingly. These reactions included explicit punishment, retribution, deterrence, incapacitation, expiation, and restitution. Although these are the classical methods still used to deal with criminal offenders in Africa and elsewhere, in addition to capital and corporal punishment, fines, and imprisonment, Iliffe (1988: 248) shows how these methods have also been used to deal with certain categories of the poor. While Africa has always had its "deserving" poor, notably the aged and orphans, who were deemed worthy of help and support, many independent regimes offered only incarceration to those labeled the "undeserving" poor. Beggars, in particular, were parasites and symbols of backwardness to modernisers without traditions of religious charity.[5]

By contrast, nonpunitive strategies of intervention include programs of relief to those seen as "deserving" aid (in the African context, of course, this applies to whole countries as well as to individuals); campaigns of moral regeneration, especially through religion; and denial of opportunity. The last named strategy presents another example of "plagiarism," especially with regard to perceived "drug problems." Following international guidelines from the United Nations and the World Health Organization (WHO) dictated largely by U.S. interests with their unrealistic agenda of "zero tolerance of drugs," many African countries have introduced legislation prohibiting the sale and possession of a range of psychoactive substances like cannabis, cocaine, and heroin. At the same time, equally harmful substances like alcohol and nicotine are not only not prohibited, but are actively marketed by both national and multinational companies, particularly to attract younger, and therefore more vulnerable, consumers. Braithwaite (1986) has also documented the "dumping" of old or unsafe pharmaceutical drugs by multinational drug companies onto unsuspecting developing countries, where citizens have also been used to test new drugs that are regarded as having risks too high for testing in developed countries. The sheer hypocrisy and blatant profiteering involved in developing strategies of intervention to deal with politically selective drug problems presents a major conundrum for African and other Third World societies concerned about the health, social, and economic costs related to *all* types of drug abuse and misuse.

From a practical viewpoint, amelioration of conditions is one of the most crucial strategies of intervention, for example, in health- and welfare-related social problems. Certainly, it is cheaper and more effective to prevent disease through measures such as universal education, public sanitation, mass inoculation, and mosquito control than to deal with its consequences and have to treat epidemics. It is interesting to note here that while malaria, spread by mosquitoes, is obviously not a *social* problem in itself, the social arrangements and policies made to deal with it—or rather the lack of them—may constitute a social problem. A basic strategy for ameliorating such basic human problems as lack of adequate health care and education provision has been clearly spelled out by Onimode (1993: 91): "African countries must make education free and compulsory up to at least primary school level and complement it with an effective adult literacy programme ... the current educational and health crisis, with falling enrolment and declining availability, must be eliminated through the allocation of some 20% of annual budgets to social services."

The means of achieving amelioration of conditions, however, is likely to be through some form of social reorganization that focuses primarily on redressing either legal or economic inequalities. The former includes legislation enacted to overthrow slavery, colonialism, apartheid, and the continuing legal dominance of women by men, particularly with regard to property rights and inheritance laws. The latter is characterized by action designed to minimize income disparities, unequal employment opportunities, and differential access to a range of services including education, health, justice, and welfare.

Ironically, social reorganization, can often be perceived as radical, and proponents of such intervention strategies may be defined as a "social problem" themselves. As such, they may find that their ideas are perceived as heretical and suppressed through "control of the press, censorship, systematic rewriting of history, jamming of foreign broadcasts, teacher surveillance, visitor control, and similar totalitarian measures" (Henshel, 1990: 103). As Mamdani et al. (1993: 104) argue, in independent Africa popular demands made manifest through social movements are likely to be identified as "problematic" by governments that follow the dubious tenets of modernization theory and a much wider "ideology of developmentalism."

Whatever the strategy of intervention that is developed, one of the most important issues for African societies is that of evaluation. To determine the effects of any planned intervention, evaluation research must be undertaken even if it contains conceptual and methodological weaknesses and inherent political problems. Certainly, such evaluation is more possible with intervention strategies based on less structural theories than those considered here. Social interaction theories, such as labeling, which are important for understanding the interpersonal dynamics involved in the process and development of social problems, inform the day-to-day work of such intervention agencies as the police, the courts, psychiatrists, development workers, and social workers, as well as more customary agents. These are the social actors who translate policies into action at the community level and whose work demands to be evaluated, no matter how problematic this process may be. In the case of those in broadly defined "help and welfare agencies," this is particularly pertinent, for one of the major problems facing Africa is that there is no real social welfare safety net for the millions who desperately need it. Indeed, "owing to chronic recession, conservative ideologies and misguided policies, many African governments, like their counterparts in America and Europe, have been advocating reduced spending on social welfare" (Rwomire and Raditlhokwa, 1996: 12). The extended family system, which has historically been the "safety net" for generations of Africans, is now becoming increasingly divided and under strain from the pressures of urbanization, the wage economy, and "the inexorable spread of greedy Western culture" (Harden, 1993: 69). This in turn weakens family bonds and loyalties as well as patterns of mutual obligations relating to personal, social, and economic support.

## CONCLUSION

It is necessary to state what has been omitted from the above framework as well as reemphasize its systematic and cogent approach for understanding social problems. The theoretical perspectives presented and the social problems and areas of Africa used as examples reflect the professional interests and personal experiences of the author rather than some objective "truth" about "social problems in Africa." The emphasis on some social problems, for example, crime, means that others have been neglected, such as Africa's staggering population explosion and problems of the environment, notably exhaustion and exploitation of natural resources, spoilage, toxicity, and pollution. Similarly, an emphasis on subregional examples, especially from Southern Africa, is at the expense of examples from Francophone Africa and Northern Africa where, for example, in Algeria's five-year civil war, more than 60,000 people have been killed.

Overall, there is little doubt that there will be an "internationalization" of social problems in the twenty-first century that will affect African countries. Social problems, as well as the activities of those who define and protest them, will become less localized, more visible in the global arena, and more likely to be "tried in the court of international public opinion." Smelser (1996: 278) suggests, perhaps correctly, that

we can expect the persistence and spread of familiar social problems associated with western market and urban development as the other nations of the world come to resemble the West and one another in economic enterprise and governmental apparatus, *despite the persistence of cultural traditions* (emphasis added).

For African people, then, there is a huge, complex, and formidable task ahead in bringing to bear the sociological imagination on understanding and interpreting their social problems as a necessary prelude to any action. Paradoxically for a chapter that has focused on structural "public issues" at the expense of more individual "personal problems," it may be true to say that the human qualities of endurance, patience, and resilience displayed by the African people in their struggles against colonialism, apartheid, and more contemporary forms of oppression and exploitation are the best hope for overcoming the social problems now facing the continent. Whether these qualities will be enough to meet the challenges of the continuing African "crisis" will depend largely on the peoples' relationship with state regimes, which remain, for the most part, omnipotent, corrupt, and repressive.

## NOTES

1. It is also necessary to raise the question of debt repayment, which can absorb up to a third of a developing country's limited government revenue. According to a recent UNDP Report (1996b: 7), "the problem is worst for the 32 severely indebted low-income countries (SILIC's), most of which are in Africa. For example, in Guinea Bissau, Mauritania, Zaire and Zambia, debt service dues ranges from three to six times public expenditure on education."

2. The African continent itself is often pathologized by commentators from other parts of the world who blame it and its peoples for the perceived dominance of crisis and disorder in its socioeconomic and political affairs.

3. In Botswana, as in other African countries, there is a phrase that ideally captures the essence of this public nature of self and identity, "*motho ke motho ka batho*" (a person is only a person within a community). It should be noted, however, that this phrase originated in precolonial times and is not so much indicative of "public" selves as it is about the absence of individualized selves.

4. The recent example of Nigeria's military dictator, General Sani Abacha, is a case in point. Toward the end of his rule, he conducted a civilian presidential campaign through GESAM'98 (General Sani Abacha Movement) based on what was described as "the forty startling inane principles of Abachaism" (*Focus on Africa*, 1997: 17) that made up "Vision 2010," his blueprint for a new social, economic and political order in Nigeria.

5. During the colonial era, for example, the main organizations that played a leading role in alleviating such social problems were nongovernmental, missionary-aligned philanthropic ones.

## REFERENCES

Achebe, C. (1958). *Things Fall Apart*. Oxford: Heinemann.
———. (1966). *Man of the People*. Oxford: Heinemann.
*African Business* (1996). (December).
Agadzi, V.K. (1990). *AIDS: The African Perspective of the Killer Disease*. Accra: Ghana University Press.
Akare, T. (1981). *The Slums*. Oxford: Heinemann.
Amin, S. (1976). *Unequal Development*. New York: Monthly Review Press.
Ankomah, B. (1993). "Out of Darkness?" *New African* (January): 13.
Barnett, T. and Blaikie, P. (1992). *AIDS in Africa: Its Present and Future Impact*. London: Belhaven Press.
Bauman, Z. (1990). *Thinking Sociologically*. Oxford: Basil Blackwell.
Becker, H.S. and Horowitz, I.L. (1972). "Radical Politics and Sociological Research." *American Journal of Sociology* 78(1).
Berger, P.L. (1965). "Towards a Sociological Understanding of Psychoanalysis." *Social Research* 32(1): 26–41.
Biko, S. (1978). *I Write What I Like*. Oxford: Heinemann.
Bloom, L. and Ottong, J. (1987). *Changing Africa: An Introduction to Sociology*. London: Macmillan.
Blumer, H. (1971). "Social Problems as Collective Behaviour." *Social Problems* 18.
Braithwaite, J. (1986). *Corporate Crime in the Pharmaceutical Industry*. London: Routledge and Kegan Paul.
Busia, N.A. (1989). *Slaves of a Culture: The Case of Domestic Servants in Ghana*. Monograph, Centre for Development and the Environment, University of Oslo.
Cabral, A. (1969). *Revolution in Guinea: An African People's Struggle*. London: Stagel.
Campbell, D. (1987). Quoted in *What Is History? A New Approach to History for*

*Students, Workers and Communities.* Johannesburg: National Education Crisis Committee (NECC).

Cohen, S. (1986). "Bandits, Rebels or Criminals: African History and Western Criminology" (Review Article). *African* 30(4).

Dag Hammarskjöld Foundation. (1992). *The State and the Crisis in Africa: In Search of a Second Liberation.* Report of the Mweya Conference, Uganda, May 12–17, 1990.

Davis, D. and Slabbert, M. (1985). *Crime and Power in South Africa: Critical Studies in Criminology.* Cape Town: David Philip.

Fanon, F. (1967). *The Wretched of the Earth.* Harmondsworth: Penguin.

*Focus on Africa.* (April–June 1997).

Foucault, M. (1980). *Power/Knowledge: Selected Interviews and Other Writings 1972–1977.* Brighton: Harvester.

Frederikse, J. (1982). *None But Ourselves: Masses vs. the Media in the Making of Zimbabwe.* Harare: Zimbabwe Publishing House.

Fuglesang, A. (1982). *About Understanding: Ideas and Observations on Cross-cultural Communication.* Uppsala, Sweden: Dag Hammarskjöld Foundation.

Gans, H.J. (1971). "The Uses of Poverty: The Poor Pay All." *Social Policy* (2).

Giddens, A. (1992). *Sociology.* Cambridge: Polity Press.

Gouldner, A.W. (1975). *For Sociology: Renewal and Critique in Sociology Today.* Harmondsworth: Pelican.

Government of Botswana. (1993). *Botswana Fact.* Gaborone: Department of Trade and Investment Promotions.

Gramsci, A. (1971). *Selection from the Prison Notebooks.* London: Lawrence and Wishart.

*The Guardian Weekly.* (December 30, 1992–January 7, 1993).

Gutkind, P. and Waterman, P. (1977). *African Social Studies: A Radical Reader.* London: Heinemann.

Haralambos, M. and Heald, R. (1991). *Sociology: Themes and Perspectives.* London: Collins Educational.

Harden, B. (1993). *Africa: Dispatches from a Fragile Continent.* London: HarperCollins.

Henshel, R.L. (1990). *Thinking about Social Problems.* New York: Harcourt Brace Jovanovich.

Hoogvelt, A.M.M. (1978). *The Sociology of Developing Societies.* London: Macmillan.

Hope, K.R. (1997a). *Structural Adjustment, Reconstruction and Development in Africa.* London: Avebury Publishers.

———. (1997b). *African Political Economy: Contemporary Issues in Development, The Africans: The History of a Continent.* Cambridge: Cambridge University Press.

Iliffe, J. (1987). *The African Poor: A History.* Cambridge: Cambridge University Press.

Jackson, B. (1990). *Poverty and the Planet: A Question of Survival.* London: Penguin.

Laakso, L. and Olukoshi, A.O. (1996). "The Crisis of the Post-Colonial Nation-State Project in Africa." In L. Laakso and A.O. Olukoshi (eds.), *Challenges to the Nation-State in Africa.* Uppsala, Sweden: Nordiska Afrikainstitutet.

Lauer, R.H. (1986). *Social Problems and the Quality of Life.* Dubuque, IA: William C. Brown Publishers.

Macdonald, D. (1996a). "Notes on the Socio-Economic and Cultural Factors Influencing the Transmission of HIV in Botswana." *Social Science and Medicine* 42(9).

——. (1996b). "Drugs in Southern Africa: An Overview." *Drugs: Education, Prevention and Policy* 3(2).

——. (1997). "Corruption and Economic Crime as Barriers to Reconstruction and Development in Southern Africa." In K.R. Hope (ed.), *Structural Adjustment, Reconstruction and Development in Africa*. London: Avebury Publishers.

*The Mail and Guardian.* (January 12–18, 1996).

*The Mail and Guardian.* (December 24, 1996–January 9, 1997).

Mamdani, M. et al. (1993). "Social Movements and Democracy in Africa." In P. Wignaraja (ed.), *New Social Movements in the South: Empowering the People*. London: Zed Books.

Memmi, A. (1965). *The Colonizer and the Colonizer*. New York: Orion Press.

Merton, R. (1968). *Social Theory and Social Structure*. New York: Free Press.

Merton, R.K. and Nisbet, R. (1971). *Contemporary Social Problems*. New York: Harcourt Brace Jovanovich.

Mills, C.W. (1959). *The Sociological Imagination*. New York: Oxford University Press.

Munslow, B. (1985). *Samora Machel: An African Revolutionary*. London: Zed Books.

Ngugi wa Thiong'o. (1981). *Detained: A Writer's Prison Diary*. Oxford: Heinemann.

Odetola, T.O. and Ademola, A. (1985). *Sociology: An Introductory African Text*. London: Macmillan.

Odetola, T.O. et al. (1983). *Man and Society in Africa: An Introduction to Sociology*. London: Longman.

Onimode, B. (1988). *A Political Economy of the African Crisis*. London: Zed Books.

——. (1993). "The Imperatives of Self-Confidence and Self-Reliance." In A. Adedeji (ed.), *Africa Within the World: Beyond Dispossession and Dependence*. London: Zed Books.

Pape, J. (1993). "Still Serving the Tea: Domestic Workers in Zimbabwe 1980–90." *Journal of Southern African Studies* 19: 387–404.

Patton, C. (1990). *Inventing AIDS*. New York: Routledge.

Purdy, J. (1996). "Post-colonialism: The Emperor's New Clothes?" *Social and Legal Studies* 5(3): 405–426.

Reid, J. and Trompf, P. (eds.). (1991). *The Health of Aboriginal Australia*. Sydney: Harcourt Brace Jovanovich.

Republic of South Africa. (1995). "Key Indicators of Poverty in South Africa." *Reconstruction and Development Plan*. Pretoria: South African Communication Services.

Robertson, I. (1980). *Social Problems*, 2nd ed. New York: Random House.

Rubington, E. and Weinberg, M.S. (1989). *The Study of Social Problems*. New York: Oxford University Press.

Rwomire, A. and Raditlhokwa, L. (1996). "Social Work in Africa: Issues and Challenges." *Journal of Social Development in Africa* 11(2).

*SAPEM (Southern African Political and Economic Monthly)*. (1996). 9(5) (February).

Schwendinger, H. and Schwendinger, J. (1970). "Defenders of Order or Guardians of Human Rights?" *Issues in Criminology* 5: 123–157.

Shaidi, L.P. (1992). "Traditional, Colonial and Present-Day Administration of Criminal Justice." In T.M. Mushanga (ed.), *Criminology in Africa*. Rome: United Nations Interregional Crime and Justice Research Institute.

Shivji, I.G. (1989). *The Concept of Human Rights in Africa*. London: CODESRIA Book Series.

Sim, J. et al. (1987). "Introduction: Crime, the State and Critical Analysis." In P. Scraton (ed.), *Law, Order and the Authoritarian State*. Milton Keynes: Open University Press.

Smelser, N.J. (1996). "Social Sciences and Social Problems." *International Sociology* 11(3): 275–290.

Sogge, D. (1992). *Sustainable Peace: Angola's Recovery*. Harare, Zimbabwe: Southern African Research and Documentation Centre (SARDC).

Soyinka, W. (1997). *The Open Sore of a Continent: A Personal Narrative of the Nigerian Crisis*. Oxford: Oxford University Press.

*The Sunday Independent* (January 19, 1997a).

*The Sunday Independent* (April 13, 1997b).

Tintner, M. (1989). *State Imperfect: The Book of Social Problems*. London: Optima.

Tungwarara, O. (1995). "Human Rights in Africa." *Southern Africa: Political and Economic Monthly (SAPEM)* 8(10): 5–7.

United Nations Development Program (UNDP). (1994). *Human Development Plan 1994*. New York: UNDP.

———. (1996a). *Human Development Report*. New York: UNDP.

———. (1996b). *Economic Growth for Human Development: Africa*. New York: UNDP.

United Nations Interregional Crime and Justice Research Institute (UNICRI). (1993). *Understanding Crime: Experiences of Crime and Crime Control*, edited by A.A. Alvazzi Frate, U. Zvekik and J.J.M. van Dijk. Rome: UNICRI.

Young, E. (1995). *Third World in the First: Development and Indigenous People*. London: Routledge.

## Part II

## Culture, Human Rights, and Democracy

Chapter 3

# Language and the Politics of Power:
# The Case of Africa

## Euphrase Kezilahabi

## INTRODUCTION

The continent of Africa has many theatrical performances of the absurd. One of them is being staged on the platform of language. The platform is raised high for everyone to see. The tragic clowns on the stage are the African intellectuals and the petty bourgeoisie of the neo-colonial states of the continent. The peasantry is the audience which does not seem to understand what is going on, but what they can hear and see makes them laugh painfully. This chapter takes this mocking laughter seriously and tries to analyze its echoes. Certainly, there has been a crisis in the whole concept of the African being. This crisis has taken place mainly because of the problem of technique and the Europeanization of the world, spearheaded by the canons of capital. There has been an intervention or intrusion by powerful nations in the African thinking process linguistically and technologically. The problem is how to come to terms with it, if not erase it. What we can say for sure is that it cannot be solved by using the same languages that caused the intervention, be it by appropriation or abrogation. The solution lies outside of them but within the concept of language as a form of consciousness.

In order to provide a balanced picture, this discussion begins by examining very briefly the problems of ethnicity and pluralism in the African context and then moves to the pertinent, sensitive problem of the "national question," its historical background and its present situation in contemporary Africa. The focus is on the diversity of African politics and the role of the OAU. After laying this background, the problem of language and the politics of power are discussed. Power is understood as the ability to influence others in making decisions and the whole thinking process (Ryan, 1984: 21–45). From there onward, the main thrust of the argument begins to reveal itself.

In many African states after independence there developed a ruling class that followed in the footsteps of its former colonial masters. This was so because it inherited what seemed to be a ready-made structure of governance. This development suited the self-centered personality of the national bourgeoisie. Armed with ambition but worried by the uncertainty of staying in power, the ruling class became apprehensive and therefore interested in the accumulation of wealth. It scrambled for resources, often using ethnicity as a rallying point. The Biafran war in Nigeria may be cited here as a glaring example. This practice of "divide and rule," which the colonial state had used as a mode of existence, did not work well in favor of the ruling class. Instead, it intensified collective consciousness and group demands based on ethnicity, race, religion, generation, and class. Uneven development of regions and uneven distribution of resources, government posts, and services (i.e., hospitals, schools, universities, roads, and even foreign aid assistance) reinforced regional solidarity. It would be futile to cite examples here because this has affected all African countries in one way or another. It is not surprising that in several African countries at this period of democratization political parties are not free from open or hidden ethnocentricity whose strong shell is language.

The elites ("modernizers") are an important group in today's postcolonial Africa. The interests and demands of this complex group often overlap with those of the petty bourgeoisie and the ruling class. It is this Westernized group which Appiah (1992: 4–5) calls "europhone intellectuals" that has compounded the problem of language in Africa with persistent allegiance to foreign languages and their discourse of power. As Ashcroft et al. (1989: 7) have observed in their analysis of postcolonial literatures, in a situation like this language "becomes the medium through which a hierarchical structure of power is perpetuated, and the medium through which conceptions of 'truth,' 'order,' and 'reality' become established."

To the Europhone intellectuals, foreign languages are magic sticks that protect their privileged positions. They distance themselves from the rest of the people and legitimize their wayward behavior with references to universality and internationalism. They sign agreements and contracts, travel abroad, establish newspapers and journals in foreign languages, and cap their "high" culture with a simulated literature of their own, written in those "prestigious" languages. Thus, there is a natural control of the flow of information which makes the public unable to critically interpret events that affect their lives. It is this gap—this distancing— that characterizes the problem of language in Africa as a struggle for power. Language becomes a class marker and an oppressive discourse of power.

Before proceeding to the second part of the argument, it is worth mentioning two cases that seem exceptional and problematic. In some parts of Africa, south of the Sahara, there are black (colored) indigenous people who speak no other languages other than those of their former colonial oppressor. In Mozambique, for example, some people speak no other language except Portuguese; and in South Africa and parts of Botswana some people speak Afrikaans as their mother tongue. In the African context, this is a complex linguistic phenomenon. For the time being we may note here that this was history made on them; they can now make theirs.

Africa has something to learn from the June 16, 1976 Soweto protest against the use of Afrikaans as a medium of instruction. Revisiting the incident, the *Sunday Times* had this to report:

On June 16, 1976, pupils in Soweto marched in protest against the use of Afrikaans as a medium of instruction; 10,000 strong, they converged on Orlando West High School for a meeting. But their protest ended in violent confrontation.

Police fired teargas and the crowd responded with stones. Police then opened fire with live ammunition, apparently first firing warning shots, killing at least one child—Hector Petersen, 13.

Riots broke out and there were several deaths on the first day.

On June 17 the government suspended all classes in the township. In the days that followed, students at schools and universities around the country demonstrated in sympathy. Rioting broke out sporadically.

By June 24, the official death toll was 140, with more than 1,000 people injured, 908 arrested and numerous buildings destroyed. (*Sunday Times*, June 16, 1996)

On their march to Orlando stadium, students were singing "Nkosi Sikilele Africa" (God Save Africa) and it was a peaceful demonstration. This incident, which centered on language, generated a chain of events that solidified political consciousness in South Africa. But what has happened to this awareness? Talk of having African languages as the media of instruction in secondary schools and universities today is greeted with derision from the europhone intellectuals, the petty bourgeoisie, and the ruling class speaking for the people. The pendulum has now swung the other way, with African countries now trying their best to reinstate foreign languages not only as means of communication but also as if foreign languages are the core of African being from which we have to find a bearing. If foreign languages are allowed to penetrate into all aspects of civil society, education, the professions, administration, commerce, parliament, and the media, then all is lost. Democratization will become a farce since there cannot be democracy without majority participation. Participation is here understood not in the sense of casting a ballot into a magic box for president, but in the sense of the majority holding the reins of their own destiny. This swing of the pendulum is disturbing to those who think we are on the wrong path.

## WHAT IS WRONG WITH FOREIGN LANGUAGES?

In the history of colonialism, language in Africa has gone through three stages. In the first stage, the colonial epoch, Africans were subjected to foreign languages through the schools. Within a short period of time, they learned to look down on their own languages and to regard the colonizers' language as superior. The elites who managed to master foreign languages became convinced that they could express themselves well only in those languages, especially in academic discussions. The colonizer, having institutionalized his own language as the content of African consciousness, was then saturated with amazing success in infusing this speaking subject with his own culture (Fanon, 1979). This period was characterized by self-denial, loss of identity, and loss of self-confidence. In most parts of Africa, this stage is long past, although some misguided intellectuals still harp on the African languages' supposed inability to express scientific concepts. But as Edwards (1985) has observed, no language has greater expressive power than the African. In addition, as Masolo, the African philosopher, points out: "Some languages are structurally more complex and present more difficulties to learn than others, but they certainly cannot be used as proofs that certain minds are more 'complex' than others" (1994: 101).

During the second stage, the African speaking subjects were enlightened by political independence. Going back to their roots, they proclaimed their language to be the best, but deep inside still believed that they could express themselves better in foreign languages. A crisis therefore occurred in which they attempted to Africanize those languages by doing violence to standard structures. The literary scene may serve as a good example, specifically, Gabriel Okara's *The Voice* and Amos Tutuola's *The Palm-wine Drinkard*. At the political level, the African speaking subjects, as a result of the unequal distribution of wealth, returned to the ethnic language as a rallying point of ethnic solidarity. For people who had distanced themselves linguistically from the majority, the call for the development of those languages could be regarded as a form of social commitment. Today, however, some Europhone intellectuals who advocate the development of ethnic languages may not be free from the disease of ethnocultural anachronism, regionalism, and the struggle for power. It has become a disease of election years when candidates find these languages useful.

In the third stage, the African speaking subjects have tried to completely abandon the predominance of foreign languages and to adopt their own languages in all spheres of life. Foreign languages are no longer taught en masse but rather are directed to specific professions as a means of communication with the outside world and as keys to knowledge available in other languages that are not necessarily those of the former coloniser. Two African countries that are struggling to get to this stage are Somalia and Tanzania.

Both countries, once inspiring examples, are now faltering. Somalia is involved in lower-level ethnic strife—the clan—and Tanzania is now stating that standards have been lowered, as if high standards were inherently English. What has gone wrong? In the case of Tanzania, the move to use Swahili as a medium of instruction in secondary schools and universities has always been blocked by Europhone intellectuals, the petty bourgeoisie, and the ruling class, who at the same time are sending their children abroad for higher studies.

These three stages reveal that foreign languages will have to lose the privileged position they now hold to allow thinking to take place. Conscientious intellectuals hoped that conscious awareness of this language crisis would accelerate when the generation that experienced colonialism was gone. But to the contrary young people are learning foreign languages more than their own indigenous languages, to the extent that they put them solidly at the center of their lives and have made them a hallmark of the modern African generation—the new generation. This has occurred because we now live in a mass media–oriented culture, and we have allowed this hegemonic culture to push our own languages to the periphery. We have failed to be creative in our own languages, and even when we succeed, we lack originality because we have not given them a chance to occupy the center of our thinking process. Foreign films and foreign videos are what the youth know. As a result, they are entering the illusory global village with nothing to contribute and are mere consumers.

Among many europhone intellectuals, indigenous languages were long pushed from the sitting room to the kitchen. Now they are being hurled from the kitchen into the bush where they supposedly belong. Parents look like ancient dinosaurs to their children when they speak these languages with their visiting relatives. They laugh at their parents' "barbarism" as they watch the latest movie from the United States. In some instances children, who happen to speak better English and better French than their parents, assume an air of superiority, disdaining their parents' grammatical mistakes and accented English or French. The number of grandparents who cannot communicate with their grandchildren is increasing. It is a painful experience to see a grandmother in tears over her failure to communicate with her grandchildren. Those who favor foreign languages must also enjoy the role of being simultaneous interpreters. It is a painful experience, and it has become a serious crisis.

The future of African languages should not be left in the hands of a few remnants of residual colonial culture who hold power. African languages will have to be at the center of our thinking process if we are to talk seriously about freedom, democracy, and technological development.

Because of the connections between language and knowledge, the use of foreign languages is not free from the hegemonic roles played by the nations to which those languages belong. Those who are aware of this fact have often proposed Kiswahili as the language capable of uniting the whole of Africa. They think that Kiswahili will broaden the horizon of understanding with which we begin in our ethnic languages. It is, hopefully, the language that will unmask the African past without bias and define properly the African's being in the world. Only African languages are able to penetrate and reach to the depth of the continent's history, behavior, and dreams long repressed by hegemonic powers. This is precisely so because language is man/woman, for it is in language that the social and historical individual is constructed and given a space in society as a human being.

Our lives as African speaking subjects encompass "the African Experience" in which the African past continually negotiates with the present. This African experience is not inert; rather, it speaks. What is needed is a language that will help Africans open themselves up so that a proper dialogue may take place. When this African experience talks to us and finds the distorted images of foreign languages as its counterpart, it withdraws, recoils, and becomes almost impenetrable. What we speak out and show to the world is only an illusory surface interpretation because proper dialogue has not taken place within our minds. Success, however, will depend on the philosophical outlook of the African who is doing the unmasking, for acts of tyranny and mystification of truth can also be performed by people using their own languages. One needs to be loyal to one's self.

Our present task therefore is to reach that underlying depth, recover the repressed areas of our life and give them a new significance. Foreign languages deal only with surface meanings of our life and culture, as does all African literature written in those languages. Our duty as African-speaking subjects is not to always accommodate foreign languages, but to develop a formidable African language so that facts of domination and oppression will be revealed freely by the now unheard voices of the "silent" majorities.

As we have already noted, foreign languages represent a direct intervention in the thinking process of most educated Africans. By accepting the predominance of foreign languages, we are giving Westerners the right to have authoritative control over our thinking process through the signifying practice of those languages. Signification has intrinsically within itself a well-defined system of valuing. By giving predominance to these languages, we automatically allow the Western world to be the center of value of our African being. As long as we use these languages, we cannot escape satisfying the demands of institutionalized codes of signification and Western values (Kezilahabi, 1985: 357–362).

Use of foreign languages distances the elite and the ruling class from the people. The declaration by some African states that French, English, and Portuguese are national/official languages is an act of betrayal of the peasantry and the working class by "their" own governments. It is also a falsification of history and truth. These languages, with perhaps the exception of English in South Africa, have never been national, and they never will be. Their predominance in Africa is a temporary phenomenon. The rehabilitation of African languages as the content of our consciousness is a necessary step toward effecting a realignment from imperialism to the peasantry. Genuine commitment means aligning oneself with one's own people. The use of foreign languages intensifies the false belief that we can bring about an African revolution from above, down to the marginalized peasantry. We can bring about rapid fundamental change only if we are properly armed with original ideas and if we speak to the people in a language understood by all. Although the use of African languages will not guarantee originality, it will facilitate ontologically our way to primordial reality and put us on the right path.

Finally, there is the question of power. Today there are many sophisticated and complex ways of exercising power. Michel Foucault (1983) left us with a history of the modes of objectification by which human beings are made subjects. He observed that the production and circulation of elements of meaning could have as their objective certain results in the realm of power. Language is one of the crucial organizational instruments that power-holders can use in controlling and managing speaking subjects so that intensive exploitation of ideas, labor, and resources may take place smoothly. Foreign languages have exerted great influence on their targets. The following are some of the indicators that have manifested themselves:

1. Foreign languages have influenced our reading and writing habits, choice of books and newspapers to read, choice of language to use in writing letters, articles, advertisements, road signs, and so on.

2. They have made some of the elite identify themselves with the power-holders, and have developed in them linguistic and cultural biases. For example, England has the best kind of education, France the best cultural values, and so forth.

3. They have intensified the cord of relationship with the power-holders to the extent that we have developed personal loyalties and sympathies for their nations; a good example is the Association of Commonwealth Countries.

4. Most europhone intellectuals have a conscious or unconscious feeling of pride in speaking these languages. This influence has persisted mainly because of the power-holders' well-organized system of rewards. Reward is one of the methods of exercising power (Kaplan, 1964).

5. Foreign languages provide opportunities for further studies both abroad and domestically: opportunities for better employment, better pay, and scholarships. The following advertisement taken from the *Daily News* (Tanzania) illustrates this idea.

**Vacancy**

Administrator and Financial Controller
Qualifications: Holder of University degree in Business Administration/Economics with computer background and a good command of English. Applications should be sent with photocopies of Certificates to:
   Tanzania Spare Manufactures Ltd.
   P.O. Box 20220
   Dar es Salaam (*Daily News*, Tanzania, August 25, 1989)

But Tanzania's language "policy" states:

The use of Kiswahili shall take precedence over any other languages in correspondence, meetings, conference, etc. Only in dealing with foreign customers and employees who do not understand Kiswahili shall English or other languages be used when discussing official matters. (SCOPO, 1984)

6. These opportunities are facilitated by the ideological institutions established by the power-holders such as the Goethe Institute, British Council, Alliance Française, and the United States Information Services. These institutions disseminate information (books, films, videos, magazines) through their libraries and make arrangements for exchange visits. Some of these institutions have the language component, which is often taught with a heavy cultural content of their own social life.

7. These institutions control the medium of instruction used in secondary schools through donations of books for teaching their languages and offering expatriate human power. The school, being an ideological state apparatus, thus becomes vulnerable.

The above-mentioned reasons argue for the rehabilitation of Africa languages. What has subjected us to these influences is the availability of "sufficient" resources on the part of the power-holder, mainly capital and its subsequent relations of production. Foreign languages have made it easy for these nations to make their presence continuously felt underneath our consciousness.

## CONCLUSION

In Africa today, the choice of national languages is an ideological issue that involves conflicts of power and power relations as embodied in the communicative process of African ethnic groups and nations. Problems of the "national question" arise mainly because of the scramble for scarce resources, the peasantry's and the working class's worsening conditions, class antagonism, ethnic demands for self-determination, discoveries of minerals and oil, agrarian and pastoral feudalism, imperialist machinations, and war among many others.

The following are some of the most sensitive "national questions" in Africa today: questions of borders, national cohesion and political homogeneity, ethnic and clan power struggles, and, most importantly, the question of management of resources. These disputes and challenges are prevalent in Ethiopia, Sudan, Angola, Mozambique, Senegal, Mali, Kenya, Nigeria, Chad, South Africa, Uganda, Sierra Leone, and the Democratic Republic of Congo. Although the historical and cultural formations that brought about these conflicts are not discussed here, all these problems point to one thing—that at present we need not highlight our differences but rather should try to bridge them by bringing to the fore our similarities through a common platform of mutual understanding.

It is here that the question of developing one African language as a facilitating and mitigating medium enters. It is acknowledged here that the existence of an intercontinental language will not solve all problems. In Burundi and Rwanda, for instance, political turmoil has long prevailed among people speaking the same African language. Thus, other factors already mentioned must be taken into account, along with the problems of language.

The continent of Africa is an amalgamation of different ethnic groups, races, and nations with diverse political forms of government struggling to survive the challenge of capital. The Organization of African Unity (OAU) is the only organ that is designed to unite the whole continent and capable of mobilizing the people consciously into one voice and making their desires and aspirations realizable. Unity could be possible if the hurdle of language were cleared.

With regard to the problem of language, the African literary scene has indicated five alternatives:

1. Acceptance of colonial languages as they are and using them as a tool to convey one's own spirit (appropriation).

2. Doing violence to foreign languages by refusing to bow to correct imperial usage. Reshaping language to suit an African culture (abrogation).

3. Developing all African languages and using them in all spheres of life (centering African languages).

4. Developing zonal languages for use: Kiswahili (Eastern zone), Zulu (Southern zone) Lingala (Central zone), Hausa (Western zone), Arabic (Northern zone) (centering five African languages).

5. Developing one intercontinental language for use south of the Sahara (counterattack).

The stand taken here is that alternatives 1 and 2 are to be rejected on the grounds of the four reasons already given. Further debate may be needed on the remaining three alternatives. To be sure, African languages should be given a chance to participate fully in the creation of knowledge rather than be on the receiving end. The use of our own languages will enable us to contribute creatively to humanity with original ideas so that we may not be bracketed out of global thought.

If we do not take this step consciously, Africa will always be an object of research and a dumping ground of outdated technology and ideas. In order to do so successfully, African languages will have to acquire the necessary tools such as technical and scientific terminology. We should be aware that English, French, and Portuguese are not inherently technological. They have been made so. Those who argue for foreign languages must realize that these languages are in fact a constraint to the African thinking process. They subsume and suffocate the creative potential and power of our own languages.

But we cannot let all flowers blossom. It is estimated that there are around 2,000 languages in Africa. Batibo (1989) has pointed out that the most extensively and routinely used languages in Africa number around 40. Definitely, a choice will have to be made. It would appear that a forcible reduction of the plurality of languages would rock the foundations of democracy, which advocates freedom of speech in whatever language. Africa will therefore have to allow a plurality of languages and values. Diversity of values will not necessarily imply conflict of values if we concentrate on the integration of those values. One does not have to build up ethnic allegiances if one's values are properly integrated into the nation and if resources are equitably distributed. This is what Africa has to do: use language as a facilitating element. This writer is skeptical of the idea of developing zonal languages, which are likely to increase the solidity of the contending groups and amplify the magnitude of the conflicts.

Africans need to have one formidable language that will integrate their values and act as a rallying point of their consciousness. European language policies toward Africa have always been directed by the politics of dominance. Africa needs one strong language that will act as a counterattack. This is possible only if the OAU takes up this challenge. The question that remains is which language? We have already hinted that Kiswahili is perhaps the most "logical" choice. But the question "why Kiswahili?" continues to resurface whenever this proposal is offered.

Batibo (1989: 29) made a typological survey of the lingua francas in Africa by looking at the prevailing factors from precolonial days to the present. Among the factors he examined are mass communication, the symbolic nature of the language at the national, racial and cultural levels, national efforts to develop the language, linguistic similarities with neighboring languages, absence of ethnic identity, demographic imbalances, emigration and nomadism, and social prestige. In his analysis, Kiswahili scored very high compared to other lingua francas except Arabic. Kiswahili is not being advocated here in terms of superiority. This would be tantamount to "linguistic imperialism" whereby "Swahili" nations will first have to conquer the whole continent of Africa. The point is that there seems to be a need to explore the avenues of "willing" that would eventually lead to what is possible.

Much has been said about the possibility of Kiswahili becoming the intercontinental language for Africa. It is necessary to join those far-sighted voices that suggest that an African language be adopted as the intercontinental language for Africa. It is further proposed that the OAU establish a center for the development of that language and other African languages. The center would train teachers of the language and conduct research on African languages. These teachers would then be sent to other African countries where they would teach it together with other African languages at secondary and university levels. The center would also train translators. This is only a quick ad hoc proposal, but linguists can work out a more elaborate proposal with necessary details if the OAU decides to take up the challenge in the interest of African unity.

Despite this seemingly insurmountable task, the development of an intercontinental language that will bridge hostilities across boundaries is actually possible because our actions are intersubjectively shared and all Africans share a subcommon stock of knowledge and experiences. Somehow, and at some point, we will have to stop that mocking laughter of the peasantry which is continually haunting us: We have to find a language in which we will be ourselves and communicate with the people so that they may participate fully in matters that affect their destiny.

## REFERENCES

Appiah, K.A. (1992). *In My Father's House: Africa in the Philosophy of Culture*. New York: Oxford University Press.

Ashcroft, B., Gareth, G. and Tiffin, H. (1989). *The Empire Writes Back: Theory and Practice in Post-Colonial Literatures*. London and New York: Routledge.

Batibo, H.M. (1989). "The Position of Kiswahili among the Lingua Francas of Africa: A Typological Survey." *Journal of Linguistics and Language in Education* 4(1): 27–41.

*Daily News* (Tanzania). (1989). August 25.

Edwards, J. (1985). *Language Society and Identity*. New York: Basil Blackwell, in association with Andre Deutch.

Fanon, F. (1961). *The Wretched of the Earth*. Harmondsworth: Penguin.

Foucault, M. (1983). "Afterword: The Subject and Power." In L.D. Hubert and P. Rabinow (eds.), *Michel Foucault: Beyond Structuralism and Hermeneutics* (pp. 208–226). Chicago: University of Chicago Press.

Kaplan, A. (1964). "Power in Perspective." In R.L. Khan and E. Boulding (eds.), *Power and Conflict in Organizations*. New York: Basic Books.

Kezilahabi, E. (1985). *African Philosophy and the Problem of Literary Interpretation*. Unpublished Dissertation, University of Wisconsin–Madison.

Masolo, D.A. (1994). *African Philosophy in Search of Identity*. Bloomington and Indianapolis: Indiana University Press.

Ryan, M. (1984). "Theories of Power." In A. Kakabadse and C. Parker (eds.), *Power, Politics, and Organizations: A Behavioural Science View*. Chichester: John Wiley and Sons.

SCOPO. (1984). *Parastatal Service Regulations*, Section E, Article F, 12–13. Dar-es-Salaam: President's Office.

*Sunday Times* (South Africa). (1996). June 16.

Chapter 4

# Cultural Incongruity in Changing Africa

## Anthonia Adindu and Norma Romm

### INTRODUCTION

This chapter develops a notion of cultural incongruity as a way of focusing on people's responses to situations that involve them in unmanageable dilemmas. The notion of cultural incongruity evokes a sense of the complexity of some of the dilemmas that people encounter as they respond to "problematic situations" in changing Africa. The chapter suggests that it is crucial that these dilemmas be seen as a matter for public discussion, as part of the process of people managing their involvement in society. This imperative in turn is linked to a specific conception of what is meant by development of a society.

Development basically requires building up and nurturing processes for meaningful involvement of people in defining possibilities for action on both personal and collective levels. It is about affording people the opportunity to make considered and responsible choices while they simultaneously take into account their involvement in the social fabric. A number of authors have concentrated on elucidating this conception of development, and this chapter will not elaborate thereon. Authors such as Braun (1991), Rwomire (1992), Chambers (1993), Long and Villarreal (1993), Mvungi (1995), Streeton (1995), Pillay (1996), and Romm (1996a) have highlighted processes of development that nurture people's *opportunities to create a manageable way of living* as being fundamental to the definition (and practice) of development. This definition of development in turn means that people's cultural resources for making sense of their reality and of their interactions with others have to become enshrined in any development effort. Accordingly, participants base development processes in the ongoing appropriation of culture.

This chapter uses the notion of cultural incongruity to highlight the need to make explicit some of the disjunctions that have come to the fore in changing Africa. The concentration is on incongruities that emerge at the interface between people's sense of their personal and family responsibilities versus their allegiance to duties that need to be performed in organizations (both private and public sector ones). The argument in the chapter is that insufficient attention has been paid to such disjunctions—and that development requires that at least the issue be elevated to the realm of public discussion. Unless this is done, the incongruities are likely to become more critical, with services that could contribute to processes of development becoming ever more hindered through the lack of attention being paid to people's personal ways of making sense of incongruous demands.

The study uses a specific case study to support some of the claims that are made (Adindu, 1995). The case study should be treated as an additional expression of what a number of other authors have argued and documented. These arguments and documents have taken many forms. Some are in the form of academic publications by authors (e.g., Oloko, 1993; Menon, 1994), and others in the form of novels (e.g., Achebe, 1960). In all these expressions, reference is made to a sense of uneasiness that arises as people find it difficult to account to themselves or to others for the way they are encountering their differing responsibilities. The strength of the case study material mentioned in the chapter is rooted in the kinds of recognition that it may evoke among readers, who themselves may be grappling with some of the issues raised. The notion of cultural incongruity is applied to show the complexity involved in addressing the issues.

Although the chapter is set in the context of a changing Africa, using some case study material to support the argument, the concept of cultural incongruity may have wider applicability. It can be used to point to any disjunctions leading to what Oliga (1996) calls "messes in collective rationality"—in whatever society or context that is under consideration. Oliga explores such "messes" in so-called modern societies by making use of Habermas's notion of social pathologies. Habermas (1987: 140) has suggested that pathological crises of modernity can take the following forms. First, crises occur when recourse to the stock of culturally available meanings in a society no longer allows people to cope with new situations (and indeed may detract from such coping ability); second, when the need to coordinate the actions of differing actors/groups is not properly catered for; and third, when the personal identity and dignity of actors have to be defended by means that run counter to social cooperation (the result being a loss of personal accountability).

Oliga (1996: 291) explains how identification of the sociopathological crises of modernity can be used to draw out the "sociophilosophical anatomy of economic recessions." He suggests that specific self-deceptions among people in regard to the functioning of the economy and polity have been allowed to perpetuate themselves in modern states. This perpetuation of self-deception generates "messes in collective rationality" (1996: 275). Although the self-deceptions remain undisclosed and unexamined (by means of collective discourse), the messes are likely to become exacerbated. This is not to say that public discussion of the "messes" will necessarily arrest the pathologies. Rather, it is to say that if they are brought under the scope of some sort of public communication, this increases the chances that together people will be able to find better ways of addressing them. Habermas posits that when people orient their arguments toward consensual understanding of situations and of how to act therein, then they can be said to be engaged in attempts at communicative action as a way of taking (some) charge over historical events.

This tenet has been questioned from a number of angles, especially by postmodernist discourse which contends that Habermas's ideal of consensus is too strong and does not cater sufficiently for continued difference, contradiction, paradox, and irony in social life. (See Romm, 1996b: 217–219, for a discussion of this matter in terms of implications for ways of seeing development.) Nevertheless, even from a postmodernist perspective, some attempt to "construct collective identities" (albeit with continuing differences and paradoxes) in the arena of public debate is not ruled out (see, for example, Schuurman, 1993: 188). In the above discussion, Oliga's reference to messes in collective rationality was introduced to lend credibility to the notion of cultural incongruity as a way of understanding development crises. The developmental crisis consists in the inability of people to engage with collective messes other than to resort to personal ways of coping and possibly self-deception for which it is difficult to account (to both themselves and to others).

Having laid this background, we will now proceed to discuss in more detail what we mean by incongruity in relation to culture, with special reference to changing Africa.

## CULTURAL INCONGRUITY AND RELATED CONCEPTS

Culture of course has a significant role to play in all societies. Its capacity to provide a sense of shared values is recognized as a binding force that holds collectivities together. It is cultural sharedness that allows people to develop patterns for living together, albeit patterns that may be subject to continued struggles as individuals respond to the demands of what they take to be cultural expectations.

African countries and perhaps other less developed countries, too, tend to place emphasis on adherence to certain upheld cultural practices. This is true even in view of the dynamic state of affairs in Africa today, characterized by inevitable and sometimes insidious Western accultura- tion, global/regional economic competition, and changing economic world markets and politics. The issue that this chapter addresses is whether all continuing cultural practices have a positive impact on in- dividual and collective development, or whether they may become merely a mode of transmitting values from generation to generation without an examination of their workability over time. It is argued that some established cultural practices that have existed over generations could create social problems and hamper development in changing Af- rica, without the introduction of measures to support an ongoing reex- amination of how these arrangements are operating.

This analysis highlights this point by considering the specific operation of the extended family system in its traditional form and its (incongru- ous) relationship to organizational involvements in the context of health services in Nigeria (the setting of our case material). Despite the evident advantages of the traditional operation of the extended family system on the level of personal care, disadvantages can accrue at other levels. We emphasize that a multileveled accounting of patterns of incongruity is crucial to the discussion of problematic issues facing people in changing Africa. Here we also draw on Weil (1997) who refers to group processes for engaging multileveled discussion via what she calls multilayering.

We do not pretend to offer any resolutions to the issues raised here (or even to suggest that our own account of incongruities is the only way of seeing the difficulties). Actually, we believe that no final way of seeing or addressing the difficulties can be established, and so our purpose in this chapter is to draw attention to the need for a public discussion of these difficulties, in which people are invited to participate in defining arrangements that could constitute an improvement (even admitting that these will be continually refined and/or redefined). Our argument is linked to a view of how culture is created and re-created.

### The Ongoing (Re-)Appropriation of Culture

Terms such as cultural beliefs, cultural practices, and cultural values are often applied interchangeably to the phenomenon called culture. All of these terms point to the idea that there is a degree of sharedness in social life which forms a basis for group or community activity. These cultural attributes could impact on the life cycle of a collectivity, affecting family structure, patterns of influence among family members, relations with others, role performance and responsibilities, sex, marriage, work, communication patterns, living and consumption, as well as health and illness behavior. This is not to say that cultural attributes remain fixed over time or that they necessarily forbid individual responses to the so-called shared patterns. Indeed, Berger (1969: 18) argues that culture cannot perfectly socialize all members of society to internalize patterns of socially accepted response. He introduces the notion of "externalization" to suggest that members of society have the propensity to "pour out" new meanings as part of their unique engagement with the world. Berger defines externalization as a moment in society when people reengage with given (or "available") cultural patterns. While they internalize ("take in") these patterns, so too can they adjust, modify, or contest them as they externalize ("pour out") alternative meanings.

Anthropologists and sociologists have proposed varying conceptualizations of culture. For example, the cognitive perspective views culture as a system of shared cognitions. In this view, culture offers a commonly accepted mode of perceiving and organizing events, emotions, and behavior. Many authors, taking this line further, concentrate on the idea of culture as patterning not only our cognition but primarily our sense of moral obligation to fulfill perceived normative expectations (for example, Parsons, 1951, emphasizes these aspects). Working with a somewhat different view, authors such as Smircich (1983), following Berger to a large extent, focus on culture as a set of symbols and meanings that facilitate sense-making among people. Although it facilitates such sense-making, it does not determine or dictate how specific people will come to construct their own realities and their sense of how to act in the world (see also Romm, 1994a, 1994b). As people appropriate culture, so too do they define their own responses to it (through a process of what may be called reappropriation).

Berger's view of sense-making accepts that some processes in society encourage individuals to internalize "available" cultural patterns. As indicated above, however, Berger simultaneously points to people's propensity for externalization, in which they pattern their own worlds. Externalization is manifest, for example, in the human quest to "beat" a system that has become oppressive in its demands (Berger, 1969: 155). The notion of externalization can also refer to moments when people begin to manipulate the system, using it for ends that they define as legitimate. For example, some people consider it as legitimate to use an organization to satisfy their own resource requirements (even though this is outside of the official, formal code of conduct for organizational members). The process of rationalizing such activities in consciousness might be part of an effort to find a way of coping in the face of what is experienced as conflicting demands.

## Juxtaposing Conflicting Demands: Personal and Social Incongruities

The following analysis argues that conflicting moral demands made within cultural patterns (as, for example, when demands to meet family obligations become juxtaposed with demands to devote time, energy, and commitment to organizational tasks) mean that the process of managing the conflict needs to be brought into the arena of public discussion. The purpose of such discussion is to find possible routes toward supporting people, so that their individual decision making does not have to be a response to fundamental "uneasiness"—to use Achebe's (1960) terminology—in the face of *unmanageable tension*. Such decision making can have dire consequences not only for the individual in the short run, but also for the collectivity (to which the individual belongs). At the individual level, if caught juggling commitments within organizational settings, the person can be accused of breaking a moral code—for example, when organizational resources are obviously being rechanneled to meet their family obligations. Furthermore, at a societal level, the services that organizations are supposed to provide (for example, those concerned with implementation of services such as health care and water provision) become inefficient and ineffective. At the societal level, social problems (perceived and admitted to be problematic because, for instance, required services are not properly rendered) then become intractable.

To address the incongruities in cultural patterns, resulting in unmanageable dilemmas on the individual level (associated with such incongruities) and in attendant social problems, we suggest that as a first step at least the incongruities must be confronted explicitly. At least, people must be prepared to submit to discussion of possible incongruities that have been identified as such. Once these incongruities are brought into the arena of public discussion, there is a possibility of looking for resolutions or options that will be experienced as better for the concerned participants. This will allow organizations to function in a better way to strive to fulfill some of their identified missions. To ignore the incongruities under discussion may mean that the issues faced become treated in a superficial way. It is this superficiality that leads to the belief, say, that it is possible to set up a functioning information management system in health care services, while glossing over the way members' allegiances are being torn by incompatible demands. This does not mean that we subscribe to a "functionalist" view of organizations as geared ideally toward ironing out paradox and inconsistency. It does mean, however, that we subscribe to the idea that any created "solutions" for organizational and social living together are "better" insofar as they bear the mark of confrontation with perceived incongruities.

The chapter investigates some of the scope for recognizing incongruity as a starting point toward rethinking (recognizing and confronting) some identified social problems in changing Africa. To enter into this discussion, we first have to consider what may be meant when we speak of a "social problem."

## Social Problems and Their Definition

A social problem may be defined as a condition that affects a significant number of people in ways considered undesirable and that may be ameliorated through collective action (Horton and Leslie, 1978). Social problems, as Horton and Leslie envisage them, therefore involve defining something as problematic and furthermore accepting that resolution cannot be achieved at a personal level alone. Resolution implies some form of collective action. By implication, substantial members of a group must view a situation as somehow problematic in order for it to be categorized as constituting a "social problem." In essence, it involves some degree of value judgment. For example, witchcraft was generally considered a social problem in early Europe, and through the measures instituted it gradually diminished. In some parts of Africa witchcraft is considered a major social problem, and only women are confirmed as witches in the society. In Ghana, for instance, once a woman is confirmed to be a witch, she is confined in an institution away from the rest of society. Other parts of Africa, however, pay little attention to witches and witchcraft.

In effect, socially endorsed cultural patterns influence the categorization of certain behaviors and the exclusion of others that are seen as constituting social problems. However, it should also be recognized that in any situation there may be lack of consensus among various interest groups or concerned parties regarding the character or even the existence of a "problem." What the issue at hand involves and what aspects of it are seen as "problematic" might vary depending on people's differing experiences and conceptualizations. Cultural incongruity has strength as a concept in that it allows us to respect the multi-vocal character of definitions of problems, at the same time as we explore issues that have been raised and that require some form of public attention. Such an exploration is compatible with Horton and Leslie's definition of a "social problem": A significant number of people experience the situation as problematic and probably would welcome some form of engagement in public forums for discussion about possible ways of addressing the issues.

Checkland and Scholes (1990) suggest that while "problems" as such cannot be said to exist independently without some categorization defining the situation as problematic, it is also true that debate to open up discussion on what some members may be experiencing as problematic normally leads to better resolutions than if this debate were not opened up. Flood (1995) in turn suggests that the language of problems, though convenient in allowing us to point to some "thing" that is recognized as requiring a solution of some sort, can just as well give way to a language that speaks about "issue addressal"—as an ongoing process of humans living together which is never completed. Issues continually come to the fore in society, requiring attention.

In the context of Africa, changing values, intergenerational differences, Western influences, changing economic circumstances, and religious and political interests may all help create moral confusion for many people in decision-making positions. As Fuller and Meyers (1941), as well as Spector and Kitsuse (1973), point out, value conflicts by implication imply some experience of issues as being "problematic"—even though the nature of the problem may not be easily definable. Simply because it is not easily definable, we suggest that people can benefit from wide public discussion in which together they build up a multilayered appreciation of complexity through juxtaposing alternative experiences (Weil, 1997).

Because human aspirations and priorities are dynamic and change over time, certain cultural values and practices must be subjected to some kind of planned positive intervention in which people seriously consider the need to encounter perceived conflicts and contradictions. However, one must also bear in mind a further complexity that arises as micro and macro political processes bear on the definition of what constitutes a problem to be addressed. Since the status quo may be to the advantage of certain interest groups, planned change is often not encouraged and is indeed (somewhat deliberately) left to chance. Perceived incongruities are dodged and left untouched. Some groups may prefer the (seeming) haphazardness that ensues from not bringing into focus the need for more public deliberation of issues faced.

It is also possible, however, that bringing such issues into focus (for example, through a pressure group's attention in the community) could meet with some degree of acceptance more generally and be taken on board as significant numbers of people begin to recognize the unsustainability of attempts to gloss them over. For instance, Flood and Romm (1996: 169–224) explore some intervention possibilities aimed at re-addressing knowledge-production processes, and their workings in the game of knowledge-power play in society. They indicate why they follow the suggestion that it is possible to nurture more widely informed decision making—despite the micro and macro political processes that often militate against participation in democratic processes. Deetz (1985: 263–265) also discusses options for raising as problematic decisions that otherwise (unless challenged) could be seen as detrimental to human development.

## SOME INCONGRUITIES

This section further develops our conception of incongruity and indicates the significance of the concept by concentrating on some incongruities surrounding the operation of the extended family system in changing Africa. Much of the discussion is based on data from Nigeria, most notably studies such as those by Oloko (1993) and Adindu (1995).

Nigeria, like many other African countries, upholds the extended family system, which ensures that members of a community are cared for by other members. Although we by no means advocate that this system cease to exist, we do propose that its workability in a changing Africa requires serious deliberation in order to support and/or modify its operation. As a starting point for this deliberation, it needs to be acknowledged that the system is creating undue pressure on individuals faced with meeting obligations, with consequent ill effects for their organizational commitments.

The assertions made here relate on the one hand to the situation in which at present, within the extended family structure, someone could be responsible for more than one wife (if the person is male), five children, parents, grandparents and other unemployed adults, nieces and nephews. Those who succeed in meeting such immense responsibilities receive approbation by members of the family and the community in general. On the other hand, in many African countries, salaries are generally meager and systems of remuneration poor, coupled with an ineffective social security system. Consequently, workers must often resort to unacceptable (or at least morally ambiguous) means of acquiring extra resources to meet their responsibilities.

Often organizational resources are diverted, or workers spend only part of their time at work. Menon (1994) points out that in so-called developing countries research appears to indicate that "employees could derive meaning from work not from the task per se, but in terms of instrumental outcomes from the work context such as status, job security, the ability to support one's family and aged parents" (1994: 108). He also observes that if workers do not identify with their tasks in the organization, it is difficult to design measures for their self-regulatory behavior therein. He indicates (1994) that workers bring into the work context factors emanating from their social environment (such as their specific sense of social duties) and that this variable is "social in nature" (1994: 111). It cannot be accounted for merely from "within" the organizational boundary. He states his claim as follows: "Being forewarned of possible context related incompatibilities, it behooves us to explicitly consider the context variable in our deliberation on work design strategies for developing countries" (1994: 85).

Menon treats the social environment (which influences the worker's sense of what is meaningful) as a "variable" that cannot be ignored when considering the extent to which work processes can be bettered in organizations. Although we would not necessarily see the variable in the same way as Menon does, his exploration offers a similar conclusion to ours: Workers' immediate social environment is a factor that impinges on the way in which they define their work commitments. If there are clashes between senses of duties, workers may resolve them in favor of what they believe will receive approbation as a community member. Ironically, as shown in this chapter, it is the services of organizations in the community that may be affected adversely when workers opt for family duty over work-related commitments.

Hence, we arrive at the suggestion that societal (cultural) expectations and responsibilities catch people up in a web of incongruity. This creates a vicious cycle that leads to organizational ineffectiveness and some of the social problems attendant thereon.

## INTERPRETATION OF RESEARCH FINDINGS

The study by Adindu (1995) was conducted to gain insight into possible factors that contribute to the intractable state of ineffectiveness within health care information systems in Nigeria. The study was set in a context in which many people assumed that a technical upgrading of the information system would "ameliorate the lack of reliable health information that has persisted since inception of modern health services in Nigeria" (Adindu, 1995: ii). The study carried out in-depth data collection with specific involvement in a chosen locality, using quantitative and qualitative approaches, from the community, state, and central levels. On the quantitative score, the accuracy, timeliness, and reliability of information were assessed, as was the training given to personnel responsible for analysis and utilization of information. On the qualitative score, interviews were undertaken with a view to gaining a sense of how people experienced their relationships with others in the system and how they perceived the management of the information system.

A decision was made to assess the information system in terms of the structure, process, and outcome model as suggested by Donabedian (1990). The assessment of "structure" involved taking into account the quantity and quality of resources available for provision of health services. This included the actual physical facilities in which services are provided, adequacy of required supplies, amount, type and condition of equipment, staffing, the number of professional and nonprofessional staff, the ratio of personnel to patients, or other responsibilities, qualifications, and experience. Structure was also seen to include provision of training, staff development, supervisory and management capability, composition of professional committees, and adequacy of systems dealing with quality measures (including recordkeeping systems). The "processes" supporting the structure were also examined. This examination involved investigating the activities carried out in the process of service provision. Finally, "outcomes" were seen as an indirect measure of quality of service, based on the extent to which changes are based on preceding services or actions.

The coordination of the information system's structure was abysmal, and this in turn affected both the quality of the process and the outcomes, resulting in organizational ineffectiveness and dysfunction. Adindu's (1995) research findings further suggested that incongruities could be seen as linked to factors in the organization that are related to incongruity in the wider social structure.

With regard to the organization, in addition to a centrally designed and information driven system, aims and missions were not delineated (or discussed) at peripheral levels, basic materials necessary for operating a simple manual system were seriously inadequate, policies implemented at peripheral levels were inconsistent with those defined at the central level, divergent (and clashing) goals were pursued by diverse groups and individuals operating the system, and the resources for operating the system were often not directed toward attainment of stated organizational objectives. These inconsistencies may be seen as linked to members' desires to acquire more resources from the organization in order to meet personal objectives, such as the extended family responsibilities discussed earlier. Oloko (1993), in a study on the ineffectiveness of both private and public enterprises in Nigeria, suggested that major causes could be related to factors in the wider society, one of which was the extended family responsibility.

In effect, the information system may be seen as ineffective and dysfunctional because of the incongruity in the behavior of workers in the organization—who in turn are influenced by inconsistent societal expectations, punctuated by immense family responsibilities, the very meagre salaries paid to workers, and the absence of mechanisms established by the government to help the unemployed and the aged. The consequences are low productivity, low standard of living, and increased social problems.

The notion of incongruity as advanced by Adindu (1995) provided an account of the health care information system which split over the taken-for-granted boundary of an "information management" system. The connection between ineffective information management and unmanageable responsibilities of organizational members allowed organizational disjunctions to be seen in the light of broader societal incongruities. Figure 4.1 offers some appreciation of how this web of incongruity is perpetuated.

Figure 4.1 indicates how incongruity in societal expectations may result

**Figure 4.1**
**Societal Incongruities**

---

1. Workers are expected to work hard and contribute to attainment of organizational objectives and societal development.

2. Salaries are meager and working conditions very poor, resulting in low morale and little commitment to the organization.

3. This is compounded by immense extended family responsibilities that lead to misappropriation of organizational resources and low productivity.

4. Workers receive approbation for misappropriating resources to meet family responsibilities.

5. The consequence is low productivity, organizational ineffectiveness, dysfunction, and stagnation in economic development, which perpetuates poverty, and the cycle continues.

---

*Source*: Adinu, 1995.

in incongruity in individual behavior, in turn leading to organizational ineffectiveness. Incongruity between individual requirements and the stated mission or function of organizations results in the lack of resources for operations of the organization. Findings in Adindu's study (1995) support those by Oloko (1993), who suggested widespread ineffectiveness in public and private organizations in Nigeria due to factors within the wider society. A complex web of incongruity ensues, resulting in and at the same time perpetuating a restriction of choices for those involved.

Of course, the account offered above is but one way of slicing through a myriad of processes that make up the society. Factors such as the structure and organization of the world market; world politics; and histories of domestic and international muting of voices of opposition (to taken-for-granted ways of thinking and acting) cannot be ignored in our understanding of development issues faced in the context studied (and in other contexts).

Nevertheless, we suggest that insofar as the notion of incongruity raises a "shock of recognition" (Wehlage, 1981) for the concerned parties in whatever context is under consideration, it might help open up a discussion in which people can participate in (re-)addressing problematic aspects of their life-worlds. It provides a good starting point for nurturing discussions in the "public mode" around the identified disjunctions. Although we have concentrated on exploring the relevance of the notion of cultural incongruity in the context of changing Africa, as indicated in our introduction, this does not imply that our argument has no relevance in other countries. The way in which the notion might engender enriched insight in a variety of contexts is a matter for continued discussion.

## DISCUSSING ISSUES IN PUBLIC MODE

Adindu (1995) indicates how her study could provide a basis for involving members of the community in defining possibilities for action, so that the constrictions of the scope for action identified in the study could begin to become dislodged. She concentrates on the engagement of community participation by offering certain recommendations in this regard. Her recommendations spring from her awareness that community discussion can be harnessed as a cultural resource in creating a "better" management information system around health care services.

Adindu suggests that to enhance people's sense that they have a stake in the way that health information management is organized, a community information resource center could be set up and managed in conjunction with members of the community (and with support from community leaders). An information system jointly operated and utilized by members of the community would, she suggests,

encourage a more efficient resource investment [and] provide a monitoring system that would enhance accountability. Following establishment of an information system that is consistent with local needs and managed with participation of the community, its success might well become the concern of the community and not just that of the Primary Health Care (PHC) department. (1995: 339)

In addition, she proposes that a health information day could be arranged and that "health workers and leaders from other communities, state, and federal health officials, as well as donor agencies could be invited to participate. Fund raising for the information system could form part of activities for the occasion" (1995: 340). In this way, people might come to understand that they can act in various ways in order to participate in defining what is relevant information and how it should be organized and accessed.

At the same time, suggestions could be advanced for putting pressure on organizations currently performing specific functions of information management to fulfill functions designated, so that their place in the community could be recognized as a development force. However, as Adindu notes, pressure for increased accountability is likely to fail unless incongruities are also brought into focus and accounted for. It needs to be brought to attention that workers may be under "constant pressure to satisfy conflicting interests" and that this often is what lies behind the "pervasive ineffectiveness and poor performance reported." This, Adindu suggests, is a "serious issue for national discussion" (1995: 356). The discussion, involving members of communities who would be rendered aware of the trade-offs that they themselves are having to make when they gloss over the pressures felt by organizational members, would need to include varying opinions concerning how to support those experiencing such pressures. As a result of these discussions, arrangements could be made (whether at the community or state level) for better forms of care, on various levels, that do not place all the responsibility with specific family members.

This is not to suggest that discussion would be a tension-free process or that arrangements that are able to iron out paradoxes and contradictions can be created (see, for instance, Gouldner, 1975, 1980). What it does mean is that new visions positing alternative ways of working and living together are given the space to come to the fore as part of the discursive process. As McKay and Romm emphasize: "The community . . . is not a unitary entity. It is a collectivity of individuals who are (ought to be) accountable to each other. Community thus does not comprise a single unitary consciousness but rather implies a revitalisation of public discourse" (1992: 109). Public discussion at least opens the space for rethinking problematic issues faced and for considering options that various concerned parties may see as more meaningful. This does not imply that their choice-making will be (or ever can be) dilemma free. Rather, it implies that their choice-making is brought within the ambit of *addressing* and *managing* dilemmas faced (Flood and Romm, 1996).

Because meaning-construction as a process in society is never "completed," proposed arrangements that might arise in processes of discourse are always open to further possibilities of discourse as people begin to work with the arrangements.

## NOTE ON THE MANAGEMENT OF INFORMATION IN SOCIETY

We have referred in the preceding discussion briefly to a view of information processing—a view implied in our discussions of the recommendations made by Adindu (1995). We wish to note that Adindu's suggestion for setting up a community resource center for the harboring of health information is significant not only for the case under consideration. Its significance lies in its claim that defining the relevance of information through organizing and interpreting it is not the preserve of those managing "information systems" (as a technical process) in society. Adindu's suggested community resource center operationalizes a vision of the importance of inviting community involvement in defining and redefining "information," along with the importance of community members participating in defining the needs that the information system should meet. This involvement can then be fed into the (more technical) operations of management information systems (for example, in specific organizations). The community dialogue through which information is rendered relevant and meaningful cannot (should not) be broken in favor of expert knowledge systems where (presumed) professional expertise alone is relied upon to generate relevant information and to interpret results of coding processes. This conception of how information should be treated is linked to a definition of development as fundamentally rooted in people's involvement in defining their realities (Romm, 1995).

## CONCLUSION

This chapter has proposed that a conception of cultural incongruity offers a way of redefining social problems in changing Africa. The chapter is directed at highlighting the web of incongruity that may be perpetuated in changing Africa, unless efforts are made to resolve problematic issues in new ways. This requires recognizing that the incongruity creates somewhat unmanageable dilemmas for individuals as organizational members, which they may try to resolve in favor of perceived family responsibilities (for which approbation is received). However, in this process they break other moral codes and have to adjust (psychologically) to this infraction. Furthermore, they may face dire consequences if as organizational members they are caught re-channeling resources or energies to meet family responsibilities.

The social cost of such decision making is that organizations find it difficult to gain their members' commitment to tasks. Work in this context may become experienced as more or less meaningless (as such). This is not conducive to the operation of organizational life and in turn leads to problematic outcomes on a social level. The chapter attempts to provide insight into how this dynamic may become perpetuated—unless broken by recognition of its problematic character. This requires multileveled engagement with the issues. The concept of incongruity is offered as a way of inviting such engagement as part of a process of public discussion. It is suggested (and hoped) that there is scope in changing African societies to put on the agenda for social discussion the dilemmatic tensions that seem impossible to address on a personal level alone.

The purpose of the chapter has been to indicate the importance of involving communities in the re-creation of culture rather than allowing the consequences of each person's individual decision making to be left unaddressed (or at least not seriously addressed). The chapter goes on to propose what social discussion around issues of concern might involve. Finally, we offer a brief account of how information processing in information management systems could be realigned to permit more discussion of its collection and interpretation as a matter of course. This means that the activities of creating, organizing, and using information become rooted in processes of social debate, in which varying interpretations can be invited, engaged, and accounted for as part of the process of "managing" information.

## REFERENCES

Achebe, C. (1960). *No Longer at Ease*. London: Heinemann.

Adindu, A.U. (1995). *The Effect of Incongruity on Quality of Health Information Systems: Bama, Nigeria PHC Case Study*. Ph.D. Thesis, University of Hull, Hull.

Berger, P.L. (1969). *The Sacred Canopy*. New York: Anchor.

Braun, G. (1991). "The Poverty of Conventional Development Concepts." In Institute for Scientific Co-Operation (ed.), *Economics*. Tübingen: Institute for Scientific Co-operation.

Chambers, R. (1993). *Challenging the Professions*. London: Intermediate Technology Publications.

Checkland, P. and Scholes, J. (1990). *Soft Systems Methodology in Action*. Chichester: Wiley.

Deetz, S. (1985). "Ethical Considerations in Cultural Research." In P.J. Frost, L.F. Moore, M.R. Louis, C.C. Lundberg, and J. Martin (eds.), *Reframing Organizational Culture*. London: Sage.

Donabedian, A. (1990). "The Quality of Care: How Can It Be Assessed?" In N.O. Graham (ed.), *Quality Assurance in Hospitals: Strategies for Assessment and Implementation*. Rockville, MD: Aspen.

Flood, R.L. (1995). *Solving Problem Solving*. Chichester: Wiley.

Flood, R.L. and Romm, N.R.A. (1996). *Diversity Management: Triple Loop Learning*. Chichester: Wiley.

Fuller, R.C. and Meyers, R.R. (1941). "The Natural History of Social Problems." *American Sociological Review* 6: 320–328.

Gouldner, A.W. (1975). *The Dark Side of the Dialectic*. Amsterdam: University of Amsterdam.

———. (1980). *The Two Marxisms: Contradictions and Anomalies in the Development of Theory*. London: Macmillan.

Habermas, J. (1987). *The Theory of Communicative Action*. Boston: Beacon Press.

Horton, P. and Leslie, G. (1978). *The Sociology of Social Problems*. Englewood Cliffs, NJ: Prentice-Hall.

Long, N. and Villarreal, M. (1993). "Exploring Development Interfaces: From the Transfer of Knowledge to the Transformation of Meaning." In F.J. Schuurman (ed.), *Beyond the Impasse: New Directions in Development Theory*. London: Zed Books.

McKay, V.I. and Romm, N.R.A. (1992). *People's Education in Theoretical Perspective*. Cape Town: Maskew Miller Longman.

Menon, S.T. (1994). "Designing Work in Developing Countries." In R.N. Kanungo and M. Mendonca (eds.), *Work Motivation*. London: Sage.

Mvungi, A.A.K. (1995). "Towards a People-Based Approach." In P. Forster and S. Maghimbi (eds.), *The Tanzanian Peasantry: Further Studies*. Aldershot: Avebury.

Oliga, J. (1996). "Economic Recession and Self-Deceptions." In R.L. Flood and N.R.A. Romm (eds.), *Critical Systems Thinking*. New York: Plenum.

Oloko, O. (1993). "Indigenising Management Concepts and Practices." *Journal of Nigerian Institute of Management* 384 (July–December): 7–15.

Parsons, T. (1951). *The Social System*. London: Routledge and Kegan Paul.

Pillay, D. (1996). "Social Movements, Development and Democracy in Post-Apartheid South Africa." In J.K. Coetzee and J. Graaff (eds.), *Reconstruction, Development and People*. Halfway House: International Thomson Publishing.

Romm, N.R.A. (1994a). "Peter Berger's Humanist Sociology." In N.R.A. Romm and M. Sarakinsky (eds.), *Social Theory*. Johannesburg: Heinemann.

———. (1994b). "Symbolic Theory." In N.R.A. Romm and M. Sarakinsky (eds.), *Social Theory*. Johannesburg: Heinemann.

———. (1995). "Participation in Defining Tanzanian Realities." In P. Forster and S. Maghimbi (eds.), *The Tanzanian Peasantry: Further Studies*. Aldershot: Avebury.

———. (1996a). "A Dialogical Intervention Strategy for Development." In J.K. Coetzee and J. Graaff (eds.), *Reconstruction, Development and People*. Halfway House: International Thomson Publishing.

———. (1996b). "Critical Theory as a Way to Understand Development." In J.K. Coetzee and J. Graaff (eds.), *Reconstruction, Development and People*. Halfway House: International Thomson Publishing.

Rwomire, A. (1992). "Education and Development." *Prospects* 22: 227–239.

Schuurman, F.J. (1993). "Modernity, Post-Modernity and the New Social Movements." In F.J. Schuurman (ed.), *Beyond the Impasse: New Directions in Development Theory*. London: Zed Books.

Smircich, L. (1983). "Concepts of Culture and Organisational Analysis." *Administrative Science Quarterly* (September 28): 339–358.

Spector, M. and Kitsuse, J.I. (1973). "Social Problems: A Reformulation." *Social Problems* 21 (Fall): 145–159.

Streeton, P.P. (1995). "Human Development: The Debate About the Index." *International Social Science Journal* 143: 23–38.

Wehlage, G. (1981). "The Purpose of Generalisation in Field-Study Research." In T.S. Popkewitz and B.R. Tabachnik (eds.), *The Study of Schooling*. New York: Praeger.

Weil, S. (1997). "Social and Organisational Learning and Unlearning in a Different Key: An Introduction to the Principles of Critical Learning Theatre (CLT) and Dialectical Inquiry (DI)." In F.A. Stowell, R. Ison, S. McRobb, J. Holloway, R. Armenson, and S. Jackson (eds.), *Systems for Sustainability: People, Organizations, and Environments*. New York: Plenum.

Chapter 5

# The Authoritarian State and Human Rights Violation in Postcolonial Africa: A Case Study of Nigeria, 1983–1995

## INTRODUCTION

Although we are now in the twenty-first century, African postcolonial states continue to experience diverse forms of socioeconomic and political crises. At the economic level, the living conditions of the populace have deteriorated rapidly, particularly following the imposition of World Bank/IMF-inspired structural adjustment programs (Ake, 1994; Nzongola, 1995; Olukoshi, 1995; Beckman, 1992; Bangura, 1992; Rudebeck, 1992; Mamdani, 1988; Mkandawire and Saludo, 1999; Mkandawire, 1995). Politically, the imposition of the reform measures has exacerbated not only social conflict and opposition from civil society, but also represssive and authoritarian tendencies on the part of the state (Olukoshi, 1995; Shivji, 1989; Leftwich, 1994; Doornbos, 1990; Rasheed, 1995; Adekanye, 1995). According to Olukoshi (1995), the socioeconomic crisis that affected most postcolonial African states in the 1980s led to the strengthening of authoritarian tendencies, diminishing legitimacy and fostering the abuse of fundamental human rights.

When most African states gained political independence in the 1950s and 1960s there was the euphoria and anticipation that African self-rule would automatically lead to remarkable improvement in the living conditions of African peoples (Nzongola, 1987). However, the anticipated socioeconomic development could not occur due to domestic instability as well as adverse international environment (Wunsch and Olowu, 1995; Decalo, 1976; Huntington, 1968; Nzongola, 1985, 1987). The democratic governments of the early independence period in Africa were either overthrown through military coups, or the dominant party transformed the political space into a one-party state dictatorship (Decalo, 1976). Simply put, authoritarian rule became the dominant pattern of regime behavior in postcolonial Africa.

In Nigeria, for example, the military junta under Buhari which overthrew the crisis-ridden second Republic government of Alhaji Shagari in December 1983, entrenched a regime whose rule was essentially based on the promulgation of repressive decrees and the suppression of fundamental human rights (Bangura, 1986). For example, the Buhari regime promulgated Decree No. 2, State Security (Detention of Persons), which allowed the then powerful chief of staff, supreme headquarters, Major-General Tunde Idiagbon to arrest and detain persons for an indefinite period without trial on the grounds of threat to state security. People arrested under this decree included two journalists, Haroun Adamu and Rufai Ibrahim, for exposing corruption at the Federal Capital Authority in Abuja (Forrest, 1993: 95–103). Other repressive decrees included Decree No. 20 (Miscellaneous Offences), which introduced the death penalty by public executions for offenses such as drug smuggling and arson of public buildings. Decree No. 4 Public Officers (Protection against False Accusation) covered accusations made in the press to bring the federal government or public officers into ridicule (Forrest, 1993: 97). Thus, the Buhari junta curtailed freedom of expression. As one analyst observed, the unpopularity of the Buhari regime "stemmed from its increasingly authoritarian tendency and a style of government in which there was little or no consultation" (Forrest, 1993: 102). Since political power was arrogated to a small group of individuals, certain sections of the officers felt alienated, hence the ruling junta split. Thus, on August 27, 1985, Major-General Ibrahim Babangida, the chief of army staff, overthrew the Buhari regime and declared himself president. As will be shown later, the intervention of Babangida marked the ascendance and ultimate beginning of the institutionalization of authoritarian rule in Nigerian politics.

This chapter examines the linkages between the rise of authoritarian states in postcolonial Africa and the implications for human rights and democratic governance. It will be argued, among other things, that with the declining capacity of the African state for development and fulfillment of the post-independence "social contract," authoritarianism has become a prevalent aspect of regime behavior, leading to abuse of human rights and constraint of the democratization process. In developing this argument, an attempt will be made to answer the following pertinent questions: What are the socioeconomic and political forces that led to entrenchment of authoritarian states in postcolonial Africa? What are the implications of authoritarianism for human rights in Africa? To what extent does authoritarianism hinder or constrain the democratization process in postcolonial Africa? More specifically in the context of Nigeria, to what extent did the institutionalization of the military in state governance promote authoritarianism? However, before getting into the empirical discussion, it is pertinent to examine some fundamental theoretical perspectives on the issues of authoritarianism, democracy, and the problem of human rights in Africa.

## THE AUTHORITARIAN STATE AND ABUSE OF HUMAN RIGHTS IN AFRICA: A THEORETICAL PERSPECTIVE

As stated earlier, most Africa states attained political independence in the 1960s, following which the citizenry thought that their new leaders who replaced the colonialists would respect the post-independence "social contract" by providing education and health programs, improving agricultural production, supplying infrastructures, and laying the foundations of African industrialization. However, after three decades of independence, African postcolonial states remain the poorest in the international system. Not only are African states the poorest, they are also the most highly indebted. According to Adekanye (1995), the total debt stock of sub-Saharan Africa stood at $55.6 billion in 1980, $89.1 billion in 1985, $171.4 billion in 1990, and $199 billion by 1993. Thus, between 1980 and 1990, the debt of sub-Saharan Africa more than tripled, while amounts spent on servicing the debts also kept increasing. Africa's current account deficit increased from $3 billion in 1990 to $11 billion in 1994 (IMF, 1994). As African countries implemented the IMF/World Bank-inspired structural adjustment economic reforms, their economies further deteriorated, leading to devaluation of national currencies, retrenchment, removal of subsidies on social services, high inflation, and national indebtedness (Bangura, 1992).

The implication of externally induced reforms not only unleashed poverty and tremendous suffering in civil society, but it also exacerbated the incidence of strikes by trade unions and generalized opposition to government policies. In a study on the impact of structural adjustment programs (SAP) on developing countries, Beckman and Bangura (1989) argued that Africa's workers and peasants are oppressed and their interests are neglected. Most workers live in unhealthy and impoverished urban slums. Most of them are unable to survive on their wages. Thus, they often respond to these oppressive conditions by organizing strikes and work stoppages. Governments, in response, become more repressive and authoritarian in dealing with such opposition. In a nutshell, therefore, SAP is not only a political contest between the postcolonial state and interest groups, but an ideological struggle as well. It is also a conflict of social forces on the basis of their position in the political economy and how they are affected by the dynamics of crisis and adjustment (Beckman, 1992). Simply put, the imposition of structural adjustment programs reinforced authoritarian and repressive tendencies by the postcolonial states and their incumbent regimes. Furthermore, the era of structural adjustment has generally been characterized by an increase in import dependency and indebtedness to international financial institutions (Wunsch and Olowu, 1995).

More specifically in the Nigerian context, the magnitude of indebtedness began to build in the 1980s. The national debt increased from $12 million in 1981 to $19.5 million in 1985 to $24 million in 1986, and by 1991 it had reached an all-time high of $33.4 million. This rapid increase in indebtedness not only exacerbated the economic crisis but also accelerated social conflict and instability in the public sector (Beckman and Bangura, 1989).

The rapid decline in the developmental capacity of the postcolonial African states clearly shows the pitfalls of modernization theorists. Advocates of the modernization perspective in the 1960s (Apter, 1965; Hungtington, 1968) argued that as African traditional societies imbibed Western values, institutions, and practices, their "primordial" orientation would gradually give way to progress and development along the lines of Western-type democracy. However, the realities in Africa today show that instead of growth, development, and improvement in the living conditions of the citizenry, Africa has witnessed diverse conflicts, underdevelopment, repression, and abuse of human rights (Adekanye, 1995; Nzongola-Ntalaja, 1995; Nzongola-Ntalaja and Lee, 1997; Bangura, 1988). Alongside the malaise of state decay are such practices as lack of accountability, primitive accumulation, obsession with holding on to political office, and prebendalization of state power for personal or sectional interests (Joseph, 1987; Bangura, 1995; Bangura, 1996; Young, 1994).

At the center of the African states' failure to chart viable paths for development is the issue of lack of accountability and hence of democracy as well. Since independence, the citizen's role in the affairs of government has systematically been reduced. The political arena has shrunk, and political demobilization has become the norm rather than the exception in regime behavior and social engineering. To rationalize and sustain political repression has been the preoccupation of most governments. All this has come about to cement one notorious but common aspect of almost all African governments: the misuse of public resources and their channelling into private gains as possibilities for viable processes of indigenous development are neglected or deliberately destroyed (Anyang' Nyong'o, 1988).

In spite of current efforts at democratization and making the transition to civil rule, the culture, values, and practices of liberal democracy have yet to take root in most of Africa. For example, in Ghana, Niger, and Chad, incumbent military rulers contested elections, and by virtue of their control of state power along with electoral institutions, they emerged as winners (Anyang' Nyong'o, 1988; "The Learning Process,"

1996). Libya, Gambia, Mali, DRC, Rwanda, Burundi, and Sudan are under authoritarian military rule, whereas Zambia, Zimbabwe, Kenya, Cameroon, Uganda, Senegal, and Côte d'Ivoire, in spite of cosmetic competitive elections, are predominantly controlled by single parties. African states such as Liberia, Angola, Burundi, Somalia, and Sierra Leone have been characterized by anarchy arising from factional disputes (Wunsch and Olowu, 1996). Regularized competitive elections along liberal democratic lines have taken place in Botswana, Malawi, South Africa, Namibia, Algeria, Mozambique, and Tanzania. On the whole, therefore, the democratization effort in Africa is still below expectation. This is because most of the states are either under direct authoritarian military rule or some form of patrimonial and personalist one-party rule where opposition is brutalized and repressed (Gibbon et al., 1992; Callaghy, 1984; Jackson and Roseberg, 1982).

As will be shown later, Nigeria provides a classic example of the African tragedy where, in spite of enormous human and material resources, very little or no reasonable economic development has taken place. In the last decade, most Nigerians have experienced not only poverty and misery in civil society following the imposition of SAP in 1986, but also the abuse of human rights and repression. The so-called oil wealth has not been translated into any meaningful socioeconomic development (Abubakar, 1986; Ihonvbere, 1993). A large part of Nigeria's wealth has been diverted into private accounts by the political class thereby generating underdevelopment at the domestic level (Forrest, 1986; Falola and Ihonvbere, 1985; Iyayi, 1986; Othman, 1984).

Thus, like most other postcolonial African states, the Nigerian state is not only the locus of political power but also the source of wealth through primitive accumulation. Individuals and social groups compete for political power to replace the incumbents, while those who are in power strive to retain it at all cost. This competition for state power within the framework of a dependent capitalist state reinforces authoritarian tendencies manifested in disregard of the rule of law and abuse of human rights.

Studies have shown that in places such as Latin America, Southern Europe, and Southeast Asia, the authoritarian state was instrumental in opening the path to socioeconomic transformation and development (Collier, 1979; Stepan, 1973; Skocpol, 1985; Robinson, 1988). In postcolonial Africa, however, the enthronment of authoritarian rule in so many countries is illustrative of the character of certain regimes whose survival depended on internal repression and consequent abuse of fundamental human rights. This observation applies to countries like Zaire/Congo under Mobutu and Kabila, Central African Republic under Bokassa, Uganda under Idi Amin and Milton Obote, Sudan under Nimeiry and Al-Bashir, Ethiopia under Mengistu, Somalia under Siad Barre and Farah

Aideed, and Nigeria under Babangida and Abacha. The concept of the authoritarian state as used here is more than just a description of a modality of rule by the regime in power. Rather, it is a sociopolitical category located in the specific historical and structural context of the reproduction of the material basis of life in peripheral societies (Thomas, 1984: 83).

As a system of repression and domination, the authoritarian state develops in peripheral capitalist societies characterized by a historically unique combination of underdeveloped productive forces and heterogeneous and multistructured modes of economic production. According to Thomas, these economies are fractured, distorted, and disarticulated, and have little capacity for self-centered, autonomous accumulation (Thomas, 1984). From the perspective of dependency theorists, peripheral societies are not only dominated by countries at the center, but are also incorporated into the capitalist world economy in such a way that they are vulnerable to vicissitudes of the international capitalist economy. Since they are fundamentally exporters of raw materials or semiprocessed agricultural products, fluctuations in prices usually affect them negatively, thereby generating balance-of-payment crises. Thus, in an attempt to restructure their economies, peripheral states are confronted with opposition from civil society. As the state responds, it increasingly becomes repressive and loses its legitimacy. As Clive Thomas rightly puts it:

the crisis of the society and the world economy together engender a crisis that threatens the continuation of the regime in power, as well as the continued social and economic domination of the class and state on whose behalf it rules. It is because of this that the Authoritarian State is the specific product of a conjuncture of world capitalism and peripheral capitalist development. Its imposition is the ruling class response to the crisis confronting the society. (Thomas 1984: 88)

Authoritarian states are characterized not only by overt and covert repression, but also by practices such as curtailing freedom of speech and assembly, and clamping down on public communication media such as newspapers, radio, and television that are critical of government policies and programs. For instance, the Babangida regime in Nigeria systematically used repression to silence opposition, *inter alia*, by closing down specific media houses that were perceived as "opponents" of the regime.

The authoritarian state is therefore a fundamental threat to the democratization process in Africa, and above all, it is a source of abuse of human rights. However, in spite of state repression, many elements of civil society, especially trade unions, students, professionals, peasants, and the urban unemployed, have mounted concerted struggles for improvement in wages, social services, and restoration of the rule of law, accountability, transparency and democratic governance in the conduct of state affairs. As Rasheed observes, although Africa's postcolonial one-party and authoritarian military regimes have over the years attempted to suppress, coopt, and discourage opposition from civil society, these tendencies have generally been unsuccessful. In fact, civil society in Africa, in spite of its limitations, constitutes an important vehicle for the expression of opposition to authoritarian rule (Rasheed, 1995).

During the Commonwealth summit in Harare in 1991, opposition groups from Kenya insisted that Western powers use the aid conditionality as a weapon to pressure the Kenya regime to introduce democratic reforms. Similarly, church leaders from Malawi called for the same strategy to be adopted against the then incumbent dictator Kamuzu Banda. Also, in February 1993, Zaire's prime minister, Etienne Tshisekedi, suggested that the Western powers intervene militarily in his country because of the failure of Mobutu Sese Seko's regime to hand over power to the civilian transitional government headed by Tshisekedi (Rasheed, 1995). In the Nigerian case, human rights groups and political movements such as the Civil Liberties Organization (CLO), the Campaign for Democracy (CD), the Committee for the Defense of Human Rights (CDHR), the National Democratic Coalition (NADECO), as well as trade unions such as the National Union of Petroleum Engineers and National Gas Workers (NUPENG), and the Academic Staff Union of Universities (ASUU), have at different times and levels since 1989 insisted on good governance, a halt to police brutality and abuse of human rights, as well as the democratization of the political system in Nigeria. Simply put, therefore, civil society in Africa, and Nigeria in particular, in spite of the repressive authoritarian state, has continued to press for democracy and human rights. There has indeed been a consistent struggle for the "Second independence," and the desire has been shown to create a democratic social order.

The Nigerian military claimed that it was committed to a transition to civil rule. The Babangida regime drew up an elaborate transition timetable between 1986 and 1993, and in spite of the elections at local, state, and federal levels, the military refused to hand over power to the supposed winner of the 1993 presidential election—Mashood Abiola—who was later locked up for treason against the state.

From the foregoing discourse, it is clear that Africa's socioeconomic crises, the imposition of externally induced structural adjustment programs, together with the declining capacity of the postcolonial state to provide necessary social services for its citizenry, led to the breakdown of the post-independence "social contract." With rising opposition from civil society, African regimes became more and more repressive. Human rights abuse became prevalent as a result of the enthronement of the authoritarian state. The authoritarian state, by its very nature, is not only undemocratic, but also an obstacle to Africa's democratization process. In the section that follows, an attempt is made to examine specifically how authoritarianism under the military in Nigeria exacerbated the abuse of fundamental human rights and stalled the struggle for democractic and good governance.

## MILITARY RULE AND HUMAN RIGHTS VIOLATION IN NIGERIA: 1983–1995

Human rights has long been a subject of debate among scholars (Shivji, 1989; Momoh and Adejunmobi, 1995; Welch, 1995; Ihonvbere and Shaw, 1998). Shivji has cogently documented the fact that despite its supposedly universalist orientation and attempts to apply it in the realm of international law and social science disciplines, the dominant human rights discourse "has essentially been a very specific ideological construct invoked at various conjunctures in history." Furthermore, he asserts that:

Human rights ideology, in its different forms, has historically played a legitimizing or mobilizing role in the struggle of classes to either rally for certain specific changes or to legitimize the status quo. And at no time, either philosophically or conceptually, has it applied to all human beings, for the very concept of "human" has varied historically and socially. (Shivji, 1989: 50)

The following analysis focuses on the concrete practice of regime behavior in terms of upholding or abusing the fundamental human rights of the citizenry. It investigates the extent to which the Babangida junta, through the use of state power, systematically abused human rights in Nigeria during its tenure. Although the regime exploited the ideological discourse of human rights to overthrow its predecessor, this era could be characterized as one of the moments in Nigeria's history when repression and authoritarian rule became the order of the day in the governance of civil society.

The Babangida regime, which came to power in August 1985, accused the Buhari-Idiagbon junta of high-handedness and repression, particularly through Decree No. 2, Detention of Persons, and Decree No. 4, Public Officers (Protection against False Accusation). Using Decree No. 2, the then chief of staff, Supreme Headquarters, Major-General Tunde Idiagbon was given the powers to arrest and detain people considered "state security risks." Furthermore, Decree No. 4 made it "an offence to make any false report in the press or to bring the federal government or public officers into ridicule or disrepute through the media" (Forrest, 1993: 97). It was under Decree No. 4 that two journalists from the *Guard-*

*ian* newspaper—Tunde Thompson and Nduka Irabor—were arrested and detained (Forrest, 1993).

Under a special Tribunal Decree No. 20 (Miscellaneous Offences), the regime introduced the death penalty retroactively for offenses such as drug trafficking, vandalizing electricity cables and oil pipelines, as well as destroying public property through arson. Using his relative popularity within the army as the chief of Army staff, Babangida cleverly evoked the concept of human rights against the Buhari-Idiagbon regime. Thus, in his maiden speech, Babangida lamented that the draconian decrees introduced by Buhari constituted violations of fundamental human rights. As he put it:

While this government recognises the bitterness created by the irresponsible excesses of the politicians, we consider it unfortunate that bitterness were applied to deal with past misdeeds. We must never allow ourselves to lose our sense of natural justice. The innocent cannot suffer the crimes of the guilty. The guilty should be punished only as a lesson for the future.

According to Babangida, as reported by Momoh and Adejunmobi:

In time . . . this government's intention is to uphold fundamental human rights. . . . we do not intend to lead a country where individuals are under the fear of expressing themselves, the public officers protection against false accusation Decree No.4 of 1984 is hereby repealed. The responsibility of the media to disseminate information shall be exercised without undue hindrance . . . the issue of decrees has generated a lot of controversies. It is the intention of this government to review all other decrees. (Momoh and Adejunmobi, 1995: 312)

As pointed out later, Babangida only appropriated the concept of human rights as an ideological gimmick to gain legitimacy. His tenure from 1985 to 1993 constitutes a dark moment in Nigeria's post-independence history. During these years, his authoritarian system became entrenched in the management of state affairs, flagrantly violating fundamental human rights, coopting the opposition, and thwarting the democratic process through the annulment of presidential elections to be held in June 1993.

The Babangida regime only paid lip-service to human rights. Nevertheless, because the regime expressed the commitment to uphold the fundamental principles of human rights, several sections of civil society expressed their support for the government, at least initially. For example, two days after Babangida's maiden speech to the nation, the Nigerian Labour Congress described the coup as a "healthy development" and affirmed that it was "particularly happy with the repeal of the obnoxious Decree No. 4." The University of Lagos branch of the Academic Staff Union of Universities (ASUU) for its part expressed "guarded optimism" that the regime was "ushering a new dispensation in the affairs of our country" (CLO, 1993a). As a CLO reporter observed, the Babangida regime worked its way into the hearts of the Nigerian populace by adopting a human rights program, or, more precisely, a human rights posturing.

Although Babangida gained acceptance and some measure of legitimacy on the platform of human rights, the regime's self-professed commitment clashed with the cold political realities of "military dictatorship characterized by awesomely wide arbitrary powers that circumscribed virtually every civil right and aborted dissent to a frightening scale. The resulting absence of legal restraints on agents of the regime gave a free reign to human rights violations" (CLO, 1993a: 6).

One of the first instances of human rights abuse by the Babangida regime was the massacre of students at Ahmadu Bello University on May 23, 1986. Among the students' grievances was their protest of the United States' flagrant invasion of Libya in mid-April 1986 and the government's "flirtation with the IMF, retrenchment of workers, cut in worker's salaries, imposition of obnoxious levies and graduate unemployment" (Mohammed, 1986: 98). The mobile police force attacked the university campus, killing five persons. Several civil organizations and professional groups condemned the government. The Nigerian Labour Congress (NLC) not only condemned the killings but also planned a peaceful demonstration for June 4, 1986 to show its solidarity with the students. As a result, the Babangida regime descended heavily on the NLC, ASUU, and the National Association of Nigerian Students' leadership, arresting and detaining them (Momoh and Adejunmobi, 1995: 322). This government action confirmed the worst fears about military rule:

Violations of human rights, including such widespread abuses as unlawful and indiscriminate arrest and detention by the police and security agents, continued. A plethora of decrees were promulgated, introducing more and more arbitrary powers and ousting the jurisdiction of the courts, mostly in cases involving violations of fundamental human rights. Intolerance and intimidation grew by the day. The adoption and implementation of structural adjustment programme created pockets of obscene affluence, worsened the living conditions of the poor and significantly undermined social and economic rights. (CLO, 1993a: 7)

As criticism against the regime continued to increase, the then minister of justice, Bola Ajibola, insisted that the violation of human rights in Nigeria was nothing compared to that in other developing countries: "there is nothing absolute about rights anywhere in the world," and "the individual pursuit of rights was subject to the right of the government to govern for the good of all and the right of society at large to preserve its corporate existence." The problem with this concept of human rights is that it arrogates the primacy of the interests of the state and those who control it in the enforcement of human rights. Simply put, fundamental human rights are subordinated to the whims and caprices of the hegemonic class in power.

The regime not only used repressive state apparatuses—the army, police, mobile police, quick intervention force—to sustain itself in power, but it also promulgated draconian decrees to insulate itself and its agents from the law of the land. For example, the detention of persons decree (No. 2) of 1984 was amended to provide for detention without trial for up to six months. Similarly, amended Decree No. 16 of 1984 banned workers from seeking legal redress following retrenchment, while Decree No. 47 of 1989 prohibited student protest. In addition, Decree No. 17 of 1986 banned senior staff associates from affiliating with the NLC.

One area in which the Babangida regime abused fundamental human rights was in that of press freedom. Specifically, in 1993 the regime closed down the following media houses: Concord Press, which belonged to Moshooed Abiola, the apparent winner of the 1993 presidential election, *Abuja Newsday*, Sketch Press, *The Observer*, the Ogun State Broadcasting Corporation (OGBC), *Punch*, the *News/Tempo*, and *Tell*. *Newswatch Magazine*, whose editor, Dele Giwa, was murdered with a parcel bomb on October 19, 1986, also suffered closures and clampdowns from the military junta. The government's opposition to the media and its arbitrary closures and arrests were motivated by what the regime viewed as reports constituting "incitement" to civil disobedience or as undermining state security. In its effort to ensure total censorship of the media, the regime promulgated Decree No. 35, which proscribed offensive publications. This decree empowered the president and commander-in-chief "to proscribe or authorize the seizure and confiscation of any publication if he was satisfied that it contained any article or material which was likely to: (i) disrupt the process of democracy and peaceful transition to civil rule; or (ii) hinder or prevent the progress and process of grassroots democracy as established by the transition to civil rule programme or disturb the peace and public order in Nigeria" (CLO, 1993a: 74). The regime also promulgated Newspapers Decree No. 48 which retrospectively legalized the closing of the media houses already mentioned. Other media houses that were later closed down under the provision of this decree included the *Guardian* newspapers and the *Reporter* belonging to Alex Ibru and retired Major-General Shehu Yar'adua, who died in detention in December 1997. Shehu Musa Yar'Adua, Nigeria's Army Chief of Staff, Supreme Headquarters (1975–1979), was arrested by General Sani Abacha, the then-head of state, on March 8, 1995, for alleged involvement in a coup plot. Yar'Adua was then tried by a military tribunal and sentenced to death. However, following appeals from leaders within and outside Nigeria, Yar'Adua's sentence was commuted to a 15-year prison sentence. In December 1995, Yar'Adua collapsed in Abakalaki prison (Eastern Nigeria) and died. It was not until after the sudden death of Sani Abacha in 1998 that the dictator's security agents confessed to murdering Yar'Adua in prison. The Abacha era (1993–1998) has been described as Nigeria's dark days because of the massive corruption, gross abuse of human rights as well as total absence of rule of law in the conduct of state–society affairs.

It is indeed ironic that, although the Babangida regime upon its inception claimed to defend human rights, its practical performance in relation to freedom of press and expression clearly demonstrates how an authoritarian regime can repress the media and coerce any dissenting opinion to maintain itself in power. Having examined the degree to which the mass media were emasculated under Babangida's authoritarian regime, it is pertinent to briefly examine violations of the human rights of minority nationality groups. The government's reaction to the Ogoni struggle against environmental degradation and the right to decent living and socioeconomic development provides a good illustration of human rights abuse by military regimes in Nigeria. The following section briefly examines the Ogoni issue with a view to demonstrating how social and economic rights have been denied to civil society within the context of Nigeria's authoritarian state.

## VIOLATION OF MINORITY AND HUMAN RIGHTS: THE CASE OF THE OGONIS

Nigeria, as a federation, has about 250 different ethnic groups dominated by three major groups: the Hausa-Fulani predominantly in the north, the Yorubas mainly in the southwest, and the Igbos predominantly in the east. These groups have dominated the politics of the country since independence (CLO, 1993b). The other smaller ethnic groups (or "minorities) have in most cases been marginalized from the control and exercise of state power. In a federation, the control of political power at the center involves access to economic resources and its allocation to states and local governments. This implies that political competition tends to be vicious and a source of instability. In addition, access to state power also involves controlling resources that could be utilized for the purposes of patronage (Joseph, 1987) as well as intimidating opposing social and political groups.

The Ogoni crisis erupted and spilled over into international politics, leading to Nigeria's suspension from the Commonwealth in 1995. It can be understood from the perspective of the struggle by social groups within an authoritarian state for the assertion of their social, economic, and environmental rights. Naanen believes that the Ogoni problem is fundamentally

that of being a minority within a country where ethnic domination takes the form of a highly competitive zero-sum contest. Their particular circumstance has placed a great historical burden upon them, and to avoid liquidation as a separate group requires constant struggle against tremendous odds. Their land, moreover, is rich in oil and natural gas, assets difficult for a small community to defend and control for their own use within a large multi-ethnic polity. The Ogoni trace their present tribulations to these natural resources the control and exploitation of which constitute an important dimension of internal colonialism against which they have to struggle. (Naanen, 1995: 64)

The Ogonis' struggle for a fair share of the wealth generated from oil and for control of environmental degradation, particularly by the Shell Oil Company, has been met by violence from the state. At the level of environmental pollution, "vast areas of terrestrial and acquatic vegetation have been destroyed by oil spills. Marine life, for which the vegetation provided a life-support system, has largely disappeared with the vegetation while oil pipelines have covered the little land available for farming" (Naanen, 1995: 66).

In pressing its demands, the Movement for the Survival of Ogoni People (MOSOP) proposed what it termed the Ogoni Bill of Rights to the federal government in which the Ogonis demanded, *inter alia* not only political autonomy but also

1. Political control of Ogoni affairs by Ogoni people.
2. The right to the control and use of a fair proportion of Ogoni economic resources for the development of the Ogonis.
3. Adequate and direct representation in all Nigerian national institutions;
4. The right to protect the Ogoni environment and ecology from further degradation. (CLO, 1993b)

Furthermore, MOSOP was authorized to make representation to international bodies such as the European Union, the United Nations Commission on Human Rights, the Commonwealth Secretariat, and the African Commission on Human and People's rights (Naanen, 1995). In addition, Ken Saro-Wiwa, the spokesman of the Ogonis, was mandated to affiliate MOSOP with the Unrepresented Nations and People Organization (UNPO). He was also instrumental in launching the Ethnic Minorities Organization of Africa (EMIROAF). Under the auspices of MOSOP, the Ogonis, with an estimated population of 500,000, organized a peaceful protest on January 4, 1993. Approximately 300,000 Ogonis participated in the protest.

Following this protest, Ogoni leaders were invited to Lagos for "very cordial talks with senior officials of the Federal Government" (CLO, 1993b). Although the president assured them that their requests would be looked into within 12 days, the government deployed troops into Ogoniland for routine patrol. Thus, clashes between security men and the Ogoni people began. In one incident, armed soldiers arrested about 37 villagers from Rumuekpe and compelled them to sign an agreement to pay for the repair of a military rifle which they allegedly damaged in a rampage (CLO, 1993b). In April and May 1993, bloody clashes broke out in Bori during which two Ogonis were shot and beaten by armed soldiers (CLO, 1993b: 332).

As the sporadic clashes in Ogoniland between the community and security men continued, the Ogonis boycotted the June 12, 1993 presidential elections. Their rationale was that any form of participation by them would amount to legitimizing the 1989 constitution, which by the provision of Section 42 (3) usurped the ownership of their land and resources. Kenuel Saro-Wiwa and two other MOSOP leaders were arrested on July 13, 1993 and arraigned before a magistrate's court on charges of sedition. They were accused of distributing "seditious pamphlets," producing the Ogoni National Flag, and printing the Ogoni anthem. They were refused bail and remanded in custody until September 20, 1993. However, the interim national government under Ernest Shonekan—to whom Babangida hastily relinquished power following the annulment of the June 12, 1993 elections—released Saro-Wiwa and the other MOSOP leaders.

At the level of the oil communities, however, violent clashes erupted between the Ogonis and the Andonis on August 2, 1993. According to MOSOP, the Andonis destroyed three Ogoni towns, which led to the displacement of about 26,000 Ogonis as well as the death of 1,200 people. The Andonis claimed that 200 of their kinsmen were killed by the Ogonis, while 50 others were abducted. The question that arises is: Why did the security men not control the communal clashes that led to killings? MOSOP, in its explanation, accused the government and Shell Oil Development Company of instigating the communal crisis and supporting the Andonis (CLO, 1993b: 337).

The climax of the Ogoni crisis was the hanging of the MOSOP leader Kenuel Saro-Wiwa and eight other human rights activists in November 1995, following their conviction by the military tribunal. Saro-Wiwa and the other eight MOSOP leaders were accused of engineering a riot involving the National Youth Council of Ogoni People (NYCOP) in May 1994 during which four Ogoni elders—chief Ignatius Kogbara, Alber Badey, Edward Kobani, and Simeon Orage—were murdered for their alleged complicity with Shell Petroleum Development Corporation. The trial of Saro-Wiwa along with the other eight accused MOSOP leaders sparked considerable controversy not only because it was conducted by a tribunal based on provisions of the draconian Decree No. 2 of 1987, but most importantly because to take legal action (e.g., by appealing) under that decree was outside the judiciary's jurisdiction. Only the Provisional Ruling Council—Abacha's highest ruling junta composed essentially of military commanders and loyalists—could look into appeals from convicted persons.

During the trial, the defense counsel led by the human rights activists Chief Gani Fawehinmi and Femi Falana withdrew from the trial alleging that "the tribunal was behaving as if it was acting on orders." Furthermore, the defense counsel was displeased because the tribunal "refused to obey a Lagos High Court which had ordered that proceedings be halted" ("Nigeria's Suspension," 1995: 21). In spite of all the protests by the defense counsel and the appeals for clemency by the international community, Nigeria's military junta confirmed the verdict of the tribunal. Following the Provisional Ruling Council meeting on the matter in November 1995, Brigadier-General Victor Malu announced that "we completely accepted the verdict. It was a case of murder and we accepted the totality of the pronouncement and verdict of the tribunal that those convicted should die by hanging" ("Nigeria's Suspension," 1995: 22). Consequently, Saro-Wiwa and the other eight MOSOP leaders were executed.

The United States and the British Commonwealth, among other countries, condemned the execution partly because the Ogoni struggle is widely conceived as a legitimate struggle by a nationality for its fundamental human rights. The swift manner in which the military junta confirmed the death sentence and ordered the execution, thereby neglecting international opinion, further exposed the insensitivity of the military dictatorship to issues of human rights. The Ogoni issue demonstrates the extent to which authoritarian rule has been entrenched in the Nigerian political system and its implications for democracy and human rights.

## CONCLUSION

This chapter has examined the character of the authoritarian state in postcolonial Africa and how it violates fundamental human rights. It has been argued that the question of human rights is related not only to Africa's economic crises but also to the question of democratization and transition to civil rule. Through the Nigerian case study, an attempt has been made to demonstrate that through the ascendance of the military, particularly under the Babangida junta, harsh economic reform policies such as the Structural Adjustment Program were introduced that dislocated civil society by exacerbating poverty and civil unrest. As civil society protested against the harsh realities of IMF/World Bank-inspired reform measures, the Babangida regime unleashed terror and violence (see especially CLO Reports of 1993 and 1994). Fundamental human rights in areas such as freedom of speech, the media, and association were severely curtailed.

Although the regime claimed that it was organizing a transition to civil rule, Babangida himself continued to make plans for perpetuating his regime in power. Lewis (1994) argues that during Babangida's final years in power, he ruled the country in an arbitrary and autocratic fashion, personalizing political authority to an extent that is unprecedented in Nigeria's history. The state security service, which acted as the intelligence apparatus of the regime, engaged in arbitrary arrests, detention, assassinations, and general abuse of fundamental human rights (Lewis, 1994).

The cancellation of the June 1993 presidential elections and the subsequent incarceration and death of the winner, Moshooed Abiola, plunged Nigeria into even deeper political turmoil, thereby giving the military room to hold on to political power. The Ogoni crisis and the execution of Saro-Wiwa, along with eight other MOSOP leaders, demonstrated the extent to which the military junta was prepared to behave autocratically and violate basic human rights. It is absolutely necessary for the oppressed classes in postcolonial Africa to continue the struggle for human rights and democracy.

## REFERENCES

Abubakar, D. (1986). *Oil, State and Power Politics: The Political Economy of Nigeria's Foreign Policy, 1960–1980*. Unpublished Ph.D. dissertation, University of Wisconsin–Madison.

———. (1995). "The Authoritarian State and the Question of Democracy in Nigeria." *Journal of Social and Management Sciences* 2(1).

Adekanye, J.B. (1995). "Structural Adjustment, Democratisation and Rising Ethnic Tensions in Africa." *Development of Change* 26: 355–374.

Ake, C. (1994). *Democratization of Disempowerment in Africa*. Lagos: Malthouse Press.

Anyang' Nyong'o, P. (1988). "Political Instability and the Prospects for Democracy in Africa." *Africa Development* 8(1): 71–86.

Apter, D. (1965). *The Politics of Modernization*. Chicago: University of Chicago Press.

Bangura, Y. (1986). "Structural Adjustment and the Political Questions." *Review of African Political Economy* 37: 24–37.

———. (1988). "The Crisis of Underdevelopment and the Transition to Civil Rule: Conceptualizing the Question of Democracy in Nigeria." *Africa Development* 8(1): 33–50.

————. (1992). "Authoritarian Rule and Democracy in Africa: A Theoretical Discourse." In P. Gibbon et al. (eds.), *Authoritarianism, Democracy and Adjustment: The Politics of Economic Reform in Africa.* Uppsala: SIAS.

————. (1995). *Reflections on Recent Patterns of Political Development.* Paper presented at a seminar on international security at the Graduate School of International Studies, Geneva, July 20.

Bangura, Y. et al. (1996). *Political Behavior.* Lanham: University Press of America.

Beckman, B. (1992). "Empowerment or Repression: The World Bank and the Politics of African Adjustment." In P. Gibbon et al. (eds.), *Authoritarianism, Democracy and Adjustment: The Politics of Economic Reform in Africa.* Uppsala: SIAS.

Beckman, B. and Bangura, Y. (1989). *African Workers and Structural Adjustment: A Nigerian Case Study.* Paper for UNRISD Conference on Economic Crisis and Third World Countries: Impact and Response. Kingston, Jamaica, April 3–6, 1996.

Callaghy, T. M. (1984). *The State-Society Struggle: Zaire in Comparative Perspective.* New York: Columbia University Press.

Central Bank of Nigeria. (1994). *Annual Report.* Lagos: Central Bank of Nigeria.

Civil Liberties Organisation (CLO). (1993a). *A Report on the Human Rights Violations of the Military Regime of General Ibrahim Babangida.* Lagos: CLO.

————. (1993b). *Annual Report on Human Rights in Nigeria.* Lagos: CLO.

————. (1994). *Above the Law: A Report on Torture and Extra-judicial Killings by the Police in Lagos.* Lagos: CLO.

Collier, D. (1979). *The New Authoritarianism in Latin America.* Princeton, NJ: Princeton University Press.

Decalo, S. (1976). *Coups and the Army Rule in Africa: Studies in Military Style.* New Haven, CT: Yale University Press.

Doornbos, M. (1990). "The African State in Academic Debate: Retrospect and Prospect." *Journal of Modern African Studies* 28(2): 179–198.

Falola, T. and Ihonvbere, J.O. (1985). *The Rise and Fall of Nigeria's Second Republic.* London: Zed Books.

Forrest, T. (1986). "The Political Economy of Civil Rule and the Economic Crisis in Nigeria 1979–1984." *Review of African Political Economy* 35: 4–26.

Forrest, T. (1993). *Politics and Economic Development in Nigeria.* Boulder, CO: Westview Press.

Gibbon, P. et al. (eds.). (1992). *Authoritarianism, Democracy and Adjustment: The Politics of Reform in Africa.* Uppsala: SIAS.

Huntington, S.P. (1968). *Political Order in Changing Societies.* New Haven, CT: Yale University Press.

Hyden, G. (1983). *No Shortcuts to Progress: African Development Management in Perspective.* London: Heinemann.

Ihonvbere, J.O. (1993). "Economic Crisis Structural Adjustment and Social Crisis in Nigeria." *World Development* 21(1): 141–153.

————. (1994). "The Irrelevant State, Ethnicity and the Quest for Nationhood in Africa." *Ethnic and Racial Studies* 17(1): 42–60.

Ihonvbere, J.O. and Shaw, T. (1998). *Illusions of Power: Nigeria in Transition.* Trenton, NJ: Africa World Press.

International Monetary Fund. (1994). *World Economic Outloook.* New York: IMF.

Iyayi, F. (1986). "The Primitive Accumulation of Capital in a Neo-colony." *Review of African Political Economy* (35): 27–39.

Jackson, R.H. and Roseberg, C.G. (1982). *Personal Rule in Black Africa.* Berkeley: University of California Press.

Joseph, R. (1987). *Democracy and Prebendal Politicis in Nigeria: The Rise and Fall of the Second Republic.* Cambridge, England: Cambridge University Press.

"The Learning Process." (1996). *West Africa* (May 4–17): 436–439.

Leftwich, A. (1994). "Governance, the State and the Politics of Development." *Development and Change* 25: 363–386.

Lewis, P.M. (1994). "Endgame in Nigeria: The Politics of a Failed Democratic Transition." *African Affairs* 93: 333–340.

Mamdani, M., et al. (1988). *Social Movements. Social Transformation and the Struggle for Democracy in Africa.* Dakar: CODESRIA.

Mkandawire, T. (1995). *Beyond Crisis: Towards Democratic Developmental States in Africa.* Paper for 8th General Assembly, Dakar, CODESRIA.

Mkandawire, T. (ed.). (1995). *The Politics of Structural Adjustment in Africa.* Dakar: CODESRIA.

Mkandawire, T. and Saludo, C. (1999). *Our Continent, Our Future: African Perspectives on Structural Adjustment.* Trenton, NJ: Africa World Press.

Mohammed, A.S. (1986). "The Aftermath of the Ahmadu Bello University Students Crisis of May 1988." *Review of African Political Economy* 37 (December): 97–104.

Momoh, A. and Adejunmobi, S. (eds.). (1995). *The Political Economy of Nigeria under Military Rule: 1984–1994.* Harare: SAPES.

Naanen, B. (1995). "Oil-Producing Minorities and the Restructuring of Nigerian Federalism: The Case of the Ogoni People." *Journal of Commonwealth and Comparative Politics* 33(1): 46–78.

"Nigeria's Suspension from the Commonwealth." (1995). *Policy Magazine* (November 20): 20–22.

Nzongola-Ntalaja, G. (1987). *Revolution and Counter-Revolution in Africa: Essays in Contemporary Politics.* London: Zed Books.

———. (1994). "The State and Democracy in Africa." *African Association of Political Science Newsletter* 17(8).

———. (1996)."Democratic Transitions in Africa." *AAPS Newsletter* 1(22): 5–9.

Nzongola-Ntalaja, G. and Lee, M.C. (1998). *The State and Democracy in Africa.* Trenton, NJ: Africa World Press.

Olukoshi, A.O. (1995). *Africa: Democratizing under Conditions of Economic Stagnation.* Paper for 8th General Assembly, CODESRIA.

Othman, S. (1984). "Classes Crises, and Coups: The Demise of the Shagari Regime." *African Affairs* 83(333): 441–461.

Purcell, S.K. and Purcell, J.F. (1980). "State and Society in Mexico." *World Politics.* 32 (January): 194–227.

Rasheed, S. (1995). "The Democratization Process and Popular Participation in Africa: Emerging Realities and the Challenges Ahead." *Development and Change* 26: 333–354.

Robinson, D. (1990). "Civil Service Remuneration in Africa." *International Labor Review* 129(3): 56–78.

Rudebeck, L. (ed.). (1992). *When Democracy Makes Sense: Studies in the Democratic Pattern of Third World Popular Movements*. Uppsala: AKIUT.

Shivji, I. (1989). *The Concept of Human Rights in Africa*. Dakar: CODESRIA.

Skocpol, T. et al. (eds.). (1985). *Bringing the State Back in*. Cambridge: Cambridge University Press.

Stepan, A. (ed.). (1973). *Authoritarian Brazil: Origins, Policies and Future*. New Haven, CT: Yale University Press.

Thomas, C. Y. (1984). *The Rise of the Authoritarian State in Peripheral Societies*. New York: Monthly Review Press.

Welch, C. E. (1995). "The Ogoni and Self-determination: Increasing Violence in Nigeria." *Journal of Modern African Studies* 33(4): 635–649.

World Bank. (1980–1991). *World Debt Tables*. New York: World Bank.

Wunsch, J.S. and Olowu, D. (1995). *The Failure of the Centralized State: Institutions and Self-governance in Africa*. San Francisco: Institute for Contemporary Studies.

Young, M.C. (1994). "Zaire: The Shattered Illusion of the Integral State." *Journal of Modern African Studies* 32(2): 247–263.

———. (1995). "Democracy and the Ethnic Question." *Africa Demos* 3(4): 24–25.

# Part III

# Poverty and Inequality

Chapter 6

# The Feminization of Poverty in Rural Sub-Saharan Africa

## Kyama K. Kabadaki

### INTRODUCTION

This chapter focuses on the poverty experienced by females who reside in sub-Saharan rural Africa. Countries north of the Sahara and the Republic of South Africa are excluded because of their relatively unique social and economic systems. While most of the information presented was obtained by document analysis, qualitative data gathered in Hoima District in Western Uganda in December 1993 and June–July 1995 is included. The purpose of that research was to gain insight into the needs and problems of rural women. Participant observation and in-depth interviews were carried out during visits to 10 villages. Altogether, 25 women were interviewed. In one village, the author attended a women's association meeting twice, and in another village three hours were spent with a Habitat for Humanity mixed work group.

#### Poverty in Sub-Saharan Africa

O'Connor (1991: 1) defines poverty as "Low level of income, whether in terms of cash or of subsistence production, and therefore, low levels of consumption of goods and services." Often an absolute approach that determines the necessary cash for sufficiently meeting basic needs and establishes the poverty line accordingly is used as a measure of poverty. Alternatively, the Human Development Index, which employs certain criteria for determining the quality of life, is utilized as an indicator of poverty. Life expectancy, literacy, and average purchasing power are part of the criteria. Whatever method is used, sub-Saharan Africa is undeniably poor. It is believed that 15 of the poorest countries in the world are found in Africa (O'Connor, 1991). A study in Malawi indicated that 55 percent of the population could be categorized as poor (House and Zimalirana, 1992). With regard to the Human Development Index, sub-Saharan Africa has the highest infant mortality in the world. The average is 95 deaths per 1,000 live births, while the average for developed nations is 10 deaths per 1,000 live births. The region has the lowest life expectancy in the world: 54 years for women and 51 years for men, on the average. Furthermore, the region has the lowest literacy rates in the world. Only 43 percent of adult women and 67 percent of adult men are literate (United Nations, 1995).

While the extent of poverty varies from country to country in sub-Saharan Africa, it also varies in individual countries on the basis of region, categories of people likely to experience it, and the degree to which it is experienced. For instance, a distinction is made between the poor and the extremely poor. The latter category is sometimes referred to as ultra-poor or core poor. Annual income for each individual in this category is less than $275. This group constitutes 30 percent of the sub-Saharan Africa population. Annual income for each person in the "poor" category is less than $370; this category constitutes 45 percent of the population. The majority of these poor individuals live in rural areas. For example, the 1980 International Labour Organization (ILO) estimates for Zambia indicated that 80 percent of rural households were below the minimum basic needs level. On the other hand, only 25 percent of urban households were below that level. In Uganda, 57 percent of the poor live in rural areas, whereas only 35 percent reside in urban areas. It is also reported that women represent the large bulk of the poor and the extremely poor (Geisler, 1992; House and Zimalirana, 1992; Uganda Government, 1994; UNICEF, 1991). It is evident that rural women are among the most vulnerable to poverty. The reasons they are trapped in poverty, the ways they are affected by it, and suggestions for effective strategies related to breaking their poverty cycle are the main focus of this chapter.

## RURAL WOMEN'S POVERTY EXPERIENCE

Although the circumstances of rural women vary, the majority of them struggle constantly for survival through subsistence farming, food gathering, and petty trading. Because of overcultivation, overgrazing, simplistic methods of farming, infertile soil, soil erosion, and occasional droughts, a number of women find it difficult to produce enough food for their households. The problem is exacerbated by the lack of adequate food storage or processing mechanisms. So while a household may have a surplus of food one season, it may experience food insecurity the following season. Women are more affected by food shortage than men are partly because it is considered their obligation to provide food for the family and partly because tradition, in many African communities, dictates that males be given the best share of food and be served first. Consequently, malnutrition and undernutrition, which are common among sub-Saharan African children, are also prevalent among rural women. It is estimated that 50 percent of African women are undernourished and 66 percent of pregnant African women experience anemia, which leaves them susceptible to illnesses, complications in pregnancy, and maternal death (Agiobu-Kammer, 1992; Cohen, 1994; Geisler, 1992; O'Connor, 1991; Topouzis, 1990).

For the extremely poor rural females, adequate clothing is not within their reach. The following excerpt from the author's journal relates to visits to villages in Hoima district: "It was an unexpected late afternoon visit to Yeneki's home. She was kneeling by the kitchen entrance as she pounded cassava. We stared at each other for a minute—she was surprised to see me—I was struggling to hold back tears. She looked thirty years older and her dress from the waist up was a mere conglomeration of strips of torn material."

Yeneki's wardrobe consisted of the dress she had on and only one other garment. The only decent clothing worn by her children were their school uniforms. However, at that time they were out of school because of problems with school fees. The family's financial situation had gotten so bad that her husband had gone to Kampala City to look for a job. Unfortunately, Yeneki's situation was not unique. Strangely, such situations were not as common 20 years earlier.

Inadequate housing and poor sanitation are problems experienced by rural women as well as rural men. These problems, combined with environment and temperatures that foster the growth of numerous microorganisms, result in the prevalence and spread of many diseases. Malnutrition, undernutrition, and improper clothing make poor women and their children vulnerable to these diseases. Consequently, being sick or caring for the sick often disrupts these women's routines. It also lowers their productivity.

Data collected through interviewing and listening to rural women in Hoima district indicated that many of them did not have any cash. Yet, in addition to being responsible for providing food for their family members and being caretakers when necessary, they had to find essential consumer goods such as salt, cooking oil, sugar, and soap. They also tended to be very concerned about children who were missing school due to lack of school fees and uniforms. A number of them cried as they described their hardships. Several of these women were married. However, some husbands did not share their income with their wives on a regular basis. Some men simply did not have the money, but others spent their money on personal needs, consuming alcohol or supporting other "wives." Rural women's lack of access to their husbands' financial resources is consistent with research done in other African rural communities (Baker, 1995; Beoku-Betts, 1990; Blumberg, 1992).

Lack of cash affects rural women in several other ways. Sometimes they are not able to seek medical care for themselves or their children either because of the lack of cash for transport or their inability to cover involved expenses. In one household, three children had severe coughs, but their mother could not afford cough mixture. In another household, two children were very sick, but their mother could not afford the minimal registration fee required at the hospital's outpatient treatment center. Sometimes hardships, conflicts, and excessive demands result in spouse abuse, especially wife-beating. Unfortunately, many women remain in these abusive situations because their weak financial position limits their options. The fear of losing their children also prevents some of them from leaving their husbands. For a few women, the stress is so excessive that they suffer from depression. The author's observations are expressed in part of her unpublished poem entitled "Cousin Ganda."

> Her eyes remained fixed on me.
> As if I had been transformed.
> I quickly reminded her
> How we grew up like sisters . . .
> How I wanted to look like her . . .
> A gentle smile was her only response
> Her once round, dancing eyes remained still.

What on the surface appeared like Ganda's normal demeanor was in essence depression, according to this writer's judgment. Very often the depression some women experience goes unnoticed.

### Norms and Tradition

The majority of sub-Saharan African societies are patrilineal. In the past, women in these societies did not own or inherit property. The most significant assets were cattle and land. A large herd of cattle was a sign of wealth. Since women did not have to pay bride wealth, ownership of cattle was not as instrumental to them as it was to men. On the other hand, women had a right to the livestock product and to the use of land. Another reason females did not inherit property from their parents was the understanding that they got married, moved away, and spent most of their lives in their husbands' lineages and clans. Males also took their responsibility of providing for their wives seriously. However, the introduction of a cash economy favored groups of people who owned property, but the norms for ownership and inheritance of property did not change. The few matrilineal societies were an exception. It is believed that females in matrilineal societies who previously had some rights for property ownership lost them at that time (Gran, 1983).

The social structure of African societies has also changed. Today there are many more women without husbands. It is believed that females head about 33 percent of the households. The percentage tends to be higher for rural areas. For instance, in Kenya, women head 30 percent of the households, but the percentage of households headed by females in rural areas is 34. The percentages are higher for countries such as Swaziland, Zimbabwe, and Botswana (UNICEF, 1992). This change is due to rural-urban migration and the death of able-bodied men as a result of political persecution and wars. On the other hand, the social protection women had in the past such as community or lineage ownership of land, and the obligation of the kings, chiefs, relatives, friends or neighbors to ensure the well-being of individuals in need and in crisis have virtually vanished.

## Limited Benefits from Agriculture for Rural Women

The agricultural sector is the backbone of most African economies. It is estimated that women are responsible for 60 to 80 percent of food production. Most of the food produced is for household subsistence, but often the surplus is sold in local markets. Women also make a significant contribution to food processing (Bates and Lofchie, 1980; Blumberg, 1992; Daddieh, 1989).

Some rural women participate in the production of cash crops. According to Guyer (1986), women provide the labor for 35 percent of tobacco production in Swaziland, 37 to 47 percent of cotton production in Malawi, and 70 percent of coffee production in Rwanda. In some countries, women work as laborers for tea picking and perform essential tasks such as weeding, mulching, and harvesting.

The money rural women get from trading agricultural products is often spent on buying essential consumer goods to ensure the well-being of their households. Although they contribute to the production of cash crops, their gain from those crops is hampered by a number of factors. First, cash crops such as rice, cocoa, and groundnuts were introduced to men only during the colonial rule. Establishing the European pattern of farming in sub-Saharan Africa was a matter of convenience. What mattered to the colonists was extracting raw materials for industries in Europe quickly and cheaply. Consequently, women did not benefit from the sale of cash crops as much as men did. Given the "separate purse" tendency alluded to earlier, women did not automatically have access to their husbands' financial resources. Subsequently, rural women were pushed further into the underprivileged class.

Second, the newly independent African countries continued with agricultural patterns established during colonial rule mainly because sale of cash crops on international markets was needed for foreign exchange, which was in turn needed for financing development plans. These agricultural policies meant favoring large-scale farming and providing support in the form of modern technology, capital for buying biological inputs, and extension services. As private ownership of land for the purpose of expanding cash crop farms increases, rural women get pushed to smaller plots and, in some cases, to less fertile areas. Not only are opportunities for extra cash from crop surplus reduced or lost, but some women struggle harder to meet food needs for their households. For instance, in some West African communities women have to weed cash crops in exchange for permission to grow food crops on their husbands' farms (Beoku-Betts, 1990; Daddieh, 1989). Baker (1995), discussing agriculture in Gambia, mentions that women buy groundnuts from their husbands or other males in their household for the purpose of trading.

Women have not benefited much from cash crops primarily because of their lack of opportunity to own or inherit land. Female heads of households in particular are negatively impacted by the scramble for land. Although married women have to do extra work such as weeding and harvesting their husbands' farms as required by custom, in addition to working on their plots for food production, they have more opportunities for limited land use. With regard to the land problem, Daddieh (1989) cites Kenya as an example. In the 1980s, only 5 percent of the women owned land. Land reforms have been initiated in a number of African countries, but still few women own land in their own right. In Uganda, only 7 percent of the women own land and 8 percent have leaseholds. The pieces of land owned by women are small. Only 3 percent of female landowners have more than two hectares each. On the other hand, approximately 84 percent of landholders are males. Eighty-seven percent of the male landowners possess more than two hectares each (Uganda Government, 1994). Some women were not able to get land titles because the process is complicated, and it requires payment of more than U.S. $50, which they cannot afford.

Even when women attempt to grow cash crops in addition to their struggle for subsistence farming, their production is limited by lack of resources. Many of them cannot afford tractors or oxen for ploughing and biological inputs. They do not have access to credit because they do not possess land, cattle, or any other property that can serve as collateral. Lack of knowledge about banking and other finance institutions also limits their chances for credit (Basgall, 1988; Guyer, 1986). A number of countries have addressed the credit problem by encouraging indigenous institutions such as women's saving associations, establishing special programs for making loans more accessible to rural residents, and setting up financial institutions aimed specifically at addressing women's needs such as the H-P Women's Development Company in Zambia. However, still a small percentage of the poor rural women are taking advantage of these programs. For instance, the Rural Farmers Scheme in Uganda was established in 1987. By 1993, only 22.7 percent of approved loans were for individual women. For the Uganda Women Finance and Credit Trust, which was established in 1984, only 200 women had received loans by 1994 (Uganda Government, 1994). None of the women interviewed in Hoima district had heard about these schemes.

Rural African women's production in agriculture has also been hampered by inadequate extension services. According to Blumberg (1992), less than 5 percent of female farmers were reached by extension services in the early 1980s. At that time, only 2.6 percent of the extension workers were women. It is believed that extension workers sidelined women partly because they were small-scale farmers and partly because the male workers avoided female farmers because of traditional attitudes. For example, government officials in Sierra Leone believed that husbands were reluctant to have male workers train their wives, that women were preoccupied with domestic responsibility, and that they were shy (Beoku-Betts, 1990). According to Ayisi's report, a female agriculture worker in Mozambique was told that women should work at home instead of being involved in programs for farmers. She was also told that women should not talk directly to men (Ayisi, 1991). Blumberg (1992) states that a number of extension workers believed that information given to husbands would get passed on to their wives. However, studies in Tanzania, Cameroon, Malawi, and Burkina Faso revealed that the information was rarely passed on to women, sometimes the women had difficulty understanding the information, and other times the information was irrelevant to their needs.

A number of governments have responded to extension service concerns by increasing the number of extension workers. By 1990, 7 percent of extension workers in Africa were females. Some countries, such as Nigeria and Kenya, have initiated strategies for delivering extension services to women's groups (Blumberg, 1992). Nevertheless, extension services are still inadequate. It is believed that increasing women's roles in decision making, administration, and research pertaining to agriculture will facilitate improvement of extension services.

Finally, many women do not benefit from agriculture because they are deprived of the right to make decisions about the marketing of crops and they are denied the right to control income from agricultural products, especially cash crops. Geisler (1992: 127) states that "men spent a much larger share of their incomes on their own personal needs. The trend seems to be more pronounced in poorer households, where husbands are also more likely to claim part of what wives earn for their own personal use."

This tendency led to a crisis for the women's association in Hoima district. It seems that the chairperson's husband spent the association's money without the chairperson's knowledge. Apparently, he believed he was entitled to his wife's "purse contents."

## CRISIS, DEVELOPMENT POLICIES, AND MARGINALIZATION OF RURAL FEMALES

By 1970, several sub-Saharan African countries had demonstrated the intent to focus on rural development. However, this effort was later stymied by economic stagnation and decline, a rise in oil prices, and the falling prices of agricultural products being exported to developed nations. Civil conflicts, wars, political instability, and the drought in the 1980s exacerbated these problems. As a result, economic decline continued at a fast pace (O'Connor, 1991).

On the other hand, in spite of declared policies for rural development, there was demonstrated urban bias in development. Timberlake (1986: 9) describes the situation as follows: "The cities where the governments live have been torn from the countryside, and development budgets have gone to filling those cities and hotels, factories, universities and cars." He goes on to say that labor and produce were "milked" from the rural people, but very little was given back to them in terms of money or support.

Aid from the developed nations was fueled into sub-Saharan Africa during the last two decades. However, its impact on the rural masses was minimal. Some scholars believed that foreign aid perpetuated the urban bias. Others felt that the developed nations gave assistance for the sake of sustaining their own economies. Conditions such as exports from donor countries and exclusive rights to the marketing of needed items were cited as proof. Other scholars and policy analysts blamed the lack of progress on experts from developed nations who were giving advice for projects that were failing. So while the policies for a basic needs approach to development were good, the implementation of designed programs was not appropriate (Agunga, 1989; O'Connor, 1991; Timberlake, 1986). According to Timberlake (1986), more than half of the annual $7–8 billion in aid went to finance the numerous expatriates. Some of the problems were attributed to the corruption and mismanagement perpetuated by African leaders and government officials.

Although rural women did not benefit greatly from development projects during the 1970s and 1980s, employment in the formal sector was not an option because there were few manufacturing industries in rural areas. Because of illiteracy, many women were at a disadvantage when they had to compete for employment. For those who were able to work, earnings were low due to lack of skills. For example, Daddieh (1989) and Rathgeber (1989) state that women's employment on commercial farms entails tedious, repetitive work such as sorting the harvest, carrying pans of manure to the fields, and carrying loads of harvest to designated locations for transportation. On the other hand, rural women benefited a little more from the informal sector. Women have ventured into such areas as beer brewing in Burkina Faso, Botswana, and Ghana, Gara dyeing in Sierra Leone, and clothing production in Ghana and Nigeria. Mostly, women are also involved in food processing and crafts such as baskets, mats, and necklaces. Unfortunately, problems related to capital, access to credit, and marketing keep levels of profit low. As in the case of agriculture, the majority of rural women who are illiterate and very poor have not been able to take advantage of credit programs set up specifically for the informal sector (Liedholm and Mead, 1986; Morewagae, Seemule, and Rempel, 1995).

The structural adjustment programs that were imposed on a number of African countries by the World Bank and the International Monetary Fund (IMF) have also contributed to rural women's increased poverty. Drastic cuts in funding for social services have affected health services and transportation, privatization and currency devaluation have resulted in soaring inflation, and reductions in consumer subsidies have increased food insecurity. Women are more vulnerable to these changes because of their responsibilities and their weak financial position (Geisler, 1992; Topouzis, 1990).

## RURAL FEMALES' LIMITED GAINS FROM EDUCATION POLICIES

Education is considered a key to upward mobility in Africa (Foster, 1980; Knight, 1990), and education policies have been geared toward expansion of education at the primary and secondary levels. Nevertheless, illiteracy and low educational attainment still characterize the rural sub-Saharan African women. For the majority of the countries in the region, 70 to 90 percent of the rural women are illiterate (James, 1992; United Nations, 1995). The reported dramatic increase in girls' access to primary and secondary schools ignores rural or urban residence as a factor in variations related to attendance patterns. For instance, a study of Mali's education system revealed that 50 percent of the children in Bamako region (city and its surroundings) attended school, but about 90 percent of the children in Timbuktu area had never received schooling. In Somalia, 70 percent of all the girls enrolled in secondary schools reside in Mogadishu, the capital. In some regions, enrollment for girls is as low as 14 percent (Adams and Kruppenbach, 1987; Hough, 1989).

A number of rural females do not attend school because of parents' bias toward educating males, whom they view as security for their future. Some parents keep girls out of school because they need help with work. For some parents, it is important for their daughters to get married at an early age instead of being exposed to ideas incompatible with their values and beliefs. A number of rural girls drop out of school at the primary level due to frustration resulting from being required to repeat classes, or lack of motivation in general. In sub-Saharan Africa, the dropout rate for girls is 8.6 percent, whereas it is 7.3 percent for boys. In Uganda, the dropout rate for primary school girls is 52 percent (Hyde, 1993; Hill and King, 1993; Uganda Government, 1994).

Even for the rural girls who complete the primary cycle, very few of them progress to the secondary cycle. This is due to lower academic achievement and the great competition for secondary school slots (Hyde, 1993). The girls' poor academic performance may be related to parents' attitude, teachers' attitude, lack of role models, and the classroom environment. The majority of teachers in primary schools are males (Bellew and King, 1993). It is believed that many of these teachers carry societal attitudes pertaining to attaching greater importance to males' education. This may result in greater expectations and support for boys (Parsons, Kaczala, and Meece, 1982). Interacting with male teachers and dealing with boys in the classroom may be difficult for some girls who interact more often with females than males in their home environment because of normative sex segregation. Although girls are socialized to respect males in their households, they sometimes see their fathers as disciplinarians and experience teaches them to regard males' superiority with reverence. Studies have also revealed that textbooks tend to depict females in domestic roles while they depict males in prestigious or professional roles (Hyde, 1993).

For the few rural girls who make it to secondary schools, many of them are concentrated in community-funded schools such as Harambe schools in Kenya because their examination scores are not high enough for government schools (Hyde, 1993). Because of limited funds, the quality of these schools is lower than the quality of government schools. Rural girls' low educational attainment is also related to the poor quality of rural schools. There are many reports of lack of desks, textbooks, teachers' books, and tools for practical subjects in a number of rural schools. Shortage of qualified teachers has also been reported (Achola and Kaluba, 1989; Hough, 1989; Mosha, 1988). The author made similar observations during visits to three primary schools in Hoima district. The poor quality of rural schools has a greater effect on girls' than boys' academic achievement because there are many barriers to girls' education.

Illiteracy and low educational attainment keep rural females locked in poverty for various reasons. First, it deprives them of employment opportunities. Second, it makes taking advantage of modern farming techniques difficult. It has been found that educated farmers achieve higher productivity than farmers who have never been to school. Although government support may account for this difference, ability is also likely to be a factor. Uneducated farmers are also less likely to participate in cooperative programs (Browne and Barrett, 1991). Yet these programs are credited with increased agricultural productivity and realization of higher returns on marketed agricultural products. Third, illiteracy and low educational attainment make it harder for rural women to take advantage of credit schemes since they lack confidence and have to deal with more barriers when information is needed. Furthermore, their ability to benefit from programs related to treatment and prevention of diseases, nutrition, and use of modern, appropriate technology is limited. Because they are less likely to participate in politics, the chances of influencing the policy-making process to ensure effective response to their needs and problems are also limited.

Women with little or no formal education tend to have many children. Most of the rural African women have six to eight children. Their high fertility is due to an early start of child bearing, the need to safeguard against infant mortality, the need to get help with work, desire for status, and lack of knowledge about family planning or lack of access to it. The relationship between low educational levels and high fertility rates has been documented (Ballara, 1992; World Bank, 1988). With large families, it is harder to meet the household members' basic needs. Furthermore, the faster the population increases, the greater the pressure imposed on the environment because of a higher demand for land, which leads to overcultivation and demand for firewood. This in turn leads to deforestation and conditions for drought. Not only do women have to struggle harder for subsistence, but they are not able to provide their daughters with the kind of quality of life that can prepare them for a better future (Birdsal, 1985; Eckholm et al., 1984).

## Current Strategies for Reducing Rural Women's Poverty

The beginning of the 1990s was marked by a variety of efforts to reduce the pain and suffering caused by poverty in sub-Saharan Africa and to promote both economic and social development in the region. To a considerable extent, rural women are beneficiaries of programs that specifically target women, some of which result in improved rural conditions.

It has been realized that in order to reduce poverty in sub-Saharan Africa, there is a need to avoid focusing on technical assistance as the only mode of development but instead to concentrate on the development process and the outcome of the development effort. People's participation in decision making related to identifying problems, deciding on the course of action, being actively involved in implementation of programs, and influencing development related to policies is viewed as an essential element of the development process. This participatory development approach tends to lead to desired results. Human-centered development which emphasizes the improvement of citizens' quality of life indicated by improved health, nutrition, education, housing, safety of water, and other amenities is also considered important (Agunga, 1990; Browne and Barrett, 1991).

As a result of the United Nations' declaration of 1975–1985 as the "Decade of Women," the subsequent International Women's Conference in Nairobi (1985), and concerns raised by feminist scholars and groups dedicated to promotion of justice, the need to improve women's economic and social conditions has received greater attention.

In order to ensure that international aid is reaching ordinary people, especially the rural masses, the donors' preference is to deal directly with local communities at the grass-roots level instead of going through governments. Nongovernmental organizations (NGOs) seem to be effective in working with disadvantaged groups, such as rural women, by supplementing government efforts in education, health, and other areas, and by providing opportunities for income-generating activities. Poultry farming, heifer projects, vegetable gardening, group ownership of grain mills, and cottage industries are some of the profitable activities (Sorensen, 1992; Ward, 1989). However, the scale of these projects is not large enough to drastically improve the economic situation of rural women. Some women are not able to participate in the projects because of household responsibilities or limited knowledge. Because of the lack of coordination among NGOs (Ward, 1989), some projects are concentrated in certain regions or districts, while others are underserved. A number of countries have attempted to improve the conditions of the rural masses through community development. This aspect of the social work profession has been defined as "[e]fforts made by professionals and community residents to enhance the social bonds among members of the community, motivate citizens for self-help, develop responsible local leadership and create or revitalize local institutions" (Harrison, 1995: 556).

Citizen participation is a significant factor in community development programs. However, with the exception of Zimbabwe and a few other countries, many African countries have not experienced success with these programs. The main problems have been the lack of coordination, funds, and recognition. For most people, community development is equated with simple government projects such as those related to water safety. For example, Gboku (1993: 170) states: "Speaking very frankly, community development in Sierra Leone has not been very effective. After many decades of community development effort in Sierra Leone, the people in the villages are still not well-educated about the purpose and meaning of community development." This observation about the ineffectiveness of community development in Sierra Leone echoes the sentiments of many community development agents.

In spite of the available information on gender analysis, governments' commitment to including women in development and promising approaches to development, rural sub-Saharan African women are still trapped in poverty. Therefore, there is a need to focus on strategies that will expedite the liberation of these women from poverty.

## CONCLUSIONS AND RECOMMENDATIONS

One of the strategies adapted to expedite the enhancement of rural women's role in agriculture is to enable them to own land, increase their access to credit, encourage their training and hiring as extension workers, and give them an opportunity to grow cash crops. Making special provision for women when mechanisms for land allocation are set up is also recommended. This may entail recognizing the right of women to own property in their own right even when they are married since household income is not shared equitably. Poor women's rights to the basic need of food, land ownership by cooperatives, or other mechanisms of community farms should be facilitated. Enforcement of inheritance laws needs to be pursued more vigorously. Devising a means of disseminating information about these laws to rural women through women's associations, churches, NGOs, adult education programs, and local centers staffed by paralegal employees or volunteers is also essential.

The number of female agricultural extension workers can be increased by getting females interested in agriculture while they are still in secondary schools, establishing special programs for training females who demonstrate a potential for extension work, and adjusting extension work to women's unique situations. Since females raised in rural areas are likely to be amenable to working in those areas, special effort should be made to recruit rural females and to locate some training centers in remote rural areas.

For women to benefit from growing cash crops, governments need to pursue agricultural policies that support both small-scale and large-scale farming. Small-hold tea growing in Kenya is a good example. Women also need assistance with marketing their crops through cooperatives or other rural institutions.

Suggestions for promoting rural females' education include the following:

- Increasing the number of female teachers at the primary and secondary level.
- Providing assistance for fees, uniforms, and the like on a need basis where free primary education is not feasible.
- Upgrading the quality of rural schools.
- Establishing academies for academically gifted girls on a regional basis.
- Expanding adult education programs.
- Giving rural schools priority when allocating resources and supplies.
- Attracting capable teachers to rural schools by paying them decent salaries and giving them fringe benefits such as housing and travel allowances.
- Attracting qualified local residents to teachers' colleges located in rural areas.

In order for girls to be motivated regarding learning and for parents to develop a positive attitude toward girls' education, females must be given opportunities to reap the financial rewards of education. It is therefore important for them to have greater opportunities for employment and fair salaries. This needs to be taken into consideration when females are guided for career choices. Encouraging and supporting girls to study subjects that are currently considered males' subjects is also necessary. These subjects include sciences, mathematics, and technical knowledge. There is also a need to explore girls' styles of learning.

Rural females are poor in part because of the oppression and discrimination they experience as a result of customs and traditions perpetuated by patriarchy. This problem needs to be addressed in order for other changes to occur. The Transformational Approach requires a critical analysis of culture instead of treating it as a sacred entity. Consciousness-raising is suggested as an effective tool for promoting gender equity. Heads of governments, government officials, women's organizations, and other nongovernmental groups need to make a conscious effort to bring out the oppressive and discriminatory aspects of the traditional attitudes, belief, and practices that pertain to women. Writers, scholars, and entertainers also need to continue engaging in consciousness-raising by using the mass media, film, drama, or other forms of entertainment, materials used in schools, and other forms of literature to analyze conceptualizations about women and to promote the needed change.

Another strategy for promoting gender equity is to increase opportunities and financial support for women's organizations. These organizations are effective in terms of giving women opportunities for income-generating activities, for controlling income, and for allowing them to practice new skills and roles such as public speaking, record-keeping, and leadership. In this way, women may be enabled to negotiate for their rights and to actively participate in the development effort. Creating opportunities for men and women to work together on community projects may enable rural men to learn new ways of sharing responsibility. The Habitat for Humanity mixed work group, observed in the Hoima district, showed cooperation and mutual respect.

Reducing poverty among rural women requires the intervention and collaboration of many ministries, departments, organizations, groups, professions, disciplines, and individuals. This integrated, multisectoral approach to rural development necessitates the establishment of structures that facilitate the coordination of plans, policies, and programs. Designating a specific ministry for rural development may serve that purpose. The social work profession may also play an instrumental role in coordinating programs and promoting Popular Participatory Development. The need to extend social work practice to rural areas by creating positions for social development specialists has already been discussed (Kabadaki, 1994). In line with the Generalist Practice Model, social workers can practice at different levels. At the macro level, they have knowledge and skills that make them capable of doing community assessments, developing programs, mobilizing citizens for participation, promoting self-help, engaging in social planning and administration, enhancing coalition building, and engaging in promotion of justice (Weil and Gamble, 1995). At the mezzo level, social workers possess knowledge and skills that make them capable of promoting the formation of groups, supporting and facilitating groups, enhancing communication, clarifying values, and resolving conflicts (Berman-Rossi, 1993). At the micro level, social workers have knowledge and skills that make them capable of enhancing the functioning of individuals by helping them to solve personal problems or meet certain needs. Counseling individuals who are experiencing spousal abuse, spousal neglect, depression, and alcohol-related problems, and connecting people with resources are examples of micro practice. This aspect of social work is essential for easing the pain experienced by rural poor women and for strengthening families as well as promoting social integration at the grass-roots level.

## REFERENCES

Achola, P.W. and Kaluba, H.L. (1989). "School Production Units in Zambia: An Evaluation of a Decade of a Presidential Experiment." *Comparative Education* 25(2): 165–178.

Adams, M.N. and Kruppenbach, S.E. (1987). "Gender and Access in the African School." *International Review of Education* (33): 437–453.

Agiobu-Kammer, I.S. (1992). "Child Survival and Child Development in Africa." *Studies and Evaluation Papers* 6. The Hague: Bernard Van Leer Foundation.

Agunga, R. (1989). "The World Bank, Rural Development, and Communication Professionals." *International Third World Studies Journal and Review* 1(2): 305–316.

———. (1990). "Development Support Communication and Popular Participation in Development Projects." *Gazzette: The International Journal for Mass Communication Studies* 45(3): 137–155.

Ayisi, R.A. (1991). "Battling the Odds." *Africa Report* 36(4): 60–63.

Baker, K.M. (1995). "Drought, Agriculture and Environment: A Case Study from the Gambia, West Africa." *African Affairs* 94(374): 67–86.

Ballara, M. (1992). *Women and Literacy.* Atlantic Highlands, NJ: Zed Books.

Basgall, S. (1988). "The Issue of Credit for Women." *Social Development Issues* 12(1): 21–30.

Bates, H.R. and Lofchie, M.F. (eds.). (1980). *Agricultural Development in Africa.* New York: Praeger.

Bellew, R.T. and King, E.M. (1993). "Educating Women: Lessons from Experience." In E.M. King and M.A. Hill (eds.), *Women's Education in Developing Countries: Barrier, Benefits, and Policies* (pp. 285–326). Washington, DC: The World Bank.

Beoku-Betts, J. (1990). "Agricultural Development in Sierra Leone: Implications for Rural Women in the Aftermath of the Women's Decade." *Africa Today* 37(1): 19–35.

Berman-Rossi, T. (1993). "The Tasks and Skills of the Social Worker across Stages of Group Development." *Social Work with Groups* 16(1/2): 69–81.

Birdsal, N. (1985). *Effects of Family Planning Programs on Fertility in the Developing World* (World Bank Staff Working Paper, No. 677). Washington, DC: World Bank.

Blumberg, R.L. (1992). *African Women in Agriculture: Farmers, Students, Extension Agents, Chiefs.* Morrilton, AK: Winrock International.

Browne, A.W. and Barrett, H.R. (1991). "Female Education in Sub-Saharan Africa: The Key to Development?" *Comparative Education* 27(3): 257–285.

Cohen, R. (1994). *Building on People's Strength: Early Childhood in Africa.* The Hague: Bernard Van Leer Foundation.

Daddieh, C.K. (1989). "Production and Reproduction: Women and Agricultural Resurgence in Sub-Saharan Africa." In J. Parpart (ed.), *Women and Development in Africa* (pp. 165–193). Lanham, MD: University Press of America.

Eckholm. E., Foley, G., Barnard, G. and Timberlake, L. (1984). *Fuelwood: The Energy Crisis That Won't Go Away.* London: Earthscan.

Foster, P. (1980). "Education and Social Inequality in Sub-Saharan Africa." *Journal of Modern African Studies* 26(2): 277–302.

Gboku, M.L. (1993). "Community Development in Sierra Leone." *Community Development Journal* 28(2): 167–175.

Geisler, G. (1992). "Who Is Losing Out? Structural Adjustment, Gender, and the Agricultural Sector in Zambia." *Journal of Modern African Studies* 30(1): 113–139.

Gran, G. (1983). "From the Official Future to a Participatory Future: Rethinking Development Policy and Practice in Rural Zambia." *Africa Today* 30(4): 5–22.

Guyer, J. (1986). "Women's Role in Development." In R. Berg and J. Whitaker (eds.), *Strategies for African Development* (pp. 393–421). Berkeley: University of California Press.

Harrison, D. (1995). "Community Development." In R.L. Edwards and J.G.

Hopps (eds.), *Encyclopedia of Social Work*, 19th ed. (pp. 483–494). Washington, DC: NASW Press.

Hill, M.A. and King, E.M. (1993). "Women's Education in Developing Countries: An Overview." In E.M. King and M.A. Hill (eds.), *Women's Education in Developing Countries: Barriers, Benefits, and Policies* (pp. 14–66). Washington, DC: The World Bank.

Hough, J.R. (1989). "Inefficiency in Education—The Case of Mali." *Comparative Education* 25(1): 77–85.

House, W.J. and Zimalirana, G. (1992). "Rapid Population Growth and Poverty Generation in Malawi." *Journal of Modern African Studies* 30(1): 141–161.

Hyde, K.A. (1993). "Women's Education in Sub-Saharan Africa." In E.M. King and M.A. Hill (eds.), *Women's Education in Development Countries: Barriers, Benefits and Policies* (pp. 116–153). Washington, DC: The World Bank.

James, S. (1992). "Transgressing Fundamental Boundaries: The Struggle for Women's Human Rights." *Africa Today* 39(4): 35–46.

Kabadaki, K.K. (1995). "Exploration of Social Work Practice Models for Rural Development in Uganda." *Journal of Social Development in Africa* 10(1): 77–88.

Knight, J. (1990). *Education, Productivity and Inequality: The East African Natural Experiment*. Washington, DC: The World Bank.

Liedholm, C. and Mead, D. (1986). "Small Scale Industry." In R. Berg and J. Whitaker (eds.), *Strategies for African Development* (pp. 308–330). Berkeley: University of California Press.

Morewagae, B.S., Seemule, M. and Rempel, H. (1995). "Access to Credit for Non-Formal Micro-Enterprises in Botswana." *Journal of Development Studies* 31(3): 481–504.

Mosha, H.J. (1988). "Assessment of the Indicators of Primary Education Quality in Developing Countries: Emerging Evidence from Tanzania." *International Review of Education* 34(1): 17–45.

O'Connor, A. (1991). *Poverty in Africa*. London: Belhaven Press.

Parsons, J.E., Kaczala, C.M. and Meece, J.L. (1982). "Socialization of Achievement Attitudes and Beliefs: Classroom Influences." *Child Development* 52(2): 322–339.

Rathgeber, E. (1989). "Women and Development: An Overview." In J. Parpart (ed.), *Women and Development in Africa* (pp. 19–31). Lanham, MD: University Press of America.

Sorensen, A. (1992). "Women's Organizations among the Kipsigis: Change, Variety and Different Participation." *Africa* 62(4): 547–566.

Timberlake, L. (1986). *Africa in Crisis*. Philadelphia: New Society Publishers.

Topouzis, D. (1990). "The Feminization of Poverty." *Africa Report* 35(3): 60–63.

Uganda Government. (1994). *The Republic of Uganda*. Country Paper Document prepared for the Fourth World Conference on Women, Beijing, 1995.

UNICEF. (1991). *Challenges for Children and Women in the 1990s: Eastern and Southern Africa in Profile* (Report). New York: United Nations Children's Fund.

United Nations. (1995). *Human Development in Africa, 1995 Report*. Addis Ababa: United Nations Economic and Social Council.

Ward, H.G. (1989). *African Development Reconsidered*. New York: Phelps-Stokes Institute.

Weil, M.O. and Gamble, D.N. (1995). "Community Practice Models." In R.L. Edwards and J.G. Hopps (eds.), *Encyclopedia of Social Work*, 19th ed. (pp. 483–493). Washington, DC: NASW Press.

World Bank. (1988). *Education in Sub-Saharan Africa*. Washington, DC: World Bank.

Chapter 7

# Measuring and Monitoring Urban and Rural Poverty in Nigeria

## Felix E. Onah

### INTRODUCTION

By the end of 1993, the World Bank had completed poverty assessments of 28 countries. The assessments analyzed a wide range of poverty issues designed to help both the Bank and national governments to gain a better understanding of the nature and extent of poverty in respective countries, as well as to identify appropriate policies and programs for tackling it. In addition, first drafts had been completed of another 20 poverty assessments. Of all these assessments and drafts, 21 were carried out in African countries, with sub-Saharan Africa accounting for 18 (World Bank, 1993).[1] Surprisingly, however, Nigeria was not one of the countries studied. Could it be that Nigeria was apparently neglected because it was regarded as a middle-income country in the 1970s, so that poverty did not constitute a serious social problem for it? If so, then the economic reversal of the 1980s should have revised this view. Moreover, the fact that Venezuela, Algeria, and Mexico (other oil-exporting countries) have attracted the attention of the World Bank weakens this line of thinking.

A more plausible explanation could be found in the absence of relevant statistical materials in Nigeria. To confirm this, the Food and Agriculture Organization (FAO) has described the various household surveys in Nigeria, spanning the period 1975–1983, as merely containing descriptive notes (FAO, 1986). Thus, the absence of statistical information appears to account for the gross lack of written materials on poverty and its alleviation in Nigeria, despite the growing literature on the subject. At a later stage, the World Bank did indeed somehow manage to conclude that, owing to the economic downturn of the 1980s in the country, the real per capita consumption of Nigerians was higher in the 1950s than in the mid-1980s (World Bank, 1990: 42). However, it is obvious that this statement needs some empirical confirmation.

The Nigerian Economic Society tried to address the problem of poverty in its 1975 Annual Conference. Most of the papers published in the proceedings of this conference ended up discussing the interpersonal distribution of income and attendant income inequality. Okigbo (1975), who contributed to the deliberations, lamented the paucity of statistical data for a thorough study of the subject. In the absence of a better alternative, he defines the poverty line in Nigeria as the median income of the population—a measure that, at the present stage in the development of empirical studies in the field, is questionable. There is therefore a need to provide more accurate poverty measures to facilitate policy orientation toward its alleviation in the country. This chapter tries to fill this gap in the literature.

## WHAT POVERTY MEANS

The main purpose of identifying the poor in the population is to orient the location and design of government policies. To do this requires, to a large extent, a good understanding of the precise meaning of poverty. Unfortunately, the definitions of poverty and their resulting indicators are numerous, and substantial disagreement exists on which are more relevant.

It should be stressed from the outset that this chapter focuses on absolute poverty, not on inequality. The two concepts mean different things. Whereas poverty is concerned with the absolute standard of living of a part of society (the poor), inequality refers to relative living standards across the whole society. Thus, poverty is concerned with the welfare characteristics of the individuals who are located below the line that separates the poor and nonpoor. In an attempt to analyze the existence and correlates of poverty, a dividing line, which is referred to as the poverty line, is introduced. This line represents the minimum acceptable living standard. Poverty is therefore defined as the inability to attain a minimal standard of living (World Bank, 1990). This, of course, begs the question of what represents a minimal standard of living.

Household income or expenditure per capita is an adequate yardstick for the standard of living as long as it includes self-production. One is deemed to be poor if one cannot afford a minimum standard of nutrition and other basic needs, and a further amount that would enable one to participate in the everyday life of the community. Thus, those households whose per capital incomes or expenditures fall below the poverty line are poor; those above are nonpoor. Absolute poverty, therefore, refers to the individual's position in relation to the poverty line, whose real value is fixed and is based on the cost of a minimum consumption basket of food necessary for a recommended calorie intake and an allowance for nonfood needs, consistent with the spending patterns of the poor (World Bank, 1994).

The poverty line is not only country specific but also dynamic. It varies from culture to culture. Also, the criteria for distinguishing the poor from nonpoor not only reflect specific national priorities and normative concepts of welfare but change over time. As a country becomes wealthier, its perceptions of the acceptable minimum level of consumption, and, hence, what Hossain (1987) refers to as the poverty threshold income or expenditure, change. However, where comparisons are needed, it is advisable to hold the value of the poverty line constant.

## SETTING THE POVERTY LINE

There are basically three approaches to measuring poverty: food poverty, overall poverty and arbitrary choice of index.

### The Food Poverty Approach

This is a "food-energy" method. Many studies, particularly for developing countries, have followed versions of this approach. Such studies include those of Osmani (1982), Greer and Thorbecke (1986), Paul (1989), and Anand and Harris (1992). This approach helps assess the success of national food policies. Moreover, it may be regarded as a proxy for estimating total poverty because of its operational advantages, which include:

• The fact that it is simple to define what constitutes a food poverty line.
• Its data needs are less than those required for estimating overall poverty lines.
• Food expenditure data are generally among the more accurate components of information collected in household budget surveys.
• The results can easily be checked against the objective standard of the physiological signs of malnutrition. (See Greer and Thorbecke, 1986.)

The first step in this method is to derive the minimum expenditure necessary to attain minimum nutritional intake, including the value of consumption from self-production. For most studies on developing countries, the FAO and WHO recommended that minimum calorie intake be used as the basis for determining the consumption expenditure. All that is required, therefore, is information on prices and energy conversion factors for different food items. These are used in calculating the food poverty line expenditure for different sectors of the national economy.

Alternatively, given information on food expenditure ($X$) and calorie consumption ($C$), such as contained in nutrition surveys, it is possible to estimate the cost of a given number of calories by using the following cost-of-calorie function (see Greer and Thorbecke, 1986):

$$\ln X = \alpha + \beta C \tag{7.1}$$

The poverty line, $z$, is the estimated cost of acquiring the recommended daily allowance of calorie intake, $R$.

$$z = e^{(\alpha + \beta R)} \tag{7.2}$$

where $\alpha$ and $\beta$ are the estimates of $\alpha$ and $\beta$, respectively. Based on the assumptions that all individuals face identical tastes and that there is a common dietary taste pattern, equation (7.1) approximates an exactly determined but unknown relationship between $X$ and $C$.

## The Cost-of-Basic-Needs Approach

At the operational level, the first step in taking this approach is to specify minimum requirements for both food and nonfood items, and then to calculate the amount of income or expenditure necessary to purchase them at current prices (Kanbur, 1987). When the purpose is to assess progress in reducing absolute poverty—defined in terms of command over basic consumption needs—then this poverty line should take on a constant value (Ravallion and Sen, 1994). Orshansky (1965), BBS (1991), Hossain and Sen (1992), and Sen and Islam (1993), to mention a few, have used versions of this approach.

Drawing from Ravallion and Sen (1994), we may set the poverty line as the cost in each sector and at each date of a normative "basic-needs" basket of food sufficient to reach a predetermined calorie requirement consistent with the consumption behavior of the poor. This is then augmented by an allowance for nonfood needs consistent with the spending patterns of the poor (Patrinos, 1994). The method is said to be preferred to the food energy method when the aim is to construct poverty measures that are consistent in terms of command over basic consumption needs.

Data requirements for this exercise include those needed for the estimation of the food energy poverty line. Information is also needed on retail price levels for items in the consumption basket in each sector or region, as the case may be. In the absence of retail price data, implicit prices obtained by dividing total expenditures on given food items by corresponding quantities are used. The major difficulty, however, is that some household expenditure surveys do not provide information on quantities consumed of food and nonfood items.

Although the concept of basic needs is appealing, this approach has some shortcomings on both theoretical and operational grounds. At the theoretical level, it pre-imposes the researcher's subjective notion of what constitutes a palatable but inexpensive diet (Greer and Thorbecke, 1986). In defense, it is possible to argue, however, that the calorie requirement used in defining the basic needs corresponds to the FAO or WHO recommended standard, which is also the nutrition anchor in the food energy method.

At the operational level, a source of discrepancy among early poverty line estimates is the choice of prices used to convert the normative minimum food consumption baskets into poverty line expenditure. For instance, in the absence of data on rural retail prices, urban retail prices for food items have been used, with an assumed fixed discount rate, to obtain rural retail price levels (Rahman and Haque, 1988). In this respect, Ravallion and Sen (1994) concede that a movement in urban prices out of line with rural prices may generate potentially large errors in the estimates of poverty measures. Moreover, the use of consumer price indices (CPI) for updating the base-year poverty line may generate errors in the poverty trends if the items on which the construction of the CPI had been based included items outside the typical consumption basket of the poor. An even more serious source of concern is the absence of price data for the nonfood component of the poverty line. To estimate the expenditure on the component, a given percentage of food expenditure is assumed, a practice that is likely to be a source of error in the estimates of poverty measures. However, this source of error is largely eliminated if the ratio of nonfood to food expenditure of the entire population is used to "gross up" the minimum required food expenditure. This method seems to capture, at the operational level, a view of poverty that relates it to the capacity to participate in all the activities of the community, on average (Orshansky, 1965; Kanbur, 1987).

### The Arbitrary Choice Approach

Sometimes, the relevant data for computing the poverty line may not be available. And even when such data are available, the researcher may wish to avoid the methodological issues associated with designing a poverty line. In either situation, the investigator may adopt an arbitrarily determined poverty line. However, the choice is often conditioned by the experiences of other countries at similar levels of development.

This consideration underlies the use of U.S.$275 and U.S.$370 per person per annum in constant 1985 purchasing power parity (PPP) prices as poverty lines in the World Bank studies (1990). The range was chosen to span poverty lines estimated for a number of countries with low average incomes, where the lower limit of the range coincided with the estimate for very low-income countries. Similarly, Psacharopoulos et al. (1992) used a uniform poverty line of U.S.$60 per person per month in 1985 PPP dollars in their analyses of poverty in Latin American countries. This value was based on the 1990 World Bank studies. In addition, rather than attempting to reformulate a new poverty standard, Patrinos (1994) employs this same U.S.$60 PPP poverty line in each of the four countries he studied. In the same way, Pfeffermann and Webb (1983), in their study of income distribution in Brazil, arbitrarily assumed two Brazilian minimum wages per family per month, or U.S.$260 per capita per annum as the poverty line. This estimate was based on Oscar Altimir's study (1982) which put the poverty line in Brazil in 1974 at U.S.$280–$260 per person per annum.

## POVERTY MEASURES

Like the issue of estimating the poverty line, the measurement of the appropriate indices of poverty has attracted a lot of debate. In what follows, the Foster–Greer–Thorbecke (1984) class of measures has been adopted. It consists of three measures, as described below.

As a starting point, Sen (1976, 1978) formulated two axioms incorporating the fundamental properties of poverty that an aggregate poverty measure ought to satisfy:

- The *Monotonicity Axiom*, which states that other things being equal, a reduction in the income of any poor individual must increase the poverty measure.
- The *Transfer Axiom*, which states that other things being unchanged, a pure transfer of income from a poor individual to any other individual who is richer must increase the poverty measure.

With these axioms in view, the following poverty measures are constructed:

### The Head-Count Index (H)

This is the most commonly used measure of poverty. It calculates the incidence of poverty as the ratio of consumption units below the poverty line to the whole population. Thus,

$$H = \frac{q}{n} \tag{7.3}$$

where $q$ denotes the number of individuals who are poor and $n$ is the entire population size.

Although the measure identifies the number of people who are poor and is easy to interpret, it fails to indicate how poor the poor are. For instance, it remains unchanged when a previously poor unit is made even poorer. It therefore does not satisfy either of Sen's axioms.

### The Poverty-Gap Index (PG)

This concept has been introduced to overcome the shortcomings of the head-count ratio. It is defined as

$$PG = \frac{1}{zn_i}\sum_{i=1}^{q}(z - y_i) \tag{7.4}$$

where $z$ denotes the poverty line, whereas $q_i$ and $y_i$ stand for the number and consumption expenditure of the $i$th group who are poor. The ratio gives the average of the poverty gap $(z - y)$ as a fraction of the poverty line. It may be interpreted as a measure of poverty "depth," indicating the monetary shortfall needed to lift the poor, on average, out of poverty.

The PG does not, however, take account of the number of the poor in the sense that if the number of poor units is, for example, doubled, then the index will still remain unchanged. Thus, it satisfies the Monotonicity Axiom but fails to satisfy the Transfer Axiom, which requires that a poverty measure be most sensitive to the well-being of the poorest of the poor.

### The Squared Poverty-Gap Index (SPG)

This index has been introduced to satisfy the Transfer Axiom. It measures the severity of poverty and is defined as

$$SPG = \frac{1}{n}\sum_{i=1}^{q}[(z - y_i)/z]^2 \tag{7.5}$$

or

$$(SPG)_\alpha = \frac{1}{n}\sum_{i=1}^{q}[(z - y_i)/z]^\alpha \tag{7.5'}$$

where the parameter $\alpha$ measures how sensitive the index is to transfers between the poor units. For $\alpha > 1$, transfers from low- to high-income units will increase poverty. Another way of interpreting equation (7.5') is that it is a weighted sum of each proportionate poverty gap $(Z - Y/$

Z), the weight being the gap itself (i.e., $(z - y/z)^{a-1}$). Indeed, equation (7.5') accommodates equations (7.3) and (7.4) as specific cases in that when $\alpha = 0$, the result is H, when $\alpha = 1$, the result is PG, and when $\alpha = 2$ it is SPG of equation (7.5).

SPG satisfies both the Monotonicity and Transfer Axioms (Foster, Greer, and Thorbecke, 1981 and 1984). Moreover, it has the property of being additively decomposable across population subgroups, according to the formula

$$SPG = \sum_{s=1}^{m}(n_s/n)(SPG)_s \tag{7.6}$$

where $n_s$ and $(SPG)_s$ are the number of people and the squared poverty gap of the sth subgroup $(S=1, \ldots, m)$. $(SPG)_s$ is measured according to the formula

$$(SPG)_s = \frac{1}{n_s}\sum_{i=1}^{q_s}[(z - y_i)/z]^2 \tag{7.7}$$

Equation (7.7) is the measure of equation (7.6) applied to the expenditure (or income) distribution of subgroups. Thus, overall respective subgroups can write poverty as a weighted sum of the subgroup poverty indices, the weights being the fractions of the population accounted for.

## ESTIMATING THE POVERTY LINE FOR NIGERIA

In this exercise, the cost-of-basic-needs approach has been chosen. The first step was to determine the energy requirement of an adult Nigerian per day. In doing this, certain options need to be considered. The World Health Organization recommended an average daily intake of 2,200 calories per adult Nigerian, with additions for special conditions such as pregnancy and lactation (WHO, 1973). On the other hand, FAO/WHO recommended a daily intake of 2,360 calories per day for an average adult in Nigeria (Latham, 1979). This latter figure is favored.

A more difficult task was choosing the items in the consumption basket that are consistent with the spending patterns of the poor. The average Nigerian's diet is built around starchy root crops and cereal food. Accordingly, the food items listed in Appendix 7.1 (at the end of this chapter) have been selected. These items are expected to provide no less than 43 to 55 grams of protein per day recommended as a safe level for Nigerians (FAO, 1993; Latham, 1979). Conversion factors have also been obtained from the same sources. To value the items, unit values at current prices were used. The consumer price index (CPI) for different

Table 7.1
Poverty Measures

|  | Head-Count Index (%) | Poverty-Gap Index (%) | Squared Poverty-Gap Index (%) |
|---|---|---|---|
| Urban 1975 (at current prices) | 50.7 | 8.1 | 0.3 |
| 1975 (at 1983 prices) | 50.7 | 9.3 | 0.4 |
| 1983–1984 | 64.4 | 24.3 | 5.4 |
| Rural 1975 | — | — | — |
| 1983–1984 | 61.3 | 12.1 | 0.9 |

Note: The rural population (adult equivalent) share for 1983–1984 is 51.2 percent.

categories of items has been used to update the base-year values presented in Appendix 7.2.

With respect to the nonfood component of the poverty line, a number of suggestions have been considered. Hossain and Sen (1992) used an allowance of 30 percent of food expenditure for this component, while Sen and Islam (1993) chose 40 percent. On the other hand, Rahman and Haque (1988) used a lower mark-up of 25 percent. The present study adopts the suggestion by Kanbur (1987) and Orshansky (1965). That is, the percentage ratio of nonfood to food expenditures of the whole population is used as contained in the household expenditure survey. For 1983–1984 this came to 42 percent, and for 1975 it was 69 percent.

Based on these percentages, the food energy allowances were grossed up to get overall monthly poverty line expenditures of ₦15 and ₦51.6 at current prices for 1975 and 1983–1984 respectively, in the urban sector. For the rural sector, ₦30 units have been estimated for 1983–1984 and ₦8.7 for 1975. There are, however, not enough relevant data for use in computing poverty measures for this sector in 1975, thus rendering impossible the computation of the poverty line for that year.

## POVERTY MEASURES FOR NIGERIA

Table 7.1 gives the estimates of poverty measures for Nigeria. Comparing the data for 1975 and 1983–1984 for the urban sector, one finds that at 1983 prices the incidence of poverty, as given by the head-count index, was higher in 1983–1984. Similarly, other indices (the PG and SPG) are all larger for 1983–1984, even when current prices are used to compute the measures.

Specifically, the head-count measures indicate that, at 1983 prices, 50.7

Table 7.2
Summary Statistics on Growth and Inequality

| Index (%) | Poverty Line (₦/person/ month) | Mean Consumption (₦/person/ month) | Mean/Poverty Line (%) | Gini Index |
|---|---|---|---|---|
| Urban 1975 (current prices) | 15.60 | 23.70 | 158 | 67.0 |
| 1975 (at 1983 prices) | 51.60 | 80.50 | 156 | n.a. |
| 1983–1984 | 51.60 | 56.90 | 110 | 57.9 |
| Rural 1975 (current prices) | n.a. | 12.79 | n.a. | n.a. |
| 1975 (at 1983 prices) | 30.0 | 41.78 | 139 | n.a. |
| 1983–1984 | 30.0 | 34.91 | 116 | 69.5 |

percent of the urban population were in poverty in 1975 as compared to 64.4 percent in 1983–1984. The poverty-gap indices show that, on the average, what was required to lift the poor out of poverty in 1975 was 9.3 percent of the poverty line or ₦4.8, as compared to 24.3 percent or ₦12.5 in 1983–1984. The corresponding severity indices are 0.4 percent and 5.4 percent. At current prices, the picture is similar. The head-count indices remain unchanged, but the poverty-gap index for 1975 goes down to 8.1 percent.

A comparison of the urban and rural sectors shows that the incidence of poverty was greater by 3.1 percent in the urban sector in 1983–1984. Similarly, the poverty gap in the rural sector was ₦3.6 compared to ₦12.50 in the urban sector. The index of severity in the latter was 18 times its level in the former. As previously mentioned, it has not been possible to compare poverty measures in 1975 in the rural sector to those for 1983–1984 owing to the lack of information relating to 1975. For the same reason, a comparison between the two sectors in 1975 is not possible.

## Causes of Changes over Time

Table 7.2 gives additional figures that could help elucidate the above results. The fourth column gives estimates of the basic-needs purchasing power of mean (adult equivalent) consumption per month. This is mean consumption ($u$) as a percentage of the poverty line ($z$). It shows that in the urban sector there was a fall in the purchasing power of mean consumption between 1975 and 1983–1984. The changes in $u/z$ track quite closely the changes in poverty measures presented in Table 7.1. When the mean rose (fell), poverty fell (rose). For instance, at 1983 prices the mean consumption expenditure in 1975 rose to ₦80.5 as against ₦56.9 for 1983–84. The corresponding values of the purchasing power of mean consumption were 156 and 110 percent, respectively. For reasons already mentioned, it is not possible to compare changes in the purchasing power of mean consumption in the rural sector at current prices. However, at 1983 prices there was a drop from 139 percent in 1975 to 116 percent in 1983–1984 in the rural sector. The declines confirm the World Bank's observation concerning a fall in the living standards of Nigerians in the first half of the 1980s.[2] Thus, changes in the purchasing power of mean consumption contribute to the changes presented in Table 7.1.

These changes were associated, however, with socioeconomic conditions that were the result of the economic and mismanagement problems experienced by the national economy in the late 1970s and early 1980s. The 1970s witnessed oil prosperity in the country following the sharp increases in oil prices in 1973–1974 and 1979–1980. By 1976 oil had become the major source of both government revenue and foreign exchange earnings, accounting for over 80 percent in both cases.

The revenue from oil provided the basis for huge government expenditure on the expansion of infrastructure and industrial projects. It also facilitated growth in institutional development, such as the creation of more states and attendant infrastructure, which was accompanied by price and wage increases. The growth of the national economy was such that in a space of six years, 1973–1979, the per capita real income in Nigeria increased from ₦115 to ₦155 per annum (Rimi, 1981).

However, in 1978 the oil market slumped. Although it quickly revived, it took another turn for the worse in 1983. From a peak of about U.S.$ 34 per barrel in 1979, the average price of Nigeria's crude oil dropped to U.S. $28.5 in 1983. As a consequence, total merchandise earnings fell from ₦10.4 billion to ₦7.5 billion over the period, while the value of imports rose from ₦6.2 billion to ₦8.3 billion (Onah, 1987). The results were, among others, a rundown of the accumulated foreign reserves and increasing balance-of-payments problems.

Meanwhile, there was a return to civilian government in 1979, after 13 years of military rule. With a new constitutional system and intensification of inappropriate macroeconomic policies, the new regime continued and intensified external borrowing. External debt, which in 1975 had stood at U.S.$1.1 billion, reached U.S.$18.4 billion in 1983 (Ajai, 1991). This led to a lot of illegal capital flight. For reasons that included being in "power" and having access to domestic and foreign money, an average of U.S.$1.4, or 1.6 percent of the GNP, left the country between

1981 and 1983. Capital flight, no doubt, intensified the shortage of foreign exchange and domestic savings that could have been used to finance investment projects at home or augmented the "real capacity" to service the already accumulated external debt.

By the end of 1981, symptoms of economic recession were noticeable, including an increasing rate of decline in the volume of production, large-scale retrenchment of workers, serious shortages of foodstuffs, reduction in real wages due to inflation, drastic reduction and higher cost of providing essential social services, and a rising crime wave. In April 1982, the government announced a crisis management package, which it christened "austerity measures," under the Economic Stabilization Act of 1982. Direct controls were imposed on prices and wages. The government formed supply companies to handle the importation and supply of essential commodities, and foreign exchange control measures were put in place. By January 1983, however, it was clear that the measures in the package were exacerbating the economy's decline.

To compound these economic problems, political instability set in. A general election held in late 1983 was marked by so much corruption and vote rigging that it provided an excuse for the military to seize power once more. This was followed by another coup d'etat in August 1985. In this way, political instability aggravated the economic hardships of the time by destroying the basic ingredients that make for normal economic activities.

With a new military government in power, policies changed and were directed toward combining austerity with adjustment. The drastic fall in oil prices in 1986 increased the urgency of reform. Consequently, the country put in place a structural adjustment program (SAP) in July 1986. The economic and social consequences of this program are well documented. The Nigerian Institute of Social and Economic Research (NISER) summarizes the adverse consequences as more retrenchment, premature retirement and underemployment, increased social and economic inequality, increased poverty, more school dropouts, and greater evidence of social alienation and social deviations, all culminating in reduced quality of life (NISER, 1988). Balogun (1993) adds such macroeconomic consequences as increases in inflation, which accelerated poverty, and exchange rate depreciation, which altered the real exchange rate in favor of agricultural workers but adversely affected the overall consumption expenditure of both urban and rural poor.

Another angle from which the data in Table 7.1 could be viewed is the sectoral imbalance in growth rates. Although mean real consumption declined by 29.3 percent in the urban sector between 1975 and 1983–1984, the drop in the growth rate in the rural sector over the same period was 16.4 percent. The implications of this imbalance in growth rates for poverty measures are greater incidence, poverty gap, and severity in

Table 7.3
Per Capita Monthly Expenditure at 1983 Prices

|  | 1975 | 1981–1982 | 1982–1983 | 1983–1984 | 1984–1985 | 1985–1986 |
|---|---|---|---|---|---|---|
| Urban Wage Earner | 107.92 | 82.12 | 97.76 | 64.39 | 42.16 | 39.13 |
| Urban Self-Employed | 56.13 | 58.70 | 65.74 | 52.98 | 36.21 | 35.20 |
| Rural Wage-Earner | n.a. | 62.09 | 90.74 | 49.97 | 28.98 | 34.49 |
| Rural Self-Employed | n.a. | 42.25 | 48.80 | 34.24 | 27.21 | 24.51 |

Note: Children are included.
Sources: Computed from FOS, 1981, 1987a, 1988; CBN, 1985: 46.

1983–1984 in the urban sector. Thus, the growth and contraction of real consumption per capita in the rural and urban sectors, respectively, may have influenced changes in the poverty measures observed.

Another important factor is the state of income (or expenditure) distribution in the economy. The fifth column of Table 7.2 gives the Gini indices of concentration by year and sector. The ratios indicate the extent to which consumption expenditures had been evenly distributed. It takes a value of zero if expenditures had been equally distributed and a value of one if they had been concentrated in one sector. The calculated values indicate that, in spite of a lower incidence of poverty in the urban sector in 1975, the degree of inequality was lower in 1983–1984. A plausible explanation for this phenomenon is that the rise in adverse economic conditions in the 1980s pushed more people into poverty while at the same time narrowing their expenditure differentials. With respect to the rural sector, the economic stabilization measures that operated from 1982 to 1985 probably succeeded in altering the terms of trade between the rural and urban sectors in favor of the rural. As a consequence, economic hardships pushed proportionately fewer people below the poverty line in the rural sector, even though the degree of inequality was higher there.

Another source of change is related to the choice of study years. Observation of the data presented in Table 7.3 reveals that, although per capita real expenditure per month fluctuated between 1975 and 1982–1983, it consistently declined after 1983–1984. Thus, the choice of 1983–1984, in which a substantial fall was recorded, may have affected the results presented in Table 7.1. If the terminal year of study had been 1982–1983 (the fiscal year that marked the end of economic prosperity in the country), the result might have been different. However, 1983–1984 is an appropriate choice since it marked the beginning of a period of continuous decline in economic welfare.

Also relevant in influencing changes in poverty measures is the choice of unit prices for valuing the poverty line. For instance, farmgate prices, instead of rural retail prices, were used in estimating the rural poverty line. This is capable of having a downward bias on the estimate of the poverty line, with obvious consequences for poverty measures.

## ANOTHER POVERTY PROFILE

Another way of looking at the structure and depth of poverty in Nigeria is presented in Table 7.3. Here, urban and rural residents are classified according to the nature of their means of livelihood, that is, according to wage-earning and self-employment categories.

When the two classes are compared in the urban sector, it will be observed that the average expenditure in each subsector (at constant 1983 prices) remained above the poverty line until and including the 1983–1984 fiscal year. The per capita expenditure was higher among wage-earners in all years both before and after 1983–1984. However, poverty struck: The average expenditure in both subsectors slipped below the poverty line, with poverty depth increasing over time. Against the poverty threshold of ₦51.6, the poverty depth (gap) was greater among the self-employed, averaging ₦15.4 – ₦16.4 compared to ₦9.4 – ₦12.5 among the wage-earning class. The implication is that in the urban sector poverty (in all its measures) was felt more by the self-employed than by their wage-earning counterparts.

The relationship between the two subsectors was similar in the rural sector. The difference lies in the resilience of the per capita expenditure of the wage-earning class. As indicated earlier, the poverty line in the rural sector in 1983–1984 was ₦30 per person per month. Against this benchmark, the average monthly expenditures in both subsectors remained above the poverty line until and including 1983–1984, after which both subsectors slipped into poverty. However, the wage-earning class quickly recovered in 1985–1986. Unlike the urban sector, the rural counterparts recorded an average poverty gap of ₦1.02 in 1984–1985 for wage-earners and ₦2.8 for the self-employed, who suffered an even greater deficit of ₦5.5 in the subsequent year.

The picture that emerges from the analysis in this section largely confirms the presentation in Table 7.1. That is, both the poverty gap and its severity in 1983–1984 were greater in the urban sector than in the rural sector. The nature of the data in Table 7.3 does not permit a clear-cut conclusion about the incidence of poverty. However, the ratio of per capita expenditure of the wage-earning class to that of the self-employed in the rural sector (146 percent) is larger than that of the urban sector (121 percent). This confirms the earlier conclusion about greater inequality in the rural sector in 1983–1984 as depicted by the Gini index shown in Table 7.2.

## CONCLUSION

This chapter set out to measure and monitor the trend of poverty in Nigeria. At the outset, it was emphasized that it was not intended to analyze income inequality. The reference to inequality was only meant to aid analysis of poverty.

In the pursuit of this objective, the conclusion reached is that a greater percentage of Nigerians were in poverty in 1983–1984 than previously. Thereafter, the level of poverty got worse. Sectoral analysis has shown that the urban sector was more adversely affected by poverty in all its measures. Of special relevance is the gap between the average expenditure of the poor and the poverty line. This represents the average amount of money required to lift the poor out of poverty. This amount has been getting larger year by year, just as the proportion of the poor has grown over time in all the sectors. The implication is that, in addition to the efforts to improve the welfare of Nigerians generally, carefully planned and targeted policy measures should be directed at improving the lot of the poor.

An area of great concern in the study has been the nature of statistical information relating to household income and expenditure patterns in Nigeria. The available data are highly aggregated and most often reported in obscure percentages, all, perhaps, in an attempt to maintain confusion. This makes research in the way of monitoring poverty extremely difficult and unreliable. The Federal Office of Statistics (FOS), which is the agency responsible for conducting and publishing statistical materials from household survey, would do well to improve on its data reporting. Data that do not facilitate improvement in knowledge and policy targeting are of no use.

Appendix 7.1
Rural and Urban Consumer Unit Values in Current Prices

| Items Included in the Mini-Consumption Bundle | Per Capita Normative Daily Requirement | | Mean Urban Consumer Unit Value (₦/kg) | | Mean Rural Consumer Unit Value (₦/kg) | |
|---|---|---|---|---|---|---|
| | Calories | Grams | 1975 | 1983–1984 | 1975 | 1983–1984 |
| Gari/Cassava flour | 1,204 | 350 | 0.26 | 1.13 | 0.13 | 0.57 |
| Yam | 118 | 100 | 0.38 | 1.57 | 0.17 | 0.74 |
| Rice | 144 | 40 | 0.40 | 1.73 | 0.21 | 0.88 |
| Maize/Guinea Corn/Millet | 345 | 100 | 0.16 | 0.67 | 0.11 | 0.47 |
| Plantain | 40 | 50 | 0.22 | 0.95 | 0.04 | 0.17 |
| Pulses | 135 | 40 | 0.18 | 0.78 | 0.24 | 1.02 |
| Beef | 14 | 12 | 1.64 | 6.48 | 1.71 | 6.48 |
| Fish (dry) | 53 | 24 | 1.60 | 6.29 | 1.66 | 6.29 |
| Oils/Fats | 177 | 20 | 0.77 | 3.47 | 0.34 | 1.40 |
| Vegetables/Fruits | 50 | 120 | 0.24 | 0.93 | 0.10 | 0.40 |
| Sugar | 80 | 20 | 0.79 | 1.95 | 0.76 | 1.95 |
| Total (calories/gm) | 2,360 | 876 | - | - | - | - |
| Poverty Line Expenditure on Food (units/person/day) | - | - | 0.297 | 1.213 | 0.188 | 0.708 |
| Markup for Nonfood Expend. (42% of Food in 1983–1984 and 69% in 1975) | - | - | 0.205 | 0.509 | 0.103 | 0.296 |
| Total Poverty Line Expend. (=/Person/Day) | - | - | 0.50 | 1.72 | 0.29 | 1.00 |
| Rural CPI for Nonfood | - | - | - | - | 100 | 188.5 |
| Urban CPI for Nonfood | - | - | 100 | 262.9 | - | - |

*Note*: Values relate to farmgate prices.
*Sources*: Computed from FAO, 1993, various pages; FOS, 1981, 1983, 1987a.

Appendix 7.2
Distribution of Sample Population According to Monthly Expenditure Group
at Current and Constant Prices

| | 1975 | | | 1983–1984 | |
|---|---|---|---|---|---|
| Adult Equivalent Population | Per Capita Expenditure | | | Adult Equivalent Population (₦) | Per Capita Expenditure (₦) |
| Urban | Current Prices | 1983–1984 Prices | | | Current Prices |
| 8,991 | 13.78 | 46.82 | | 2,746 | 30.76 |
| 4,334 | 24.26 | 82.43 | | 2,937 | 46.78 |
| 1,481 | 28.31 | 96.20 | | 1,730 | 68.81 |
| 1,847 | 37.61 | 127.80 | | 933 | 75.94 |
| 494 | 64.80 | 220.20 | | 479 | 188.78 |
| 577 | 82.43 | 280.10 | | — | — |
| 17,724 | 23.70 | 80.50 | | 8,825 | 56.90 |
| **Rural** | | | | | |
| n.a. | n.a. | | | 5,671 | 26.37 |
| n.a. | n.a. | | | 2,394 | 37.10 |
| n.a. | n.a. | | | 581 | 51.71 |
| n.a. | n.a. | | | 429 | 65.07 |
| n.a. | n.a. | | | 174 | 152.91 |
| n.a. | n.a. | | | 9,249 | 34.91 |

*Note*: Children 0–14 years of age have been converted to adult equivalents by the ratio of
a weighted average of calorie intake per child per day to adult intake (1,386/2,360 for
1975 and 1,846/2,360 for 1983/984).
*Sources*: Computed from FAO, 1993, various pages; FOS, 1981, 1983, 1987a.

## NOTES

1. Assessments had been completed for Malawi, The Gambia, Ethiopia, Ghana,
Mali, Namibia, Sierra Leone, Uganda, and Mozambique, while the first drafts
have been completed for Algeria, Egypt, Morocco, Burkina Faso, Burundi, Cape
Verde, Chad, Guinea Bissau, Kenya, Madagascar, Mauritania, and Senegal.

2. The World Bank (1990) reports that, as a result of the economic reversal of
the early 1980s, per capita consumption in Nigeria dropped by 7 percent a year
and standards of living became lower in the mid-1980s than in the 1950s. Calorie
intake also showed no improvement between 1952 and 1985. How these figures
were arrived at, however, is not disclosed.

## REFERENCES

Ajai, S.I. (1991). *Macroeconomic Approach to External Debt*. Nairobi: Initiative Publishers.

Altimir, O. (1982). *The Extent of Poverty in Latin America*. World Bank Staff Working Paper No. 522. Washington, DC: World Bank.

Anand, S. and Harris, C. (1992). "Issues in the Measurement of Undernutrition." In S.R. Osmani (ed.), *Nutrition and Poverty*. Oxford: Oxford University Press.

Atkinson, A.B. (1975). *The Economics of Inequality*. Oxford: Oxford University Press.

Balogun, E.D. (1993). "Economic Reform and the National Question: The Effects of Structural Adjustment on Poverty and Inequality in Nigeria." In *The National Question and Economic Development in Nigeria*. Proceedings of NES 1993. Ibadan: Annual Conference.

Bangladesh Bureau of Statistics. (BBS) (1991). *Report on the Household Expenditure Survey 1988–89*. Dhaka: BBS.

Central Bank of Nigeria. (CBN) (1985). *Annual Report and Statement of Accounts*. Lagos: CBN.

Federal Office of Statistics (FOS). (1981). *FOS National Integrated Survey of Households 1975*. Lagos: FOS.

———. (1983). *Retail Prices for Selected Items*. Lagos: FOS.

———. (1987a). *National Integrated Survey of Households, 1985*. Lagos: FOS.

———. (1987b). *Social Statistics of Nigeria, 1985*. Lagos: FOS.

———. (1988). *Social Statistics of Nigeria, 1988*. Lagos: FOS.

Food and Agriculture Organization (FAO). (1986). *Review of Food Consumption Surveys, 1985*. Rome: FAO.

———. (1993). *Food and Nutrition in the Management of Group Feeding Programmes*. Rome: FAO.

Foster, J., Greer, J. and Thorbecke, E. (1981). *A Class of Decomposable Poverty Measures* (Working Paper No. 243). Ithaca, NY: Department of Economics, Cornell University.

———. (1984). "A Class of Decomposable Poverty Measures." *Econometrica* 57(3).

Greer, J. and Thorbecke, E. (1986). "A Methodology for Measuring Food Poverty Applied to Kenya." *Journal of Development Economics* 24(1): 59–74.

Hossain, M. (1987). *The Assault That Failed: A Profile of Absolute Poverty in Six Villages of Bangladesh*. Geneva: United Nations Research Institute for Social Development.

Hossain, M. and Sen, B. (1992). "Rural Poverty in Bangladesh: Trends and Determinants." *Asian Economic Review* 10: 1–34.

Kanbur, S.M. Ravi. (1987). "Measurement and Alleviation of Poverty." *IMF Staff Papers* 34(1): 60–85.

Latham, M.C. (1979). *Human Nutrition in Tropical Africa*. Rome: FAO.

Nigerian Institute of Social and Economic Research (NISER). (1988). *Social Impact of the Structural Adjustment Programme* (Monograph Series No. 1). Ibadan: NISER.

Okigbo, P.N.C. (1975). "Interpersonal Income Distribution in Nigeria." In O. Teriba (ed.), *Poverty in Nigeria* (pp. 313–325). Proceeding of 1975 Annual Conference of the Nigerian Economic Society. Ibadan: NES.

Onah, R.C. (1987). *Forced Retirement in Anambra State Primary School System: A Cost Benefit Analysis*. Unpublished M.Sc. Project, Nsukka, University of Nigeria.

Orshansky, M. (1965). "Counting the Poor: Another Look at the Poverty Profile." *Social Security Bulletin*. Washington, DC: U.S. Social Security Administration.

Osmani, S. (1982). *Economic Inequality and Group Welfare*. Oxford: Oxford University Press.

Patrinos, H.A. (1994). "Methods and Data." In G. Psacharopoulos and H.A. Patrinos (eds.), *Indigenous People and Poverty in Latin America: An Empirical Analysis*. Washington, DC: World Bank.

Paul, S. (1989). "A Model of Constructing the Poverty Line." *Journal of Development Economics* 30.

Pfeffermann, G. and Webb, R. (1983). "Poverty and Income Distribution in Brazil." *The Review of Income and Wealth* 29(2). New Haven, CT: International Association for Research in Income and Wealth.

Psacharopoulos, G. et al. (1992). *Poverty and Income Distribution in Latin America: A Story of the 1980s*. Washington, DC: World Bank.

Rahman, A. and Haque, T. (1988). *Poverty and Inequality of Bangladesh in the Eighties: An Analysis of Some Recent Evidence* (Research Report No. 91). Dhaka: BIDS.

Ravallion, M. (1994). *Poverty Comparisons*. Chur, Switzerland: Harwood Academic Publishers.

Ravallion, M. and Sen, B. (1994). "When Method Matters (Policy Working Paper No. 1359)." In *Toward a Resolution of the Debate about Bangladesh's Poverty Measures*. Washington, DC: The World Bank.

Rimi, A.A. (1981). "Governor's Address." In *Income Distribution*, Proceedings of NES Symposium at Kaduna, Ibadan, Economic Society (NES).

Sen, A. (1976). "Poverty: An Ordinal Approach to Measurement." *Econometrica* 44(2): 219–231.

———. (1978). "Three Notes on the Concept of Poverty." *Research Working Paper (World Employment Programme)*. Geneva: International Labour Office.

Sen, B. and Islam, Q.T. (1993). "Monitoring Adjustment and Poverty in Bangladesh: Issues, Dimensions, Tendencies." In *Monitoring Adjustment and Poverty in Bangladesh* (Report on the Framework Project, CIRDAP Study Series, No. 160). Dhaka: URDAP.

The World Bank. (1990). *World Development Report*. Washington, DC.

———. (1993). "Poverty Reduction and the World Bank: Progress in Fiscal 1993." *World Development Report, 1990*. New York: Oxford University Press.

———. (1994). *World Tables, 1994*. Baltimore, MD: Johns Hopkins University Press.

World Health Organization (WHO). (1973). "Energy and Protein Requirements." In *WHO Report No. 522*.

Chapter 8

# Determinants of Labor Migration to Gaborone, Botswana

## Oludele A. Akinboade

### INTRODUCTION

Gaborone was selected as the site for the new capital of Botswana in 1962. At that time, its population was about 3,800. It was also the administrative center for the Gaborone District, the site of the Central Prison and Police Headquarters, whose buildings were laid out in a government camp called "the village." In addition, there was a hotel and a few houses at the railway station and a small airstrip. A master plan for the new capital of the country was prepared in 1963 and approved by the colonial administration. Construction work on the town began in 1964, and the first government buildings were ready for occupation by February 1966. Administration was finally shifted from the erstwhile administrative capital city of Mafikeng to the capital of Gaborone in December 1969.

Plans called for Gaborone to have a minimum assured population of about 5,000 people by the time the seat of government was transferred in 1969, increasing to 7,500 people within 20 years. It was expected that additional growth induced by net immigration would increase the population to 10,000–15,000 by 1990. Thus, the ultimate planned size of the town would be about 18,000 or 20,000, including the village.

Contrary to these expectations, by 1971, the population of Gaborone was already 17,700; it had nearly attained the ultimate planned population in just five years. Gaborone's population increased to 31,255 in 1976, and 44,500 in 1978, far in excess of the master plan. Gaborone, which was more like a cattle post in the 1960s and 1970s, is now the largest city in Bostwana, with the largest population in the country—

Table 8.1
Probability of Adults Being in Wage or Self-Employment, by Sex, in
Selected Towns/Cities

|  | Probability of Wage Employment | | Probability of Self-Employment | |
|---|---|---|---|---|
| Location | Males | Females | Males | Females |
| Gaborone | 0.77 | 0.57 | 0.03 | 0.07 |
| Lobatse | 0.70 | 0.35 | 0.04 | 0.12 |
| Selebi-Phikwe | 0.74 | 0.31 | 0.04 | 0.13 |
| Francistown | 0.69 | 0.27 | 0.05 | 0.08 |

*Source*: GOB, 1982: 250.

about 180,000. Only recently, however, has it acquired the official status
of a city. According to Evans (1996: 54),

While there were no more than 3,000 people living in Gaborone at independence,
today (1996) there are about 160,000. Although it is still a tiny city by international standards, the rate of growth of the population has been astonishing: an
estimated 18 per cent per year.

Gaborone, as the seat of government, offers the most extensive government employment opportunities and pays quite well even for un-
skilled labor. Private nongovernment employment is also booming,
especially in the service sector. As Table 8.1 illustrates, many Batswana,
especially men, stand a good chance of getting jobs in Gaborone and
other major towns in the country.

Employment in Gaborone increased from 1,500 in 1964 to 7,000 in 1971
and 16,000 in 1978. By 1991, 66,820 people were employed in the city,
representing about one-third of total urban employment in the country
(GOB, 1995).

In 1973, total enrollment in primary schools in Gaborone was 2,889.
There were 79 teachers and only 38 overcrowded classrooms. Enrollment
in primary schools increased rapidly by 15 percent in 1970–1971, 9 percent in 1971–1972, and 22 percent in 1972–1973. Accordingly, government
made plans to build more schools. By 1985, eight primary schools had
been built in Gaborone, and two more were scheduled to be built during
the Sixth Development Plan. Of a total population of 118,253 who, in
1991, were engaged in full-time primary education in the urban areas of
Botswana, about 16 percent (19,216) were from Gaborone. The city also
accounts for a quarter of the urban population involved in full-time sec-

Table 8.2
Gaborone's Population Growth, 1971–1991

|                  | 1971   | 1981   | 1985   | 1991    |
|------------------|--------|--------|--------|---------|
|                  | 17,718 | 59,659 | 87,346 | 134,800 |
| % All Towns      | 32.56  | 39.77  | 44.59  | 48.49   |
| % National Total | 2.97   | 6.34   | 8.01   | 9.93    |

Source: GOB, 1985.

ondary education and about 50 percent of those involved in tertiary education in 1991 (GOB, 1995). There are now many more primary and secondary schools throughout Gaborone. The University of Botswana, also located in the city, had a student population of almost 7,000 in 1998.

The 1979–1985 National Development Plan (GOB, 1979: 84) noted the tendency toward unequal development of towns and villages in Botswana where most modern sector activities are concentrated in the towns, especially Gaborone. This situation encourages the drift of population to the city, which is reasonably modern and has beautiful houses, a growing number of restaurants, and many entertainment facilities. Banking, health, and educational facilities are better developed in the city than in the country's other towns. Some of these facilities are not even available in rural areas. Migration to Botswana cities has continued to be very rapid, with Gaborone showing the fastest rate of urban growth.

Of course, there is no guarantee that everyone who migrates to Gaborone enjoys these benefits. Although the city is reasonably modern, pockets of slums and ghettoes, with significant population concentration, remain. Many migrants end up living in these areas, where they are supported by relatives while they are waiting to secure gainful employment; some commute from there to work in small informal businesses. Those job seekers who fail to obtain employment may resort to crime to support themselves.

## Background of the Study

Associated with Botswana's rapid population growth is a change in settlement patterns. Gaborone has been growing even faster, so that whereas about a third of the total urban population lived in the city in 1971, this proportion rose to almost half in 1991. Only a small proportion (3 percent) of the total Botswana population lived in Gaborone in 1971. The figure rose to about 10 percent in 1991 (see Table 8.2).

The agricultural share of Botswana's gross domestic product declined from 40 percent at independence to 7 percent at the beginning of National Development Plan 6 and 3 percent in 1989. In 1966 the agricultural sector contributed P124 million of the P578 million total GDP; in 1983, P150 million of P2677 million; and in 1989, P149 million of P4115 million. Although there has been an increase in the absolute values, the agricultural share of GDP has decreased steadily over the years. This decline is partly due to recurrent drought, rural-urban migration, and to the faster growth of other sectors of the economy.

The discovery of minerals in the 1970s resulted in a significant shift of resources from agriculture as people migrated to mining towns such as Orapa, Jwaneng, and Selebi-Phikwe, and undertook other nonagricultural activities. This migration away from rural agriculture contributed to the decline of the sectoral share of GDP as increasingly smaller numbers of people were retained in the sector (GOB, 1991a).

Some economic constraints and natural disasters, including low and variable rainfall, poor soils, limited underground and surface water, and poor access to credit and economic resources, have caused people to abandon the agricultural sector and look toward the towns for their livelihoods. The asset base of many households was eroded by the 1981–1982 to 1986–1987 drought, which wiped out livestock in the process, reducing rural incomes and consequently pushing many people below the poverty line. This resulted in many people migrating from rural to urban areas in search of means to sustain their families (GOB, 1991a).

Rural-urban migration may lead to the lowering of rural incomes. These migrants are generally young adults who are relatively better educated. Their movement involves a large transfer of human capital out of the rural sector, which may adversely affect agricultural production and incomes. Such movements result in agricultural stagnation (Oberai and Singh, 1983).

The government of Botswana responded to problems in the agricultural sector by strongly emphasizing rural development. Several assistance programs were put in place, including the Financial Assistance Policy (FAP), the Accelerated Rural Development Program (ARDP), the Drought Relief Program (DRP), and the Accelerated Rainfed Arable Program (ARAP), in the expectation that rural-urban migration would decline significantly. The rationale is that providing gainful employment in rural areas would prevent large-scale migration to the cities. Unexpectedly, however, rural-urban migration continues at a very high rate.

Rural-urban migration plays an important role in the internal population dynamics of every country. Identifying migration streams, however, and measuring them accurately is of paramount importance, though in most cases, such accuracy cannot be attained because of draw-

Table 8.3
Migrants in 1980–1981 aged 12+, by Sex and Education

|  | No. of Male Movers | Population (%) | No. of Female Movers | Population (%) | Total Number | Population (%) |
|---|---|---|---|---|---|---|
| No School/ Unknown | 24,198 | 19.7 | 18,836 | 15.1 | 43,034 | 17.4 |
| Some Primary | 17,752 | 22.3 | 22,091 | 19.4 | 39,843 | 20.0 |
| Completed Primary | 10,590 | 30.7 | 12,842 | 26.6 | 23,432 | 28.3 |
| More than Primary | 7,884 | 37.2 | 6,793 | 35.2 | 14,677 | 36.2 |
| Total | 60,424 | 23.4 | 60,562 | 18.5 | 120,986 | 21.2 |

*Note*: The % columns show migrants as a percentage of migrants and nonmigrants for each
   row category.
*Source*: GOB, 1983.

backs and limitations in the migration data utilized. This issue is discussed later in this chapter.

This chapter examines what attracts labor to a capital city, with Gaborone as the case study. Specifically, it looks at the extent to which
people (by gender) migrate to the city for employment purposes and
take advantage of average income differential between rural (agricultural) and urban (nonagricultural) sectors of the country. Consideration
is also given to the significance of the age of migrants by gender in
determining their decision to migrate.

## RURAL-URBAN MIGRATION IN BOTSWANA

Schapera's migration surveys (1947) showed that the highest proportion of migrants in Botswana were able-bodied men aged between 15
and 44 years of age. It also showed that more unmarried men tended to
migrate than married men. After Botswana's independence, a new pattern of migration from rural areas to towns emerged. In 1964, the three
existing towns (Gaborone, Lobatse, and Francistown) had a combined
population of 20,845. By the 1981 census, the total population of the six
principal towns had grown to 150,021, about 16 percent of Botswana's
total population of 941,027. Persons who had moved in the year before
the census were more likely to have done so the more educated they
were. Table 8.3 shows data from the 1981 census which indicate that

Table 8.4
Migrants in 1980–1981 Aged 12 and Over, by Sex and Economic Activity
Status

| | No. of Male Movers | Population (%) | No. of Female Movers | Population (%) | Total Number | Population (%) |
|---|---|---|---|---|---|---|
| Employee | 25,421 | 29.7 | 10,231 | 27.0 | 35,652 | 28.9 |
| Self-Employed | 1,079 | 18.4 | 583 | 16.1 | 1,662 | 17.5 |
| Periodic Piece Work | 917 | 20.9 | 468 | 21.6 | 1,382 | 21.1 |
| Family Agriculture | 11,946 | 15.4 | 10,745 | 16.3 | 22,691 | 15.8 |
| Actively Seeking Work | 4,052 | 27.4 | 4,101 | 23.3 | 8,153 | 25.3 |
| Economically Inactive | 16,948 | 24.5 | 34,411 | 18.7 | 51,359 | 20.3 |
| Total | 60,363 | 23.5 | 60,539 | 18.7 | 120,902 | 21.3 |

*Note*: The % columns show migrants as a percentage of migrants and nonmigrants for each
    row category.
*Source*: GOB, 1983.

more than one-third of those with at least a primary education had
moved. In all educational categories, men were slightly more likely to
migrate than women, but the difference was substantially smaller at the
highest level. For both men and women, those with no education or only
an incomplete primary education were less likely to move, while those
with a complete primary education or more than primary education
were more likely to move.

Table 8.4 shows that employees and those actively seeking work are
well represented among both male and female migrants. For men, the
economically inactive are also quite substantial among migrants. This is
explained by the rapid expansion of secondary and postsecondary education opportunities in towns. In addition, in order to take advantage of
educational opportunities at this level, most students must migrate to
towns or large villages in the absence of such opportunities in rural settings.

Those females who were in the "periodic piece jobs" category (i.e.,
those who were casually employed) were quite substantial among migrants. The explanation here is that young women tend to migrate in-

dependently to towns, and when they are unable to find jobs or sufficient support from relatives or partners, they resort to menial activities for survival. An econometric analysis of the National Migration Survey (NMS) data convinced Lucas (1982) that, under Botswanan conditions, the creation of an extra urban job induces more than one adult migrant to move to town, adding to the nonemployed adults in town.

The 1981 census also found that employment was the main motivation for migration. The three new towns (Orapa, Selebi-Phikwe, and Jwaneng) are mining towns to which most people migrate seeking employment opportunities. Among the young, continuation of education is a frequent reason for migration. Family reunification is almost certainly one of the reasons for migration. James Cobbe (1983) found that although the practice of maintaining two residences is very widespread, a proportion of male migrants to towns are eventually joined by their wives and children.

Migration has transformed the structure of Botswana over the last 20 to 30 years. The capital city, Gaborone, has grown from a small government post and rail stop to a city of 180,000 people. What was formerly the main town in the southern part of the country, Lobatse, has gone into decline as its economic attractions have diminished relative to those of Gaborone. Three entirely new towns, based on mining, have risen from bare land. Francistown, located close to the Zimbabwe border, has grown rapidly and added some manufacturing (mostly textiles) to what was formerly a commercial center and railhead for the neighboring freehold farms.

At the same time, the rural settlement pattern has been changing. The old pattern was based on a network of villages, fitting into a hierarchy from quite small to surprisingly large. However, the smaller villages have lost population while the larger ones have gained, and a rising proportion of the rural population is living permanently where agricultural activities take place or in new, small hamlets not yet recognized by governments.

The 1984–1985 Labor Force Survey classifies the Botswana population into three groups based on migration. About 40 percent, the vast majority of whom live in rural areas, have never moved. Of the 60 percent who have moved, a small proportion is presumed to be permanently settled in their new location, typically either on "permanent land" or among the more securely and better paid employed in towns. However, the 1981 census found that nearly one in five of the population had moved in the previous year. Some of these are classic circular migrants moving between jobs (often in towns) and rural bases. Others are those moving temporarily in search of education or perceived better economic or social conditions.

That a capital city attracts rural-urban migrants is not peculiar to Gaborone. Using lifetime migration data from the 1969 census, Sly and Wrigley (1986, in Nam, Serow, and Sly, 1990) have established that rural-urban migration accounted for about one-third of all movements in Kenya. The phenomenon is demonstrated by the importance of Nairobi, the capital city, and Mombasa as the primary destination of migrants from rural districts. Nairobi receives population from Kirinyana, Muranga, and Nyeri (three of the five districts) in Central Province; all districts in Eastern Province; and two of the districts in Western Province. Mombasa is a primary destination for migrants originating from Coast Province. Mombasa itself loses population to Nairobi (the only inter-urban migration).

In 1969, 70 percent of the male population in the Nairobi metropolitan province were lifetime migrants compared to 59 percent of females. Kenyan data also show that in the national rural-urban migration survey of eight major towns, migration peaked at 20 to 24 years. In the three other surveys, the peak ages were 25 to 29 years. This suggests that the age bracket 20 to 29 years is a crucial one. After age 30, the percentage of migrants drops, suggesting that population mobility occurs steadily up to the 40s.

In Tanzania, the net annual rural-urban migration shift during the half-century prior to 1948 was very small. The total population of the six regional centers in 1948 was 62,500. Between 1948 and 1971, the population of these urban centers nearly quadrupled, implying an average annual growth rate of 6 percent. Over 175,000 more people were living in the six towns in 1971 than in 1940. The population increase of the six towns due to natural growth was 48,000 per 1,000 people, and nearly 130,000 were people who had left their birthplaces to go to the six towns. Eighty-six percent of the increase in Arusha was due to migration, while in Tabora, natural population growth contributed as much as migration to the town (Sabot, 1979).

The population of Dar-es-Salaam, the capital city, grew very quickly. Seventy-eight percent of the total population increase of 242,000 during the period 1948–1971 was due to migration. Dar-es-Salaam's population in 1948 was greater than the combined total for the six towns. After urbanization began in the nineteenth century, the choice of Dar-es-Salaam by most migrants in the postwar period perpetuated the high primary characteristic of the urban hierarchy in Tanzania. Migrants left primarily in search of employment opportunities. The increase in the rate of in-migration to the six towns was not uniform. In 1948–1971, the population growth rate was less than 2 percent in Arusha and in Dodoma, while Mwanza grew by 15 percent per year. Eighty-three percent of the total adult population of both Dar-es-Salaam and the six towns were born elsewhere (Sabot, 1979).

An urban resident was classified as a migrant in this study on Tanzania only if the individual had come to town after the age of 13. Approximately two-thirds of the seven towns' population qualified as migrants, and nearly 90 percent of these towns' migrants come from rural areas. Rural-urban migration is therefore the predominant factor in the growth of Tanzania's towns. However, the pace of urbanization is considerably slower than the rate of urban growth, and Tanzania remains one of the least urbanized countries in the world. Migration in Tanzania has been predominantly male dominated. A little more than half of the migrants in 1971 were male (Sabot, 1979).

In Sabot's study, a high proportion of male migrants (70 %), indicated that the search for employment was their main reason for coming to town, with only 9 percent of female migrants giving the same reason. Sixty-six percent of the migrant women indicated that they had come to town to live with their husbands as economic dependents. Most of the migrants were aged between 14 and 30 years, and most of these migrants were males (Sabot, 1979).

The present study therefore seeks to contribute to the understanding of the determinants of rural-urban migration in Botswana, using Gaborone as a case study. Discussion of Kenya and Tanzania's experiences is useful in guiding this study, especially in determining the age grouping of migrants, sex (gender), preference for a capital city, and motivation for migration among others.

## SURVEY OF THE LITERATURE

### Underlying Causes of Rural-Urban Migration

Migration is an old topic in social science and various aspects of it have been widely studied and discussed. Work by Bilsborrow et al. (1984), Adepoju et al. (1994), and Appleyard (1998) examines the importance of various attributes of the migration decisions such as education, uncertainty, age and gender. Moreover, intersectoral labor migration is the centerpiece of the dual economy analysis by Lewis (1954) and subsequent works by Fei and Ranis (1964) and Jorgenson (1961). These studies reveal that in the process of development, labor must move from the traditional to the modern sector. However, inherent in this idea is the notion that the modern sector faces a perfectly elastic labor supply, originating from the traditional or rural sector. As Larson and Mundlak (1995) contend, this view is inconsistent with the ideas that migration is determined in response to varying income differentials and that labor is productive in all sectors of the economy. When labor migrates in response to income differentials, the dynamics of the economy is determined by the economic environment and is also affected by economic policies.

Numerous studies show that migrants respond to economic incentives and are affected by the presence of friends and relatives and by distance from the home site. Most econometric studies have included direct policy variables such as wages and employment into model specifications in order to provide some policy prescriptions. The intention could be to examine whether increased wage differentials motivate people to move out of places of origin or to attract others to a target destination. Policy prescriptions could therefore emerge from such studies stemming from the significance of the examined wage variable.

Most studies on rural-urban migration are cross-sectional studies. These include Beals and Moses (1967) for Ghana, Huntington (1974) for Kenya, and Barnum and Sabot (1975) for Tanzania, just to mention a few African examples. As cross-sectional studies, they highlight point-to-point migration, usually between regions and states.

The basic form which the migration functions specified is log-linear. Typical independent variables used include wage or income levels, un-employment rates, and degree of urbanization for population in particular areas; distance between the origin and places of destination; and presence of friends and relatives in target destinations. These studies utilize structured questionnaires administered to rural-urban migrants in order to generate primary data, which upon analysis are used to derive the significance of these variables.

Most econometric work confirms that people move from poorer areas to wealthier ones for economic gain. As such, differences in average income or wage levels between two places are significant variables in affecting migration between locations. When wage or income differentials between two places are included as variables, the migration rate increases with the size of the wage/income differential. Barnum and Sabot, among others, have confirmed this point for Tanzania. This is the approach that has been followed in this study. Other studies have included average wages or income levels separately. The result has been that migration is positively related to the wage/income level in the target destination and negatively related to the wage/income levels in places of the migrants' origin.

Some studies have included the chances of securing an urban job as an explanatory variable (Harris and Todaro, 1970, in Todaro, 1994). Todaro proposed a well-known rural-urban migration model which postulates that migration occurs in response to urban-rural differences in expected income rather than actual earnings. The model states that migrants consider different labor market opportunities available to them in rural and urban sectors and choose the one that will maximize their expected gains from migration. Expected gains are measured by the difference in real incomes between rural and urban work and the probability of the migrant obtaining an urban job. The theory assumes that potential migrants compare their expected incomes for a given time horizon in the urban sector (the difference between returns and costs of migration) with prevailing average rural incomes and migrate if the expected income is greater than the average rural incomes. The migrant would, of course, seek the higher paying urban job. In this case, the exclusive emphasis is the income differential as the determinant of the decision to migrate.

Some studies have linked migration to such factors as the increasing commercialization of the agricultural sector of many low-income countries. The increased demand for modern consumption goods has resulted in shifts in production from subsistence to cash crops. The commercialization of agriculture has generally increased competition among rural producers, which has increased inequality in land distribution. With greater access to technology, large landowners have become richer while small farmers who cannot afford the new technology are forced to lag behind. Since a massive increase in productivity and output brings down prices, those farmers using traditional forms of production and small farmers experience declining incomes. Many are compelled to sell their land and quit production altogether. When the number of landless people increases, they may move to cities in search of nonagricultural jobs (Oberai, 1983).

Other studies show that migrants are attracted to cities in search of better entertainment or better educational facilities for their children. As Oberai (1983), and Bilsborrow, Standing, and Oberai (1984) have observed, such factors as the presence of friends and relatives in urban areas to provide initial assistance also affect migration. Destination contacts have a positive effect on migration to a specific area. The approach adopted in the present study is to stretch this variable to include the presence of migrant spouses in Gaborone. The presence of a spouse in the city is expected to positively affect the decision to migrate.

The present study utilizes secondary data published by the Central Statistics Office. Where other data are not available, missing data were generated. As such, the analysis is restricted to migration to Gaborone differentiated by gender and age. The study is unable to capture return migration and multiple moves within the period under study. In addition, the analysis is restricted to a single case study so that it could be more focused. The study is unable to include distance as an important variable in the model, for it would have required utilizing primary data on migrants' source areas and the average distance to Gaborone.

A time variable has been used to capture other variables explaining the attractiveness of Gaborone as a city. As noted earlier, migrants might move to the city in search of educational opportunities or entertainment or because the city is more urbanized than others. The average Gaborone dweller has more access to pipe-borne water sewage connections, electricity, modern medical care, and better schooling opportunities than an average rural dweller. Other attractions could include better living conditions, a wider variety of shopping, availability of social and recreational facilities, and so on. All these factors might stimulate migration to Gaborone. Measuring some of these variables could have posed serious difficulties. Therefore, the time variable has been used to capture them in the econometric specification.

Traditionally, the migration variable used in some studies is measured either as people who have moved from one region/state to another during a particular year or as people in a particular state/region in a particular year who were born in that state/region. These data are generated from census data or questionnaire surveys. The approach here involves the use of secondary published data essentially to look at the growth rate of Gaborone city and deduces what is expected to be the city's natural rate of growth. The difference has been attributed to immigration, consistent with the government of Botswana's approach.

Accurate income measures are not easy to come by. Hence, published wage and income data are used, taking the average agricultural income as indicative of rural incomes. A simple average of sectoral incomes is used to derive incomes obtainable in the nonagricultural sector in Gaborone. This could be applied to other cities as well.

At the individual and household levels, considerable concern has been expressed about the effects of migration patterns in Botswana. Much of this has been in the context of unaccompanied male migration (especially to South Africa), which sometimes has deleterious effects on wives and children left behind, despite substantial remittance flows from the bulk of such migrants. The National Migration Survey data on both internal and South Africa remittances have been analyzed in detail by Lucas and Stark (1985). Unaccompanied male migration has similar effects whether the destination is domestic or foreign.

Concern has also been expressed about the effects of migration on agricultural productivity. Another concern centers on the social impact of migration to towns of young unaccompanied females, particularly unmarried mothers and their children. Most of these women have insecure sources of economic support, raising questions about their own welfare and that of their children (Nam, Serow, and Sly, 1990).

## RESEARCH METHODOLOGY

This rural-urban migration study seeks to examine the cause of migration to a capital city, employing income rather than wage differentials and other factors to determine migration. Wage and income differentials are likely to be correlated, and hence only one of the measures is used. Following Larson and Mundlak (1995), it is assumed that the decision to

Table 8.5
Example of Rural-Urban Migration Data Construction

|                          | 1981–1986 | 1986–1990 | 1991–1996 |
|--------------------------|-----------|-----------|-----------|
| Growth Rate of Gaborone  | 9.68%     | 7.78%     | 6.48%     |
| Rate of Natural Increase | –5.56%    | –4.46%    | –3.63%    |
| Net In-migration         | 4.12%     | 3.32%     | 2.85%     |

migrate is based on lifetime income, and so the age of the individual is important. Larson and Mundlak argue that, other things being equal, the younger the person is, the longer the period during which he will benefit from the higher income in the new occupation. They also suggest that the costs and benefit of migration may relate to other specific attributes of the individual such as gender. The present study examines these issues in relation to migration to a particular city, Gaborone.

The analysis relies on published secondary data to provide consistent time series trends for use in the analysis. Where missing values are encountered, corresponding values are generated, especially for net immigration to Gaborone and the differential between agricultural and nonagricultural incomes.

## DATA CONSTRUCTION

The data set covers the 1978–1993 period. Published data on rural-urban migration are available only for the years 1978–1981, 1986, and 1991. Therefore, other data on Gaborone's population were used to find missing numbers by subtracting the natural rate of increase of Gaborone from the overall growth rate of this area, thus obtaining the net migration rate for the years for which official data were not available. In so doing, the researcher obtained immigration rates of 4.12 percent and 3.32 percent for 1982–1985 and 1987–1990, respectively, which were used to calculate net immigration to Gaborone for those years, simply by multiplying the population of Gaborone in a particular year by the appropriate rate of immigration. The rate for 1991 was found to be 2.85 percent, so the numbers of immigrants for the years 1992 and 1993 were derived by multiplying the total number of immigrants for the year 1991 by 2.854 percent to get the total for 1992, which was further multiplied by the same growth rate of immigration to get the total immigrant population for 1993. The net immigration rates derived in the study are shown in Table 8.5.

Thus, growth rates of 4.12 percent, 3.32 percent, and 2.85 percent (as calculated above) were used to find the missing values for both males and females migrating to Gaborone for 1982–1985, 1987–1989 and 1992–1993. Central government employment as a proportion of total formal employment is obtained from published data. The sectoral income differential was calculated by subtracting average agricultural income from average nonagricultural income.

## DATA ANALYSIS AND INTERPRETATION

This econometric analysis utilizes the ordinary least square (OLS) method to estimate total male and female migration as a function of age, availability of government employment, differential between agricultural and nonagricultural incomes, and time trend.

As such, four main models are presented. The first model examines the relationship between annual migration, growth in sectoral income differentials, growth of government employment, and time trend. This relationship is examined by age classification and gender. It is anticipated that the willingness to migrate may be influenced by age groupings in response to the income-earning opportunities presented by growth in government employment and sectoral income differentials. A time trend is specified to capture other variables such as city attractiveness and search for educational opportunities.

The second model examines annual migration flow by gender and specifies lagged differential in sectoral income, time trend, and growth in share of government employment in total employment. The ratio of agricultural and nonagricultural incomes is used as another measure of income disparity in a variant of this model. In introducing a lag of sectoral income differentials, the intention is to evaluate the influence of past income differentials on current migration decisions. If this differential is quite substantial, it is expected that a potential migrant might determine that future involvement is not worthwhile in the sector where income-generating opportunities are low.

The third model seeks to examine the effect of migration on average agricultural incomes. The intention is to examine the controversy in the literature that migration out of agriculture could lead to an increase or decline in average rural agricultural income, especially if the movers are the most productive.

The implication of migration for government recurrent expenditure is the focus of the fourth model. This is to capture the budgetary implications of the process. Development expenditures, an alternative that was considered, was rejected on the ground that they reflect more of the long-term vision of city growth consequent upon its expected natural increase. Recurrent expenditures are used instead to capture immediate government response to migration.

## MODEL RESULTS

The analyst ran a number of separate regressions, the results of which are presented in Tables 8.6–8.9. The Schwartz Criteria (SC) and the Akaike Information Criteria (AIC) were used to select the models presented. These are in addition to the familiar criteria for determining model performance.

### Model 1: Determinants of Annual Migration to Gaborone

Table 8.6 presents the results of a simulation of annual migration to Gaborone by age distinguishing mainly between the 15–29 age group (described as young) and 30–49 age group (described as much older). The results show that growth in sectoral income differential discourages the migration of the young, both male and female, to Gaborone. The result, significant at the 10 percent level, is perhaps not surprising. Growth in sectoral income differential may provoke a more active migration of more elderly individuals to Gaborone, reducing the chances that the younger ones will perform well in the Gaborone labor market. Growth in government employment is not significant in explaining the migration of the young to Gaborone.

The results also show a strong positive relationship between time and youth's migration to Gaborone. The 1981 and 1991 censuses confirm the prevalence in towns of secondary and postsecondary education opportunities and the total absence of these opportunities in villages. It is therefore not surprising that the youth movement to Gaborone might be motivated by the desire to seek educational opportunities. This we have captured under time trend in the absence of better indicators such as secondary/postsecondary school enrollment, which would have been preferred.

In deciding to migrate to Gaborone, the much older male migrants appear to be motivated by growth in sectoral income differential regardless of whether or not such income differential can be obtained in government employment. This finding shows that in deciding to leave the rural areas, the much older male migrants are motivated by the prospect of bettering their income positions. This does not appear to be the case with much older female migrants moving alone. Whereas when older females move with much older men (as spouses), growth of sectoral income differential is quite crucial, as is the preference for government employment with the associated employment security that it carries with it. Growth in sectoral income differential, however, discourages competitive joint migration to Gaborone, whereas the growth of government employment promotes it. That the coefficient of joint migration between the much older males and females is significant in the models shows the

Table 8.6
Determinants of Annual Migration to Gaborone

Dependent Variable—Annual Migration (Log)

| Independent Variables | Females | 1# | 2 | Males | # |
|---|---|---|---|---|---|
| | Young | Much Older | | Young | Much Older |
| Constant | 6.3264 (319.3) | 157.73 (41.99) | −7.7165 (−6.886) | 6.6263 (636.6) | 331.02 (76.97) |
| Joint Migration with Much Older Males | | | 2.2091 (11.49)*** | | |
| Income Differential Growth | −0.055977 (−1.444)* | −0.00584 (−0.615) | −0.03972 (−2.295)** | −0.032646 (−1.603)* | 0.01603 (1.476)* |
| Growth of Govt. Employment | 0.055882 (0.3756) | 0.00024 (0.665) | 0.11765 (3.213)*** | 0.10185 (1.303) | −0.000038 (−0.0938) |
| Time | 0.041427 (30.6)*** | 10.055 (8.88)*** | −0.01426 (−2.983)** | 0.03761 (52.9)*** | 10.487 (8.091)*** |
| **Test Statistics** | | | | | |
| Adj $R^2$ | 0.9894 | 0.9991 | 0.9992 | 0.9965 | 0.9989 |
| Durbin-Watson | 1.9019 | 3.1592 | 2.2564 | 1.6335 | 1.8337 |
| F | 313.39 | 3740.59 | | 937.69 | 2981.5 |
| SC | 0.000303 | 1.696 | 0.0000242 | 0.0000836 | 2.224 |
| AIC | 0.000262 | 1.468 | 0.0000202 | 0.0000724 | 1.924 |

* Statistically significant at 10%; ** Statistically significant at 5%; *** Statistically significant at 1%.
Figures in parentheses are the corresponding $t$-statistics.
2 After correction for autocorrelation.
# values not expressed in logs.

importance of spousal migration once employment is secured. Although individual migration to Gaborone will increase over time, joint migration will ultimately be discouraged.

## Model 2: Determinants of Annual Migration Flow

Table 8.7 shows the results of the model on the flow of annual migration to Gaborone. Total migration is considered, classified by gender. The

Table 8.7
Determinants of Annual Migration Flow

**Dependent Variable—Annual Migration Flow**

| Independent Variables | Total Female | Total Female | Total Male | Total Male |
|---|---|---|---|---|
| Constant | 3.8221 (3.018) | 1.667 8 (0.5673) | 4.0672 (3.360) | 0.94939 (0.8951) |
| Growth in Share of Government in Total Employment | 0.87673 (2.243)** | 2.0095 (36.38)*** | 0.81195 (2.172)** | 1.3066 (3.561)** |
| Agricultural/ Nonagricultural Income Ratio | | −0.33946 (−0.5138) | | |
| Lagged Differential in Sectoral Income | −0.85411 (−2.899)*** | | −0.90678 (−3.220)*** | |
| Growth in income Differential | | | | 0.52594 (1.931)** |
| Time | 0.091288 (2.518)** | 0.028131 (0.5673) | 0.09601 (2.771)*** | −0.10439 (−1.10) |
| **Test Statistics** | | | | |
| Adj. $R^2$ | 0.9952 | 0.9918 | 0.9957 | 0.9937 |
| F | 793.73 | 459.58 | 877.33 | 603.82 |
| Durbin-Watson | 2.3361 | 1.8071 | 2.3316 | 2.2790 |
| SC | 0.023337 | 0.040203 | 0.021318 | 0.030931 |
| AIC | 0.019321 | 0.033286 | 0.017650 | 0.025609 |

* Statistically significant at 10%; ** Statistically significant at 5%; *** Statistically significant at 1%.
Figures in parentheses are the corresponding $t$-statistics.

variables under consideration included the growth in the share of government employment as a proportion of total employment, the ratio of agricultural and nonagricultural income, and lagged differential in sectoral income differential. The table shows the overwhelming significance of growth in government employment's share in total employment and the lagged differential in sectoral income. Whereas this growth promotes migration to Gaborone, lagged income differential discourages it. This may indicate that migrants are not positively influenced by lagged

Table 8.8
Impact of Migration to Gaborone on Agricultural Incomes

| Dependent Variable | Average Agricultural Income | |
|---|---|---|
| Independent Variables | (1) | (2) |
| Constant | -6.159 (-1.797)** | -7.348 (-2.213)** |
| Male Migration | 1.4444 (3.125)*** | |
| Female Migration | | 1.6192 (3.58)*** |
| **Test Statistics** | | |
| AdjR² | 0.859 | 0.868 |
| Durbin-Watson | 1.8339 | 1.8597 |
| SC | 0.05152 | 0.04818 |
| AIC | 0.046777 | 0.04375 |

*Note*: Results were corrected for second-order autocorrelation using the Cochrane-Orcutt procedure.
Figures in parentheses are the *t*-ratios.

income differential but are more influenced by growth in sectoral income differential. The ratio of agricultural and nonagricultural income is not significant in the model of total female migration and does not help explain total male migration; hence, it was excluded.

### Model 3: Effect of Rural-Urban Migration to Gaborone on Average Agricultural Income

The results presented in Table 8.8 indicate that migration to Gaborone, both male and female, increases average rural agricultural incomes for nonmigrants. As people move out of agriculture, average incomes must increase for those remaining if they are to be retained on the farms. The results are significant at the 1 percent level.

### Model 4: Effect of Rural-Urban Migration to Gaborone on Government Recurrent Expenditures

The results presented in Table 8.9 show that migration increases recurrent government expenditures on security, law and order, urban in-

Table 8.9
Impact of Migration to Gaborone on Recurrent Government Expenditure

Dependent Variables: Recurrent Expenditure on

| Independent Variables | Security/Order | | Urban Infrastructure | | Health | |
|---|---|---|---|---|---|---|
| | (1) | (2) | (1) | (2) | (1) | (2) |
| Constant | -23.89 (-11.29) | -26.35 (-14.2) | -31.5 (-19.88) | -34.1 (-26.7) | -23.78 (-7.62) | -27.3 (-11.5) |
| Male Migration | 3.65 (12.83) | | 4.132 (19.4) | | 3.65 (8.68) | |
| Female Migration | | 4.03 (15.98) | | 4.53 (26.06) | | 4.16 (12.9) |
| Test Statistics | | | | | | |
| AdjR² | 0.939 | 0.938 | 0.955 | 0.9602 | 0.926 | 0.93 |
| Durbin-Watson | 1.98 | 1.86 | 2.098 | 2.04 | 1.94 | 1.96 |
| SC | 0.075 | 0.076 | 0.068 | 0.061 | 0.095 | 0.091 |
| AIC | 0.068 | 0.069 | 0.062 | 0.055 | 0.086 | 0.083 |

Note: Results were corrected for second-order correlation using the Cochrane-Orcutt procedure. Figures in parentheses are the $t$-ratios. All variables are significant at the 1 percent level.

frastructure, and the health sector. These are significant at the 1 percent level.

## CONCLUSION

Rural-urban migration has been of interest to many social scientists, especially economists. It has been associated with the process of development in the more industrialized countries. Lewis (1954), for example, postulated the necessity for the rural traditional sector to free disguisedly unemployed labor for employment in the modern urban sector. This means that the category of labor whose marginal contribution to the overall output is zero or negative will be released from the traditional rural sector to the urban modern sector where it will become more productivity engaged. Other authors such as Todaro (1969) have examined the application of this theory in less developed countries (LDCs) and found that the modern urban sector usually does not grow sufficiently to allow all rural migrants to obtain productive employment.

This study has attempted to enhance our understanding of the rural-urban migration process in LDCs. Botswana is a developing country with a rapidly growing urban population, high per capita income, and a democratic form of government that permits free movement of people from rural to urban areas within the country.

Gaborone, the capital of Botswana, is the seat of government and possesses all the features needed to attract rural population. The city has been growing at a very rapid rate, but not all this rate of increase can be attributed to natural forces. A significant proportion is due to rural-urban migration, which is the focus of this study.

The regression analysis utilizes secondary data on population, age of migrants, sectoral wage rates, and central government employment as a proportion of total formal employment. Some of these data had been subjected to additional manipulations in order to obtain estimates of net immigration to Gaborone by gender and age groups. The analysis involves the use of estimated monthly agricultural earnings to reflect average rural incomes. The nonagricultural income was calculated as a simple average of monthly earnings across sectors. The traditional OLS econometric technique was applied to test the significance of a number of variables in determining male, female, and total migration. Four models are presented here. The results show that when the sectoral income differential between agricultural and nonagricultural earnings widens, rural-urban migration to Gaborone will be encouraged, especially by the older male migrants. However, it discourages competitive joint migration by both genders. Male migration has a pull effect on female migration as spouses come to join their husbands and on the very young who accompany their parents, as dictated by the place of employment. This is consistent with a priori expectations, as female (spouses) migration and those of the very young are incidental on male migration. In other words, it is to be expected that wives and children migrate with their husbands and fathers, respectively, and not the other way around. Growth in sectoral income differentials discourages the migration of the young to Gaborone regardless of gender.

Growth in the share of central government employment as a proportion of total formal employment encourages migration to Gaborone. Growth in government employment is not significant in explaining youth's migration to Gaborone but it promotes joint migration with spouses.

With time, migration to Gaborone will always take place, as shown in the models. This might be in response to varying sectoral income differentials, attraction to the city, or the search for educational opportunities.

The results of the present study apparently support Kanbur's findings (1981) that rural development does not immediately result in reduced migration. The government of Botswana has spent large sums of money on rural development over the years, but still migration continues to increase. The study shows that notwithstanding these development efforts, rural-urban migration to Gaborone will increase over time.

On the positive side, migration, both male and female, increases average rural agricultural incomes for nonmigrants. As people move out of agriculture, average incomes must increase for those remaining if they are to be retained on the farms. However, migration increases government recurrent expenditures on security, law and order, urban infrastructure, and the health sector. Resources meant for other uses may therefore be diverted to cater for incoming migrants.

The government of Botswana must invigorate its incomes policy in order to reduce widening sectoral disparities in income earnings between the agricultural and nonagricultural sectors.

Educational opportunities and social amenities should not be concentrated in particular cities, for this will increase the attractiveness of the cities, promoting rural-urban migration. If educational opportunities become available in rural areas, and if social amenities are provided in the immediate locality, youth's migration to Gaborone (and indeed other cities/towns) will decrease, regardless of gender.

The government should also promote private sector development and thereby reduce reliance on government employment. Government administration should be decentralized to other parts of the country. When government employment is seen as a guarantor of employment security, then it should not matter where the job is located. This approach may reduce the pressure on Gaborone.

## REFERENCES

Adepoju, A. and Oppong, E. (eds.). (1994). *Gender, Work and Population in Sub-Saharan Africa*. London: James Currey Publishers.

Appleyard, R. (ed.). (1998). *Emigration Dynamics in Developing Countries. Vol. 1: Sub-Saharan Africa*. Aldershot, England: Ashgate.

Barnum, H. and Sabot, R.H. (1975). *Education, Employment Probabilities, and Rural-Urban Migration in Tanzania*. Paper presented to the Third World Congress of the Econometric Society, Toronto, Canada.

Beals, R.M.L. and Moses, L. (1967). "Rationality and Migration in Ghana." *Review of Economics and Statistics* (49): 480–486.

Bienefeld, M. and Sabot, R. (1971). *The National Urban Mobility, Employment and Income Survey of Tanzania (NUMEIST)*. Dar es Salaam: Ministry of Economic Affairs and University of Dar es Salaam.

Bilsborrow, R.E., Oberai, A.S., and Standing, G. (1984). *Migration Survey in Low Income Countries*. London: Croom Helm.

Chenery, S. (1988). *Handbook of Development Economics, Volume 1*. Amsterdam: North-Holland.

Cobbe, J. (1990). *Internal Migration in Botswana*. Quoted in C.B. Nam, W.J. Serow, and D.F. Sly, *International Handbook on Internal Migration*. Westport, CT: Greenwood Press.

Evans, R. (1996). "Gaborone, Africa's Fastest Growing City: Growing Pains." *Focus on Africa* 7(3): 54–56.

Fei, J.C.H. and Ranis, G. (1964). *Development of the Labour Surplus Economy: Theory and Policy*. New York: Irwin.

Ghatak, S. (1995). *Introduction to Development Economics*. London: Routledge.

Government of Botswana (GOB). (1979). *National Development Plan 5*. Gaborone: Government Printers.

———. (1982). *Migration in Botswana: Patterns, Causes and Consequences*. Final Report. Gaborone: Central Statistics Office (CSO).

———. (1983). *1981 Population and Housing Census*. Gaborone: CSO.

———. (1985). *National Development Plan 6*. Gaborone: Government Printers.

———. (1986). *1985 Statistical Bulletin*. Gaborone: CSO.

———. (1987a). *1986 Labour Statistics*. Gaborone: CSO.

———. (1987b). *Population Projections 1981–2011*. Gaborone: CSO.

———. (1988a). *Household Income and Expenditure Survey 1985/86*. Gaborone: CSO.

———. (1988b). *1987 Labour Statistics*. Gaborone: CSO.

———. (1990). *1989 Labour Statistics*. Gaborone: CSO.

———. (1991a). *National Development Plan 7*. Gaborone: Government Printers.

———. (1991b). *Population of Towns, Villages, and Associated Localities*. Gaborone: CSO.

———. (1993). *1991/92 Labour Statistics*. Gaborone: CSO.

———. (1995). *1994 Statistical Bulletin*. Gaborone: CSO.

Harvey, C. and Lewis, S.R. (1991). *Policy Choice for Development Performance in Botswana*. London: Macmillan Press Ltd.

Huntington, H. (1974). *An Empirical Study of Ethnic Linkages in Kenyan Rural-Urban Migration*. Unpublished Ph.D. Thesis, SUNY, Binghamton.

Jorgenson, D. (1961). "The Development of a Dual Economy." *Economic Journal* 71: 309–334.

Kanbur, R. (1981). Quoted in S. Ghatak, *Introduction to Development Economics*. London: Allen and Unwin, 1995.

Kerven, C. (1979). *Rural-Urban Migration and Agricultural Productivity in Botswana*. Gaborone: Ministry of Agriculture.

Larson, D. and Mundlak, Y. (1995). *On the Intersectoral Migration of Agricultural Labour*. World Bank Policy Research Working Paper No. 1425. Washington, DC: The World Bank.

Lee, E.S. (1966). "A Theory of Migration." *Demography* 3(1): 47–57.

Lekwape, V. (1996). *Factors Influencing Rural-Urban Migration: A Case Study of Gaborone*. Project in Applied Economics Submitted in partial fulfillment of the requirements of the Bachelor of Arts Degree.

Lewis, W.A. (1954). *Economic Development with Unlimited Supplies of Labour*. Manchester, England: School of Economic and Social Studies.

Lucas, R.E.B. (1982). "Outmigration, Remittances and Investment in Rural Areas." In Government of Botswana, *Migration in Botswana: Patterns, Causes and Consequences*. Gaborone: Central Statistics Office.

Lucas, R.E.B. and. Stark, O. (1985). "Motivations to Remit: Evidence from Botswana." *Journal of Political Economy* 93(5): 901–918.

Mukras, M.S., Oucho, J.O., and Bamberger, M. (1985). "Resource Mobilization and Household Economy in Kenya." *Canadian Journal of African Studies* 19(2): 409–421.

Nam, C.B., Serow, W.J., and Sly, D.F. (1990). *International Handbook on Internal Migration.* Westport, CT: Greenwood Press.

Oberai, A.S. (ed.). (1983). *State Policies and International Migration: Studies in Market and Planned Economies.* London: Croom Helm.

Oberai, A.S. and Singh, H.K.M. (1980). "Migration, Remittances and Rural Development: Findings of a Case Study in the Indian Punjab." *International Labour Review* 119(2): 229–241.

———. (1983). *Causes and Consequences of Internal Migration: A Study in the Indian Punjab.* Delhi: University Press.

Oberai, A.S., Standing, G. and Bilsborow, R.E. (1984). *Migration Surveys in Low Income Countries: Guidelines for Questionnaire Design.* London: Croom Helm.

Oucho, J.O. (1990). "Internal Migration in Kenya." In C.B. Nam, W. Serow, and D.F. Sly (eds.), *International Handbook on Internal Migration.* Westport, CT: Greenwood Press.

Peek, P. (1980). "Agrarian Change and Labour Migration in the Sierra of Ecuador." *International Labour Review* 119(5): 609–623.

Ravenstein, E.G. (1885). "The Laws of Migration." *Journal of Royal Statistical Society* 48(2): 167–277.

Sabot, R.H. (1979). *EconomicDevelopment and Urban Migration: Tanzania 1900–1971.* Oxford: Oxford University Press.

Schapera, I. (1947). *Migrant Labour and Tribal Life: A Study of the Conditions in Bechuanaland Protectorate.* Oxford: Oxford University Press.

Sly, D.F. (1972). "Migration and the Ecological Complex." *American Sociological Review* 37: 615–628.

Sly, D.F. and Wrigley J.M. (1986). "Migration and Decision and Migration Behaviour in Kenya." In J.F. Fawcett (ed.), "Migration Intentions and Behaviour: Third World Perspective," *Population and Environment* 8(1–2) (Spring–Summer): 78–97.

Speare, A.J. (1974). "Urbanization and Migration in Taiwan." *Economic Development and Cultural Change* 22(1): 302–319.

Stark, O. (1991). *The Migration of Labour.* Oxford: Basil Blackwell.

Todaro, M.P. (1969). "A Model of Labour Migration and Urban Unemployment in Less Developed Countries." *American Economic Review* 59: 138–148.

———. (1994). *Economic Development,* 5th ed. New York: Longman Publishing Co.

Yap, L. (1977). "The Attraction of Cities: A Review of the Migration Literature." *Journal of Development Economics* 4(3): 239–264.

# Part IV

# Conflict and Violence

Chapter 9

# Social and Political Aspects of Violence in Africa

## Tibamanya mwene Mushanga

### INTRODUCTION

The changes that have taken place in Africa in the last 150 years are phenomenal. Among the root causes of those changes was the European scramble for the continent in the nineteenth century. The Europeans' main aims were to establish "spheres of influence," to access, monopolize, and ensure a steady supply of raw materials, to control and structurally compel African labor to produce raw materials cheaply, and to establish and control markets in Africa for goods manufactured by the industries of the competing European powers.

Military confrontation which these competing interests might well have provoked was averted through the Berlin Conference of 1884. Presided over by the German Prince Otto von Bismarck, the conference culminated in the partitioning of Africa into exclusive spheres of influence for the major European powers of the time, particularly England, France, Belgium, and Germany. Conspicuously absent from the conference was Portugal which had been entrenched in Angola and Mozambique since the fifteenth century.

The Berlin Conference was the prelude to the participating countries' colonization of Africa. In some cases, even a few individuals acquired huge portions of Africa as private property. For instance, King Leopold of Belgium was "given" the territory now called the Democratic Republic of Congo (DRC), one of the largest and most mineral-rich countries in Africa. In other cases, nationals of the European country who were party to the conference assumed permanent residence in the acquired spheres of influence. They took over the most fertile land and confined the indigenous people to barren reserves where they could barely survive, following which the settler Europeans exploited their labor to the maximum for near-zero pay. That was the case in Kenya which some called a "white man's country" (Edgerton, 1989).

Many explanations of the scramble for Africa have been offered. For some the competition was about opening up the "Dark Continent" to infuse Christianity, foster civilization, and promote commerce. Even if we were to accept the so-called civilization factor and other explanations, however, besides converting most of sub-Saharan Africa to Christianity, the benefits from contact with Europe were invisible and in many respects remain so to most Africans. That was the case even following independence. Africans are still underdeveloped technologically, economically, and socially. With regard to commerce, raw materials from Africa are still extracted and exported with little or no value added, as was the case centuries ago. Most Africans remain as exploited today as they were during colonialism. As Eitzen and Zinn (1993: 56) argue, Africans "are poor . . . because they have been and continue to be dominated and exploited by powerful nations that have extracted their wealth and labour."

Introducing a new belief and legal system, as well as political, economic, and administrative processes and structures, and arbitrarily "uniting" but treating heterogeneous populations differently, planted the seeds of social upheaval for the continent and its people.

The following discussion examines the historical factors, processes, and contexts that have contributed to the violence that has so profoundly rocked Africa. The focus is on two types of violence: social and political. The chapter uses examples from various African countries, namely, Uganda, Rwanda, Burundi, Sudan, Nigeria, South Africa, Angola, and Mozambique, the countries that have experienced some of the most excessive political violence of recent times.

## TWO FACES OF VIOLENCE

The incidence and categories of violence in Africa must be examined from the contexts of the brutal changes in history the continent has been subjected to and is still experiencing. As Clinard and Abbott (1973) argue, countries undergoing rapid social, political, and economic changes tend to have high rates of crime, especially property crimes. Modernization and industrialization and the accompanying urbanization process that tends to break down traditional social control mechanisms during the process of change help create conditions that are conducive to crime. As a result of abrupt social, cultural, economic, and political changes, crime and violence have increased across Africa. Social violence, or violence with a so-called social face, is commonly committed by individuals during the course of social interaction. Such violence is culturally defined. According to the literature, some types of violence, such as those with a social face, result from cultural definitions of situations by individuals and groups (Mushanga, 1974: I). Thus, different cultural groups may react to social situations differently. Even subgroups with well-defined subcultures react differently to social situations. They define some situations as "requiring," and others as "not requiring," violence in settling disagreements or differences (Wolfgang and Ferracuti, 1982).

Current criminological studies generally underestimate cultural factors in assessing criminality and criminal trends. Their emphasis is shifting toward economic determination and social disorganization, or what Edwin Sutherland and other theorists called differential association (Sutherland and Cressey, 1994; Clinard and Meier, 1992).

Sutherland's theory of differential association has replaced most earlier theories, especially those of the Italian positivist school as proposed by Cesare Lombroso. Lombroso challenged Cesare Beccaria, who had earlier postulated that only conduct deemed dangerous to the state or to other people should be prohibited by law and that punishment should be no more severe than necessary to deter persons from committing certain crimes. Instead, Lombroso argued that criminal tendencies were hereditary and that "born criminals" could be identified by their physical characteristics (what he called stigmata). According to Lombroso, "born criminals" were atavistic or a throwback to an earlier, more primitive species of humans; they constituted a distinct type (Haskell and Yablonsky, 1974: 452–453).

Reliable criminological data is scarce, especially in African countries where it is mostly inadequate and inaccurate. In many cases, homicides, attempted homicides, suicides, or cases of arson are not properly recorded or clearly classified. This is not to mention the many cases of homicide or aggravated assault that occur in very close domestic circles and are rarely reported to the authorities. Nevertheless, a few studies conducted on the continent show that African societies have relatively high rates of violence, especially homicide.

In Africa, both studies and general observations locate the pattern of criminal homicide in the social category. With regard to homicides, women are more often the victims than the offenders, and housewives and lovers tend to be the most common victims in cases of domestic violence. This kind of violence, whose origins may often be found in the social structure of the African family, has been on the increase due to the breakdown of traditional values (Mushanga, 1974, 1977–1978).

An increase in the use of firearms has also been noted. However, in a Ugandan study of 501 cases, in only four cases or 0.07 percent were firearms used (Mushanga, 1974: 70). This finding reflects the relatively limited availability of firearms at the time of the study. If a similar study were conducted today, however, it would definitely show an increased use of guns in homicides and other aggravated assaults, primarily because availability and access to guns have increased in Uganda. In other words, people tend to use the commonly available tool that the culture in question defines as an offensive weapon. In the United States, for example, 66.3 percent of its 21,505 homicide cases in 1991 were committed with firearms (Federal Bureau of Investigation [FBI], 1991: 17).

The role of the availability of firearms in committing criminal acts is quite controversial, especially in the United States. Siegel (1993: 83) reports: "The use of firearms is a continuing source of controversy in the United States. Yet, there is little question that they play a major role in the commission of crime." According to the National Crime Survey (NCS), in 1989, firearms were involved in 20 percent of robberies, 10 percent of assaults, and 6 percent of rapes. During the same year, the FBI reported that 12,000 people were murdered with firearms. Most of these weapons (80 percent) were handguns. Despite these grim statistics, gun control remains a hotly debated issue.

The majority of homicide cases in Africa involve young male adults' murders of young adult female lovers. People between 20 and 30 years of age are frequently the offenders as well as the victims, although the offenders tend to be a little younger than their victims when the victims happen to be males. Moreover, the old and the young are rarely involved in homicide situations; if and when they are, they are more likely to be victims than offenders. In most homicide cases in Africa, the victim and the offender are related or are known to each other.

Alcohol is often a common factor in homicides in Africa, with the offender or the victim having been drunk or having consumed some alcohol. Furthermore, in some cases, homicide may be precipitated by either the offender, the victim, or a third party. This implies that it is not always the offender who precipitates and/or perpetrates commission of homicide. The victim could bring about his or her own killing (Wolfgang, 1958). For illustrative purposes, let us now focus on political violence in selected African countries, beginning with Uganda.

## UGANDA

The world was aghast, Africans were flabbergasted, and Ugandans died at the rate of 100 to 150 a day (Lamb, 1985: 88). The two decades from 1966 to 1986, especially during Idi Amin and Apollo Milton Obote's rule, were years of extreme strife in Uganda's history. During that period, Ugandans were subjected to and suffered brutality, torture, imprisonment, and all conceivable forms of degradation. This gross abuse of basic human rights came from the very state security personnel who were supposed to protect them. Political opponents and/or rivals (real or suspected), particularly those from "hated" ethnic groups were hunted and murdered by state agents day and night. From the west of the country to the east, from the central to the southern regions, people were taken from their houses at night and others were taken from offices and other workplaces, while many were trapped at roadblocks set up in an ad hoc manner, in broad daylight. Murder and torture centers were set up in residential quarters, in government hotels, and in offices. One of the most beautiful hotels in the center of Kampala, the national capital, served as a notorious center of torture or murder. Few ever came out alive. They "disappeared," as the Ugandans describe the state-inspired deaths.

Rape was a source of special entertainment and amusement for the intoxicated and undisciplined soldiers. Both old women and young girls were often indiscriminately raped by unruly government soldiers, and the rapes were often the prelude to torture and murder. There were numerous reports of armed soldiers attacking villages, raping wives in front of their husbands, mothers in front of their children, and children in front of their parents. School girls no longer felt safe to go to school (Mushanga, 1988).

Amnesty International reported similar atrocities in "Violation of Human Rights in the Republic of Uganda" (Index AFR59/21/85, June 1985). For Ugandans, violence was a daily experience. Well over 1 million people may have been killed during the dictatorships of Amin and Obote, and another 1 million are estimated to have gone into exile in neighboring Kenya, Sudan, and Tanzania, while others went as far as Zambia, South Africa, Canada, the United States, and Papua New Guinea. Yet another 1 million or so were internally displaced (Mushanga, 1992: 57–81).

One British medical doctor working in Uganda at the invitation of the government reported the state-inspired violence in the country to British ministers on returning to his country:

I dearly loved the country and the people from its many different tribes. However, I grieve very much for the gross abuse of human rights that is going on in Uganda. My main concern here is not the restriction of basic liberties but mass murder. Uganda reflects the problems facing all African countries, the collapse of democratic government ... but it is an expression on the scale of not only killing of political opponents but the mass murder of innocent people. From my experience in Uganda, the Obote regime is guilty of the crimes of Amin. ... I base this on having worked in one area for a year and subsequently working and travelling around a majority of the country. (Kanyeihamba, 1988: 75–76)

The British doctor's observations on the atrocities of his host government were not isolated. Another doctor made the following statement to the French newspaper *Le Croix*: "What was new for me, wasn't the poverty or the violence, but the daily and accepted terror. Ugandans live by the day and their own hope is that they survive. . . . When in 1980 Milton Obote returned to power aided by Tanzanians, it was believed that Uganda would be coming out of the nightmare where Idi Amin had plunged it. Four years later, the opinion finds that the country is sinking deeper into murderous chaos" (Kanyeihamba, 1988: 75).

Among the root causes of the discord leading to political violence in Uganda during 1966–1986 was political sectarianism. According to this practice, the leadership, exploiting the heterogeneous character of the country, sought to govern use of divide and rule tactics such as pitting ethnic group against ethnic group, political faction against political faction, religious denomination against religious denomination, and region against region. During the period in question, the top leaders in the government and in the security forces in Uganda, owing to a complex mix of factors and processes, set in motion since colonial rule, came from Nilotic ethnic groups in the north of the country and beyond. Those leaders, beginning with Presidents Obote and Amin, systematically sought from the time of independence to dominate the more numerous (in the ratio of 3:1) economically and historically politically powerful southern Bantu ethnic groups, especially the Baganda and Banyankore. When the latter groups resisted their systematic exclusion and marginalization from the political and economic processes, violence erupted between them and government security agencies, in particular the army and the police, complemented by the secret police and party vigilantes.

This state of affairs escalated and persisted until January 1986 when the National Resistance Movement (NRM), led by Yoweri Museveni, forced dictator Obote, and later his military brass, Tito Okello Lutwa, out of office following a protracted guerrilla war. The new broad-based leadership that was formed has since then been trying to restore security, the rule of law, and normalcy, and to reconstruct the infrastructure to revive the economy. State-inspired violence has been relatively reduced and political stability somewhat restored. As of 1998, the economy was regarded as one of the fastest growing in Africa.

## RWANDA AND BURUNDI

Rwanda and Burundi, both former Belgian colonies, have populations of about 8 and 6 million people, respectively. Both are inhabited by two races. As defined here, race refers to a group of people with common physical characteristics inherited from generation to generation which distinguish them from other groups (Hunt, 1967: 288). The two races in Rwanda and Burundi are Bahutu and the Batutsi. The Bahutu are the majority in each country, and the Batutsi are in the minority. The ratio of Bahutu to Batutsi is 85:14, with Batwa making up the remaining 1 percent.

According to oral and written history, the Batutsi migrated from territories forming present-day Ethiopia and Somalia (Maquet, 1961; Seligman, 1966) and are historically pastoralists. They have been the rulers in the two countries, with their domination over the agriculturalist Bahutu and Batwa well documented. Their ruthlessness and oppression were evident both before and after colonialism. Since independence in the 1960s, there have been repeated outbreaks of violence between the Bahutu and the Batutsi in Rwanda and Burundi. The recent genocidal tragedies in these countries, as well as in the Democratic Republic of Congo, are well known.

Because of the long-standing, deep-seated hatred between the Bahutu and the Batutsi, a hatred augmented and entrenched by the differential treatment of the Batutsi over the Bahutu during Belgian rule, it is unlikely that the two groups would ever wish to live side by side. This is especially true in light of the recent violence of genocidal proportions in those countries. Apart from language, the Bahutu and the Batutsi share mutual distrust, hostility and duplicity. They could live together only in the unlikely possibility that they would agree to share power through genuine democratization of the social, economic and political institutions and would live together within the same territories that they occupy.

The establishment of an international tribunal by the United Nations Security Council in 1994 to prosecute the perpetrators of the genocide in Rwanda might have heightened fears of revenge, exacerbated animosities, and set the stage for further vicious cycles of revenge between the two antagonistic racial groups.

The best way to restore and ensure sustained peace in Rwanda is to achieve a general amnesty, followed by a roundtable conference to develop a mutually acceptable program of power sharing. Genuine reconciliation, built on and manifested in a broad-based and nonsecretarian kind of politics practiced in Uganda since 1986, could be beneficial to all parties engulfed by the conflict and violence. Reconciliation and legal retribution cannot be meaningfully implemented simultaneously. Tolerance and demonstrated willingness to live together would be the most cost-effective, viable alternative.

Recently, the situation in Burundi has deteriorated dramatically. The Batutsi continue to terrorize the Bahutu. The majority Bahutu resents domination and oppression by the minority Batutsi. Time and again, violence has erupted in that country since independence in 1960. Sometimes thousands of people have been killed. Two decades ago, *Newsweek* reported the following.

In terms of sheer brutality, few events in the post–World War II history can equal the massacre that took place last year in the beautiful Central African Republic of Burundi. At the time, members of the country's population rose up against the towering Batutsi overlords who have dominated them for centuries. The insurrection failed, and the "Tutsi" government of Col. Michael Micombero exacted a frightful vengeance—slaughtering up to 250,000 "Hutu" men, women and children. Some died from bullets or razor-sharp panga knives, others from long nails driven through their heads. (Mushanga, 1988: 24)

Twenty years after the *Newsweek* piece was written, Burundi was again plunged into violent conflict in which a democratically elected Hutu president, Melchoir Ndadaye, was assassinated by Batutsi soldiers who now dominate the centers of power, including the military. In an attempted coup d'etat only six months later, his successor, Cyprien Ntaryamira, was also assassinated with Rwanda president Juvenal Habyarimana when their plane was gunned down over Kigali on April 6, 1994, sparking the genocidal violence in Rwanda outlined above. The Rwanda scenario is being reenacted in Burundi.

Resolving the conflict in Rwanda and Burundi lies in working out a democratic and acceptable political program. Such a program would guarantee the minority groups equal participation in decision making and freedom as defined by the United Nations. No group in those countries should be left in fear for its future. Proper guarantees based on the rule of law, respect for human rights, and reverence for human life must be spelled out before the two antagonistic races can live together. As a prerequisite to sharing political and economic power, there is a need to determine and address the root causes of conflict in the Great Lakes region. To ignore this need is to gloss over fundamentals and postpone viable solutions.

## THE SUDAN

The Sudan is physically the largest country in Africa with a population of about 30 million people. The conflict situation in this country presents yet another case of interracial conflict, which feeds on and is aggravated by religious differences. The racial element in the conflict is between Africans located in the south who are Christians or animists, and Arabs located in the north who are Muslims. The Africans are the majority, the Arabs the minority.

The Arabs have ruled the Sudan since independence in 1956 and have consistently excluded Africans from access to political and economic power. In recent times, the Arab-led government in Khartoum, headed by Muslim fundamentalists, introduced the Sharia, or Koranic law, as the basic law of the country, but the Africans have rejected and resisted the Sharia. Mobilized under the Sudanese People's Liberation Movement (SPLM), the Africans have advocated the "removal of religion from politics on the grounds that there is no room for religion in the politics of multicultural, multi-ethnic and multi-racial and multi-religious state" (Malwal, 1992: 8). The SPLM has repeatedly stated that it is not a sepa-ratist movement and that it is striving for a Sudan in which "no one race, especially a minority race, nor a religious grouping, especially the Islamic fundamentalists, are able to dominate political and economic power" (Malwal, 8).

Historically, the present troubles in the Sudan are the result of colonial policies whereby the British unwittingly incorporated the two groups, the Arab Muslims and the Africans, in one country. In addition, the British successfully converted some of the Africans to Christianity. To the legacies of colonial policies, which were insensitive to or ignorant of history and the local context, must be added certain precolonial factors. The Africans in the Sudan are frightened of Arab rule for good historical reason: In the past, the Arabs traded hundreds of thousands of Africans across the desert into Arab lands and beyond. In contemporary times, the media have published articles describing how the Arabs have traded Sudanese African children, partly as a result of war-induced famine.

The international community has attempted to bring the conflicting factions in the Sudan to a round table and to negotiate peace. The United Nations and the Organization of African Unity (OAU) have both been involved in those efforts, but little has been achieved so far. One reason for this dismal failure is that these agencies have overlooked a funda-mental point, as they have in the case of Rwanda and Burundi. That is, they have failed to address the fundamental causes of the conflict. The best approach would be to delineate the origins of the conflict, for if a disease is to be cured, its cause must first be diagnosed. Emissaries, peace talks, peacekeeping and the like, are all important, but to resolve the conflicts, their root causes must be identified and addressed.

## NIGERIA

According to Blaine Harden (1990: 283), Nigeria is a geographical and historical fluke. It is about a third of the size of the Sudan and has an estimated population of about 120 million people, which makes it the most populous country in Africa. Among Nigeria's salient characteristics are its ethnic, cultural, and religious diversity and divisiveness. For ex-ample, Nigeria has about 395 languages and not just dialects. The three leading ones are Hausa in the north, Yoruba in the southwest, and Igbo in the southeast.

Violence in Nigeria has erupted periodically. For example, at inde-pendence the federal leaders from the northern region, to whom power was transferred, were assassinated on a single day. Those leaders in-cluded the federal prime minister, Tafawa Balewa. After this incident, the Igbo, who are some of the most sophisticated people in Africa, foresaw the impending conflict between the southerners and the northeners and attempted to secede from the federation. They established their own republic, Biafra. Confrontation to end the secession plunged Nigeria into a civil war in which about 1 million people reportedly died. Unlike the situation in Rwanda, Burundi, and Sudan, the war in Nigeria was neither racially nor religiously motivated; it was civil in the sense that one region tried to pull out of the federation. The Igbo as a nation now number over 20 million people.

The conflicts in Nigeria led to one the most vicious civil wars in Africa and are as diverse as they are complex in their origins. For example, Moshood Abiola was widely believed to have won the June 1993 presidential election but was subsequently detained and presumably assasinated by the Abacha regime. This violence is traceable to ethnic conflict and political divisions in Nigeria. Abiola, a Muslim, would have been acceptable to the Muslim northeners, but he is also a Yoruba, from the south. For this reason, he was deemed unacceptable to northeners who still control the levers of power, including the military establishment.

The origins of the conflicts in Nigeria thus reflect the social, cultural, geopolitical, and economic diversity of that country. The sources of the conflicts include, first and foremost, religion. Northern Nigerians are mostly Muslims, whereas the Southerners are mostly Christians. Second, during colonial rule, the British practiced what Lord Lugard, the former colonial ruler of Nigeria, called indirect rule. That policy was inconsistent even within a single colony. Indirect rule encouraged conservatism and traditionalism in northern Nigeria but did just the opposite in the south where Western education, modernization, and democracy were introduced and promoted. Third, the economy has been a major source of conflict in Nigeria. The country has substantial oil resources. According to Harden (1990: 275), "Below ground, there are about forty years' worth of oil and a century's worth of natural gas." The country ranks sixth among the largest oil producers in the world and fifth in natural gas reserves. In the early 1970s, Nigeria had the strongest economy in Africa. However, with the fall in prices coupled with gross economic mismanagement, it has since slipped considerably behind South Africa, Algeria, and Egypt.

Since independence, the southerners, including the Yoruba and other kindred groups, have realized that the northern Hausa-Fulani Muslims are determined to dominate the political and military organs of the state to further their economic ends. Oil is the main focus in the struggle for domination and the conflicts in Nigeria. Each of the large national groups would like to be in control of that vital resource, which happens to be located in the southern part of the country. It has been predicted that, politically, Nigeria may have to split; otherwise it will continue to be unstable and ungovernable.

## SOUTH AFRICA

Conflict and violence in South Africa, with a population of about 40 million inhabitants, have been largely racial in origin. When the Europeans settled, acquired, and monopolized political and economic power in South Africa, they systematically excluded Africans from meaningful and beneficial participation in the political and economic processes.

When the Afrikaner National Party came to power under Dr. F.M. Malan, apartheid, whose main objective was *Baaskap* or keeping black people in their place, became the official policy. The architect of apartheid was Dr. Hendrich F. Verwoerd who became prime minister of South Africa in 1958. Whatever its manifestations, apartheid was about avoiding and preventing Africans, who account for some 70 percent of the population, to ever rule over the minority whites, who are just about 18 percent of the 40 or so million people. (The remaining 12% of the population of South Africa is made up of people of East Indian origin and the coloured, as South Africans of racially-mixed parentage have been historically classified.)

Even as the winds of change were blowing across Africa, Whites in South Africa were devising more tactics to hold onto power. Using divide and rule and exploiting local differences, the Whites instigated and fueled violence by and among Africans. The goal was to prolong minority rule and make the country ungovernable (except with Whites as the rulers).

Violence in South Africa intensified even with the release of Nelson Mandela. The Zulu began to agitate for a special status for their kingdom. Whites, and Boers in particular, demanded an autonomous state, as did the nominally independent Bantustans, formerly the scattered reserve-like territories created under the policy of apartheid as independent states for Africans, but which were never internationally recognized outside South Africa.

Much of the violence in South Africa was inspired by the racially based, White-dominated apartheid regime. This was evident especially when Nelson Mandela was sworn in as the new president. Thereafter, violence among Africans declined quite considerably. The Whites who had been threatening the country and the world with a rebellion that would lead to a bloodbath have since retreated. Ever since 1994, they have tried to negotiate deals with the Mandela as well as the Thabo Mbeki-led administrations.

Without more agitation and support from White extremists, the mainly Zulu Inkhata militants are unlikely to pursue their campaign of hostility toward the African National Congress and its members. South Africa, the last bastion of racially based European domination in Africa, could become the model of reconciliation for the rest of Africa to emulate.

## ANGOLA AND MOZAMBIQUE

Angola and Mozambique, with populations of 14 million and 17 million inhabitants, respectively, became Portuguese dependencies in the fifteenth century. These countries contributed enormously to the wealth of Portugal, which exploited and traded both human and raw material resources originating in these countries. Long-term harm was done to the development of these countries even after Portugal relinquished control over them in 1975 following nationalist guerrilla activities. Their economies were left in shambles. Illiteracy was high, and no attempts were made to prepare the indigenous people for the possibility of assuming leadership. According to the Portuguese authorities, Angola and Mozambique were destined to remain Portuguese provinces; only they were located overseas.

The political violence that characterized the two Portuguese dependencies differed in some important details from those in most of the countries examined so far. One salient difference is that in both countries the groups involved in the violence were not racially or religiously differentiated or motivated. As in Uganda, the contending groups tended to organize themselves around ethnic and/or territorial concerns.

Perhaps most unique to the conflicts in Angola and Mozambique is that the nationals of those countries have been fighting other people's wars, at least in a more open manner than elsewhere in Africa. In both countries, foreign interests have been considerable and critical in fueling and sustaining the conflicts (Museveni, 1992). In the case of Angola, the Americans and South Africans incited and openly supported the National Union for the Total Independence of Angola (UNITA) forces of Savimbi to fight the Soviet-backed Popular Movement for the Liberation of Angola (MPLA) forces under Presidents Neto and his successor dos Santos. The Americans and their allies were using Angolans to fight among themselves to dislodge the Soviets from a Western sphere of influence, following the unplanned departure of Portugal, which had created a power vacuum in Southern Africa in the broader context of the Cold War. In the same Cold War context, the Soviets had supported MPLA since the struggle for independence, with a view to establishing a niche in the Western spheres of influence. It cannot be a coincidence that with the thawing of the Cold War, despite the continuing war in Angola, we are witnessing reconciliation and efforts to install mechanisms for democratic processes in these two former Portuguese dependencies.

## CONCLUSION

No survey, however extensive, can exhaust the pervasive violent political conflicts in Africa. Even if such an attempt were made, it would be outdated almost immediately with the outbreak of violence somewhere in one of the over 50 independent African states. It is virtually impossible to provide an exhaustive and comprehensive analysis of the conflicts that have occurred in Africa. It is clear that the turmoil and often-violent conflicts in Africa are due to sectarian politics, which are motivated by the desire of one or more groups to dominate and oppress another, or others combined. In addition, attempts to resist such tendencies have led to violence. Sectarianism—feeding on emotionally charged factors such as racial and ethnic prejudice and discrimination, religious fanaticism, territorial ambitions, and language differences—constitutes the root causes of the numerous conflicts across Africa.

Conflict in general and violent conflict in particular have been enhanced by foreign powers pursuing their own interests in Africa and beyond. Some of the conflict situations in Africa are simply extensions of European conflicts. However, instead of fighting each other, since the Berlin Conference some European countries have used and pitted African against African. Perpetuating the conflict have been European involvement in African affairs and the provision of arms and ammunition to contending indigenous groups in the hope of retaining and/or asserting spheres of influence for, *inter alia*, economic reasons.

In the cases examined here, racially based inequalities have been a major factor in stimulating conflict, especially in countries like Rwanda, Burundi, South Africa, and the Sudan. Ethnic as well as religious or regional factors have been at play in the conflicts, as the cases of Nigeria and Sudan show. Foreign interests, historical and present, have generally fueled and sustained conflicts. Angola and Mozambique are cases in point.

These contributory factors to conflicts notwithstanding, some of the conflicts in Africa are part and parcel of the broader process of state formation and nation building. Historically, few countries in the world have emerged and survived without engaging in waging wars. Without war, the United States, Germany, Russia, or even Japan may never have become mighty nations. Some African nations have gone to war in an attempt to create nations out of many ethnic groups that need consolidation as nation-states.

War is not a hobby engaged in for its own sake. Rather, it is part of an attempt to solve a problem that has eluded formal and informal political and administrative processes. In general, war is condemnable rather than condonable. There have been far too many wars in Africa. No effort should be spared to find the least costly and mutually acceptable solution to the issues contributing to conflict and violence. Nevertheless, to achieve such a goal in any conflict situation, the real causes of the conflict must be determined, delineated, and addressed in a way that is appropriate for all the parties involved. In some cases, the sources of conflict can be identified easily but may be difficult to correct because these sources may be deeply entrenched and because even in conflict there are beneficiaries. To resolve this problem, there is a need for a high degree of political commitment, tolerance, reconciliation, and readiness to share power, as well as a willingness to live together in spite of whatever factors may have precipitated even the most vicious hostilities in human history.

## REFERENCES

Amnesty International. (1985). Index AFR59/21/85. June. London: Amnesty International.

Clinard, M.B. and Abbott, D. (1968). *Crime in Developing Countries: A Comparative Perspective*. New York: John Wiley.

Clinard, M.B. and Meier, R.F. (1992). *Sociology of Deviant Behaviour*. Fort Worth, TX: Harcourt Brace.

Doornbos, M.R. et al. (1992). *Beyond Conflict in the Horn of Africa*. London: James Currey.

Edgerton, R.B. (1989). *Mau Mau: An African Crucible*. New York: Ballantine Books.

Eitzen, D. and Zinn, M.B. (1993). *Social Problems*. London: Allyn and Bacon.

Everett, S. (1978). *History of Slavery*. London: Bison Books.

Federal Bureau of Investigation (FBI). (1991). *Uniform Crime Reports*. Washington, DC: FBI.

Hansen, B. and Twaddle, M. (eds.). (1988). *Uganda Now: Between Decay and Development*. Nairobi: Heinemann.

Harden, B. (1990). *Africa: Dispatches from a Fragile Continent*. Boston: Houghton Mifflin.

Haskell, M.R. and Yablonsky, L. (1974). *Criminology: Crime and Criminality*. Chicago: Rand McNally.

Hunt, E.F. (1967). *Social Science: An Introduction to the Study of Society*. London: Macmillan.

Kanyeihamba, G. (1988). "Power That Rode Naked Through Uganda under the Muzzle of the Gun." In H.B. Hansen and M. Twaddle (eds.), *Uganda Now: Between Decay and Development*. Nairobi: Heinemann.

Lamb, D. (1985). *The Africans*. London: Methuen.

Malwal, B. (1992). *The Sudan: A Second Challenge to Nationhood*. New York: Lilian Barker Press.

Maquet, J.J. (1961). *The Premise of Inequality in Rwanda*. London: Oxford University Press.

Museveni, Y.K. (1992). *What Is Africa's Problem?* Kampala: NRM Publications.

Mushanga, T.M. (1974). *Criminal Homicide in Uganda*. Kampala: East African Literature Bureau.

———. (1977–1978). "Wife Victimisation in East and Central Africa." *Victimology: An International Journal* (3–4): 479–485.

———. (ed.). (1992). *Criminology in Africa*. Rome: United Nations Interregional Crime and Justice Research Institute.

———. (1994). *Genocide and Suicide in Rwanda and Burundi: A Response to Centuries of Racial Inequality*. Unpublished Paper, Ottawa.

————. (1998). *Crime and Deviance: An Introduction to Criminology*. Nairobi: Kenya Literature Bureau.

National Resistance Movement (NRM). *The Political Program*. Kampala: NRM Publications.

Oberg, K. (1962). "The Kingdom of Ankole in Uganda." In Fortes M. and E.E. Evans (eds.), *African Political Systems*. Oxford: Oxford University Press.

Pakenham, T. (1991). *The Scramble for Africa: White Man's Conquest of the Dark Continent from 1876 to 1912*. New York: Avon Books.

Roger, J.A. (1961). *Africa's Gift to America*. New York: Civil War Centennial.

Seligman, C.G. (1966). *Races of Africa*. Oxford: Oxford University Press.

Siegel, L.J. (1993). *Criminology*. New York: West Publishing Co.

Sutherland, E.H. and Cressey, D.R. (1994). *Criminology*, 10th ed. Philadelphia: Lippincott.

Wolfgang, M.E. (1958). *Patterns in Criminal Homicide*. New York: John Wiley.

Wolfgang, M.E. and Ferracuti, F. (1982). *The Sub-Culture of Violence: Towards an Integrated Theory in Criminology*. Beverly Hills, CA: Sage.

Chapter 10

# Nigeria's Armed Robbery Problem

## Emmanuel U.M. Igbo

### INTRODUCTION

Armed robbery as defined here involves the use of firearms such as rifles, pistols, and submachine guns as well as other dangerous weapons such as daggers and clubs to dispossess persons or corporate organizations of their money or property. The targets are not only unarmed persons, but also fairly well-defended individuals, banks, and armored vehicles believed to contain large amounts of cash or other valuables.

Post–civil war Nigeria has witnessed disturbing incidents of armed robbery or robbery with violence. Before the civil war (1967–1970), incidents of armed robbery were isolated and less violent and so did not constitute a serious social problem. After the civil war, armed robbery not only became widespread but extremely violent.

Although highly unreliable and suspect, police statistics on crime indicate that there were 1,446 incidents of "robbery and extortion" in Nigeria in 1965, 2,370 in 1966, and 1,070 in 1970. It is not clear how many cases of robbery and extortion are subsumed in these figures. However, these figures fell drastically to 733 and 619 in 1968 and 1969, respectively (Government of the Federal Republic of Nigeria, 1980: 15). The government attributed these sharp declines to the exclusion of the breakaway "Biafran" territory which was the theatre of the Nigerian civil war. Another factor was that many members of the age group of the population from which most armed robbers are recruited joined the armed forces (the Army, Air Force, and Navy) as fighting soldiers.

As soon as the civil war ended in January 1970, however, and with the reunification of the country as well as the demobilization of former

Table 10.1
Armed Robbery Offenses in Nigeria, 1987–1996

| Year | Number | % Increase/ Decrease |
|------|--------|------------------------|
| 1987 | 1,241 | — |
| 1988 | 1,338 | +7.8 |
| 1989 | 1,316 | –1.6 |
| 1990 | 1,937 | +47.2 |
| 1991 | 1,056 | –45.5 |
| 1992 | 1,568 | +48.5 |
| 1993 | 1,975 | +25.9 |
| 1994 | 2,044 | +3.5 |
| 1995 | 2,109 | +3.2 |
| 1996 | 2,419 | +14.7 |
| Total | 17,003 | |

*Source*: Nigeria Police Force (NPF), *Abstract of Crime and Offenses Statistics, 1987–1991 and 1992–1996* (Lagos: NPF Headquarters).

soldiers, armed robbery (which was separated that year from extortion) increased dramatically. Thus, a total of 1,994, 1,483, and 1,083 incidents were recorded for the years 1970, 1971, and 1972, respectively (Government of the Federal Republic of Nigeria, 1980: 14). Since then, the rate has remained more or less stable. In a keynote address at a seminar on "Crime and Crime Control in Nigeria" in August 1987, the then federal attorney-general and minister of justice, Prince Bola Ajibola, declared that Nigeria had recorded an average of 1,500 armed robbery incidents over the previous 10 years (*West Africa*, August 10, 1987: 1553). Again, the last available Annual Report of the Nigeria police force shows that there were 1,700, 2,064, and 1,568 armed robbery incidents in 1990, 1991, and 1992, respectively (*Annual Report of the Nigeria Police Force*, 1993: 85).

The year 1992 witnessed a sharp increase in armed robbery offenses (48.5% above that of the previous year). Since then, armed robbery offenses have been rising steadily over the years 1993–1996 (see Table 10.1).

The seriousness of armed robbery as a social problem in Nigeria does not depend on its overall annual rate (since it is subject to underreporting and official manipulation) but on the use of actual violence and victim fatality. Many of the victims are shot to death, some are maimed for life, and others are seriously injured. Although there are no reliable and up-to-date statistics to verify this point, available records show that in 1982, for example, a total of 93 persons were killed and 234 seriously injured in armed robbery attacks. Similarly, in 1983 a total of 159 persons were killed and 246 seriously injured, while in 1984 a total of 142 persons lost their lives and 241 others had serious injuries from various armed robbery operations across the country (Dansanda, 1985: 6; *The Guardian*, April 14, 1985: 4).

Armed robbery statistics recently released by the police show that between 1990 and 1994 a total of 532 armed robbery suspects were killed in shoot-outs with the police, while the robbers, in turn, killed a total of 123 policemen and 276 civilians within the same five-year period (Dansanda, 1995: 1). Bearing in mind the problem of underreporting, or the "dark figures," as well as official manipulation of available statistics, these figures can be said to constitute only the "tip of the iceberg."

The inclination of armed robbers in Nigeria to use actual violence contrasts sharply with the bulk of evidence from the more industrialized Western countries. Research findings in the United States and Britain, for example, show that the use of actual violence during robbery is either rare or "an isolated episode" (Normandeau, 1968; Letkemann, 1973; Repetto 1974; and Walsh, 1986). In corroborating the findings of these authors, Gunn and Gristwood (1976: 60) have observed that the more professional robbers are somewhat less violent, and that when they use violence, they do so judiciously or only as a threat. This seems to suggest that armed robbers in Nigeria are predominantly "amateurs" rather than "professionals," hence the widespread use of actual violence.

Threats may or may not work, however. According to Walsh (1986: 93), if the threat works, violence is not necessary, but if it does not work, "running away and escaping are more practical ways to cope than violence." What is more, "were it to be the case that in some areas the police shoot-to-kill, robbers will avoid these areas" (Walsh, 1986: 98). This is not true of Nigeria. In addition to the death penalty and long prison sentences for convicted offenders, the police are also empowered to shoot robbers on sight while they are engaging in the act or suspected to be on the run. Despite these harsh measures, armed robbery does not appear to have declined or to have become less violent. Rather, indications from the police, the media, victims, and witnesses are that it is not only on the increase but has become extremely violent.

What is worse, the Nigeria Police Force (NPF), which is statutorily charged with maintaining law and order and protecting life and property, appears to be losing the war against armed robbers. This has led to the establishment of joint police and military patrols. However, the police themselves often bear the brunt of the attacks by armed robbers. In their many encounters with armed robbers, they are often said to take to their heels because of the criminals' daredevil attitude and superior firepower. For example, "Anini" and his gang (reputed to be one of the most violent gangs in post–civil war Nigeria) killed a total of 10 policemen in Bendel State in the second half of 1986, and also shot and wounded the state police commissioner in the nose (Omotunde and Oroh, 1987: 14–15). The same year in neighboring Anambra State, armed robbers killed eight policemen and seriously wounded two others within a period of just six weeks (*Daily Times*, May 31, 1986: 2). These are frightening news items. Indeed, at the end of the civil war in 1970, the first celebrated armed robber, "Dr." Ishola Oyenusi, had warned a police officer ordering him about, when he was arrested and in handcuffs, that "People like you don't talk to me like that when I am armed, I gun them down" (Ekpu, 1986: 12). This appears to be the general attitude of most armed robbers in Nigeria.

Worried about the escalating rate of armed robbery in Nigeria, many state governors have either set up or hired the services of "vigilante groups" to complement the efforts of the embattled Nigeria Police Force in the fight against crime. A good example of these vigilante groups is the Aba-based "Bakassi Boys," whose arrival in the crime-infested towns of Nnewi and Onitsha in Anambra State has caused armed robbers to relocate to the neighboring Enugu and Imo States of Nigeria.

Scott and Al-Thakeb (1980: 4) have pointed out that a society's perception and evaluation of its "crime problem" are more relevant than its actual crime rates or patterns as to consequences and policies. Similarly, Rossi et al. (1974: 24) have drawn attention to the fact that "To be of practical use, a measure of crime 'seriousness' requires that a society show consensus about the order of seriousness of specific criminal acts. This consensus should be reflected in the criminal codes, the behaviour of judges and juries and the actions of law enforcement agencies."

Suffice it to say that in the Nigerian context no other crime involves the use of so much terror and deadly violence; no other crime has generated so much fear, anxiety and a general feeling of insecurity and helplessness; no other crime has aroused such fierce and bitter public resentment; and caused so much embarrassment and concern to successive Nigerian governments, since the end of the civil war, as armed robbery. This chapter examines the various background factors associated with the emergence, nature, and persistence of this crime in Nigeria. It also discusses the practical response of both the government and private citizens to this seemingly intractable problem and concludes with the implications of the problem for other African countries.

## BACKGROUND TO POST–CIVIL WAR ARMED ROBBERY

The use of physical force to dispossess people of their property or belongings is not an entirely new phenomenon in Nigeria. What is new is the extreme violence and general sophistication of the robbers who now use automatic and semiautomatic weapons, and are motorized and better organized than previously.

Among the traditional Hausa-Fulani in the North, cattle-raids were common. Among the Igbo in the Southeast, there were "bandits" and plunderers, some of whom had been warlords, accomplished wrestlers, or exceptionally strong men who often mounted roadblocks at strategic junctions, exacting tributes of food items and other valuables from travelers. This explains such Igbo names as "Ochedike" (one who waylays the strong) and "Ebubedike" (one who instills fear in the strong). Travelers who offered resistance were subjected to physical beatings as a show of strength. But the use of extreme violence was rare or used only in self-defense. In addition, traditional societies had few articles of great value that could be stolen or exchanged easily by robbers, and transportation was fairly difficult. Consequently, robbery was not as common as it is today (Igbo, 1990).

Furthermore, robbers in traditional society operated mostly alone rather than in well-organized groups. They rarely attacked their victims in their homes, for this was likely to attract the attention of the able-bodied in the community to the rescue of the victim. Such actions usually ended in the lynching of the attackers. But because of the increased firepower and ruthlessness of post–civil war robbers, few (if any) persons would rush to rescue a relation or neighbor under attack by armed robbers.

The early beginnings of present-day armed robbery can be traced to the incorporation of Nigeria into the world capitalist system with associated individualism and unbridled quest for wealth. More specifically, some of the factors that encouraged robbery before the civil war include the introduction of a "cash economy" versus "trade by barter"; the mass importation of portable and sophisticated manufactured goods (radios, television sets, cars) which were in high demand in relation to supply; and urbanization with all its social and economic complications. This era was dominated by highway robberies which were carried out mostly at night—hence the Igbo name for armed robbers, "abali di egwu" (night marauders).

Before the civil war, most robberies involved the "use of muscles" and "strong-arm tactics," or were simply muggings. This explains why robbery was lumped together with extortion, which, in police crime statistics, has since 1970 been further classified as "demanding with menace." During this period, one of the restraints to the use of deadly violence in robbery was perhaps the strong influence of the traditional aversion to "spilling of innocent blood." Spilling of innocent blood was believed to bring about terrible woes and tragic consequences to the actor and his immediate family. However, the civil war appears to have changed this belief, thus transforming robbery from the "use of muscles" to a highly violent offense.

## Explaining Armed Robbery in Post–Civil War Nigeria

Two major factors facilitated and encouraged armed robbery after the Nigerian civil war that ended in January 1970: (1) the civil war itself and (2) the socioeconomic condition of the post–civil war years.

## THE CIVIL WAR AND ITS CONSEQUENCES

As argued elsewhere (Igbo, 1994: 109–121), the Nigerian civil war can be seen as the watershed between ordinary robbery and armed robbery. Three major fallouts from the civil war considerably influenced armed robbery after the war: (1) the military subculture of violence, (2) military commandeering, and (3) easy availability of firearms.

### The Military Subculture of Violence

The civil war caused most able-bodied young men to enlist, either voluntarily or by conscription, into the armed forces as fighting soldiers. These included the unemployed and underemployed, school-leavers, and dropouts as well as some members of the criminal population. These new recruits learned how to use rifles, machine guns, and other firearms against their opponents. They also learned military discipline and became accustomed to the use of verbal commands, intimidation, and brute force against opponents or subordinates. In short, they internalized the military subculture of violence and thereby abandoned the traditional aversion to "spilling of innocent blood." While on the war-front they killed, or were encouraged to kill, their opponents; at the rear, they brutalized and easily shot their colleagues and others on the least provocation (Igbo, 1990: 159–160).

### Military Commandeering

Einstadter (1969: 77) has pointed out that military experience readily lends itself to robbery. One aspect of military experience that appears to have facilitated armed robbery in Nigeria is military commandeering. This involves the forceful seizure of money or property of nonmilitary persons (generally referred to as "idle civilians") by military personnel. Military commandeering was especially common in breakaway Biafra where, because of economic blockade, everything was in short supply and the struggle for survival was desperate. Passenger and goods trucks were commonly commandeered to convey fighting troops to the war-fronts. Cars, bicycles, and whole buildings were also commandeered, which sometimes involved consultations between military authorities and the owners of such property. This was official commandeering.

But unofficial commandeering was generally organized by "stragglers," runaway soldiers, and other irresponsible military personnel. It was usually carried out under the pretext of official commandeering, and the identities of those involved were often unknown. Items commonly commandeered included cars, food items, bicycles, transistor radios, beds and mattresses, and other household goods that served the personal and selfish interests of the commandeering soldiers. This type of commandeering was often accompanied by bullying, intimidation, threats, and, sometimes, actual violence.

At the end of the civil war, military commandeering gave way to a new wave of "civilian commandeering" in the form of armed robbery as demobilized soldiers gave up their uniforms and joined the ranks of the so-called idle civilians. This means that post–civil war armed robbery was encouraged by the internalization of the military subculture of violence and that of commandeering. More importantly, it was facilitated by the easy availability of firearms.

## The Easy Availability of Firearms

The civil war not only led to a proliferation of firearms through importation on both sides of the conflict, but it also stimulated the local manufacture of arms (Rotimi, 1984: 124). At the end of the war, many defeated and demobilized soldiers did not surrender their weapons to federal authorities (Nkpa, 1976: 72). Some of these weapons were abandoned at the war-fronts, while others were either buried underground or carefully concealed in bushes to make them easily retrievable if and when the need arose. Such need could be for resistance against federal authorities in the form of guerrilla warfare or for criminal purposes, as in the case of armed robbery.

In addition, some serving policemen and military officers who went back to the barracks at the end of the war sometimes gave out their officially assigned weapons to persons with criminal intent. Furthermore, wealthy and well-connected businessmen began to specialize in the lucrative trade of illegal importation of pistols, shotguns, and double-barrelled rifles. These weapons were in great demand for self-protection against armed robbers, and as such they found ready markets among law-abiding citizens as well as criminals. This aggravated the crime problem, especially armed robbery.

## SOCIOECONOMIC INFLUENCES

The escalation and persistence of armed robbery in the years following the end of the civil war can be attributed to two major factors: (1) economic hardship and (2) the oil boom.

### Economic Hardship

The sudden demobilization of former fighting soldiers, without any plans for rehabilitation, subjected thousands of young men and their families to untold hardship. Many young men, who were working before the civil war, were not reabsorbed by their former employers on grounds that they had "abandoned" their jobs to join the secessionist army. These young men included former federal civil servants, former policemen, as well as former armed forces personnel in the Army, Air Force, and Navy. Most of these officers had to roam the streets in search of new jobs that often never materialized.

In addition, the prewar unemployed, for whom the civil war was a "blessing in disguise" in terms of employment, were once again thrown into the streets and the job market. There were also many young persons whose educational careers were abruptly disrupted by the war. Some joined the Army. Many of these youths became confused and disillusioned with the sudden end of the war. A good number refused to go back to school and instead joined the large army of unemployed persons eager to make "quick money" by any means. With massive unemployment everywhere in the former secessionist areas, many breadwinners could not fend for their families. Some had to resort to begging to make ends meet.

These factors may help explain the high incidence and violent nature of armed robbery immediately after the civil war. These incidents were more or less confined in the war-devastated secessionist area, particularly the East Central State—the heartland of the resistance. A careful analysis of police robbery statistics shows that for six years (1970–1975) following the end of the civil war, East Central State consistently recorded the highest rate of armed robbery among the existing 12 states in the country at that time (see Igbo, 1994: 116).

### The Oil Boom

The other major socioeconomic influence on post–civil war armed robbery in Nigeria was the so-called oil boom. Nigeria enjoyed unprecedented prosperity from the sale of crude oil, particularly during the 1973 Gulf Crisis up to about 1976. During this period, oil revenues increased dramatically while financial discipline declined drastically. The government embarked on a number of eye-catching and flamboyant projects such as the building of fly-overs, construction of stadia and expressways, and the multibillion dollar Iron and Steel Complex at Ajaokuta, among others.

The oil boom facilitated the emergence of a new group of wealthy Nigerians—the "young millionaires" and "Cash Madams," "importers and exporters," "manufacturers' representatives," and other bogus businessmen (and women). For politicians and those in government service, corruption reached alarming and staggering proportions and brought in large financial fortunes for themselves, relations, and friends. The few privileged and "lucky" Nigerians basked in their often fraudulently or ill-gotten wealth. At the same time, the vast majority of civil servants, the poor, the unemployed, and the underemployed as well as the peasants were subjected to a series of belt-tightenings and austerity measures and were asked to make "sacrifices" in the face of rising inflation. In short, while the rich and powerful became richer, the poor and powerless became poorer. This situation aggravated inequality and social injustice in Nigerian society.

As those who had suddenly become wealthy, directly or indirectly, from the "oil economy" showed off with their flashy and expensive cars, palatial residences, and indulged generally in an extravagant lifestyle, a "get-rich-quick" epidemic seemed to take hold of most Nigerians. Armed robbers were not left out. They, too, joined the rat race in their own way, if only to pick the proverbial "little crumbs" that fall from the master's table.

Mankoff (1976: 187) aptly points out that "it is the same institutional structure that produces great wealth and comfort and choice of lifestyle for some and that drives others to kill." Speaking to newsmen before he was publicly executed for armed robbery in Jos, Nigeria, on October 20, 1984, George Enahoro blamed Nigerian politicians in particular for looting the nation's treasury while millions of youths had no jobs and no future. He stated that if he were an illiterate, he would not have read the newspapers to learn how, between 1979 and 1983, "politicians were daily changing their lifestyle as well as becoming millionaires overnight while a majority of the youths had no means of livelihood (*Daily Times*, October 24, 1984: 32).

The persistence of armed robbery in Nigeria must therefore be understood within the context of an economy that concentrates the nation's wealth and resources in a few hands while subjecting the vast majority of the population to the indignities of poverty, inequality, deprivation, unemployment, and underemployment which aggravate the struggle for scarce resources. It would appear that this struggle is a matter of life and death for armed robbers in Nigeria, considering the risks they face during and after robbery (on conviction).

## GOVERNMENT RESPONSE TO THE ARMED ROBBERY PROBLEM

Before the Nigerian civil war, robbery was legally defined as "stealing with violence." Chapter 36 of the 1958 Criminal Code made a distinction between "ordinary robbery" and "aggravated robbery. Ordinary robbery involved the actual use or threat of violence and was punishable with a maximum of 14 years imprisonment. Aggravated robbery, on the other hand, involved the use of dangerous weapons leading to physical injuries to victims and was therefore punishable with life imprisonment, with or without whipping. This section of the Criminal Code was replaced by the Armed Robbery and Firearms Decree of 1970.

The end of the civil war in January 1970 witnessed the emergence of a more violent type of armed robbery executed with automatic and sophisticated weapons or "firearms" such as rifles, pistols, and submachine guns. This change tended to raise the level of violence across the country. The federal military government responded to this increasing violence by enacting the notorious Robbery and Firearms Decree "to protect life and property" across the country, and at the same time instituted some extralegal measures to deal with the increasing incidence of armed robbery in the country.

### The Robbery and Firearms Decree

Immediately after the Nigerian civil war, the federal military government promulgated the Robbery and Firearms (Special Provision) Decree, No. 47 of 1970, to deal with the problem of armed robbery. The Decree was designed to eliminate, temporarily or permanently, known and convicted armed robbers, deter others, and reduce drastically the number of firearms in public circulation. Section 2 of the Decree provides that:

If (a) any offender . . . is armed with firearms or any offensive weapon or is in company of any person (b) at or immediately before or immediately after the time of the robbery, the offender wounds or uses any personal violence to any person, the offender shall be liable, under this Decree, to be sentenced to death.

This was the first time capital punishment was prescribed and used for convicted robbers since the introduction of the Western legal system in Nigeria. Previous use of capital punishment was for the offense of murder only.

The Decree further provides that a convicted robbery offender may be executed "by hanging the offender by the neck till he be dead or by causing such offender to suffer death by firing-squad as the Governor may direct." In the 1970s, the predominant mode of inflicting the death penalty for armed robbery was by the military firing squad or what has become generally known as public execution whereby members of the public were invited to come and witness "the show" at the Bar Beach or some other public places.

The decree also prescribes between 14 and 20 years of imprisonment for "attempted robbery." However, if an offender convicted for attempted robbery was armed with firearms or dangerous weapons at the time of the crime or was in the company of any other person so armed, such an offender is liable to life imprisonment. Similarly, mere possession of firearms (without lawful authority or valid license) is an offense punishable with a fine of N20,000 (20,000 Naira) or imprisonment for not less than 10 years, or both.

Apart from being too harsh, the Robbery and Firearms Decree makes no provision for the offender to be reformed. More importantly, there is a high possibility of executing innocent persons on trumped-up charges or perhaps on mere circumstantial evidence such as "being in company of any person so armed." What is worse, persons convicted under this Decree have no right of appeal in the light of fresh evidence, as is the practice in most Western legal systems. So far, the Decree has undergone several amendments (in 1971, 1974, 1977, 1979, 1984, and 1986) without addressing these crucial issues.

At the end of September 1971, a total of 103 convicted armed robbers had been executed by firing squad (Nkpa, 1976: 82), and by July 1972 the figure had reached 143 (Sanwo, 1984: 5). With poor recordkeeping and with each of the 30 states of the Federation ultimately responsible for its armed robbers, the nation appears to have lost count of the total number of armed robbers executed to date, either publicly or by hanging in the enclosure of the prisons.

Over two decades since the introduction of this Decree and the strict enforcement of the provisions, particularly the death penalty, armed robbery does not appear to have declined. Rather, the indications are that it has increased significantly, with the robbers becoming more vicious, "believing that it is either their victims' lives or theirs" (Ekpenyong, 1989: 25).

### Extralegal Measures

Apart from the Robbery and Firearms Decree, two extralegal measures have been introduced to deal with the seemingly intractable problem of armed robbery in Nigeria. The first measure is a policy that many state governments instituted, particularly in the 1970s, whereby convicted armed robbers were shot in public, in their local and rural communities, before their relatives, friends, and loved ones. This was meant to serve as a deterrent to potential robbers and to humiliate families and close relatives of convicted offenders.

The second measure is a standing federal government directive that authorizes the police and other law enforcement agents to shoot suspected armed robbers on sight. This shoot-to-kill policy is increasingly favored in police circles as the quickest, cheapest, and most effective response to the armed robbery problem. It discharges the law enforcement agents of the responsibility placed on them by the due process of law. The danger inherent in this policy is that it is subject to abuse by policemen, some of whom have already dispatched innocent and law-abiding citizens to their early graves because of poor judgment and over-zealousness. It is also subject to manipulation by witch-hunters, score-settlers, and others parading as law enforcement agents. In such instances, the police combine the roles of prosecutor, judge, and executioner.

## PUBLIC RESPONSE TO THE ARMED ROBBERY PROBLEM

Many researchers have stressed the relationship between the criminal and his victim, emphasizing that in many instances the victim, directly or indirectly, instigates the process leading to victimization (Hentig, 1967; Schafer, 1968; Reckless, 1973). With particular reference to post–civil war armed robbery in Nigeria, Nkpa (1976: 75–81) identifies several ways through which victims can be said to have contributed to their victimization. These include public display of wealth, playing the role of the "Good Samaritan," taking reckless chances in the face of danger, loose talk in the midst of strangers, and sheer carelessness. Potential victims should therefore embark on forward-looking measures to deter or reduce the risk of victimization.

Nigerians have realized, rather painfully, that despite the government's various draconian measures, armed robbery is far from abating. Consequently, they have learned to protect themselves through both individual and collective measures and strategies to frustrate or discourage armed robbery—notably, changes in lifestyle, neighborhood policing, and other self-protective measures.

### Changes in Lifestyle

The social life of many Nigerians has undergone drastic changes as a result of the activities of armed robbers. This point is best illustrated by Chinua Achebe's (1958: 20) reference to the "Eneke" bird which "since men have learnt to shoot without missing, he has learnt to fly without perching." This signifies a serious and sustained effort to reduce vulnerability.

Hindelang et al. (1978) have observed that there are high-risk times, places, and people and that lifestyle determines one's exposure to crime, both directly and through personal associations. Accordingly, most Nigerians have made adjustments in their lifestyle. Many, for example, no longer stay out late at night. Even the much-talked about traditional African spirit of "being our brothers' keepers" has lost its appeal. Motorists no longer offer rides to stranded passengers and those in need for fear of losing their cars and their lives to car-snatchers. House-owners no longer offer temporary accommodation to stranded travelers for fear of harboring armed robbers.

Several reports from the police, the media, witnesses, and victims indicate instances of people masquerading as "Reverend gentlemen" and dressed in priestly robes, clerics who have turned out to be armed robbers. Similarly, not everyone dressed in gowns and skirts turn out to be females. Consequently, people have become more cautious and suspicious of others and their intentions; they are no longer as open and "large-hearted" as they used to be.

## Neighborhood Policing

Many urban centers as well as rural communities in Nigeria have witnessed the emergence of neighborhood watch and vigilante groups in response to the armed robbery menace. Residents of many communities, neighborhoods, and streets in urban centers now hold regular meetings and contribute money to maintain their security. In Lagos, Ibadan, and other large cities, for example, street gates, bumps, and other barricades have become a common feature, preventing strangers and undesirable persons from gaining access to the areas at odd times in the night (see *Sunday Concord*, April 22, 1984).

In many urban centers, residents of many streets either pay for night guards or take turns guarding their areas at night. It has also become customary for paid night-guards, vigilante groups, and individual residents to deliberately disturb the usually quiet nightlife with noise from whistles, bells, drums, and gongs as a way of scaring away armed robbers and other nocturnal criminals. These groups are commonly armed with bows and arrows, catapults, cutlasses, and iron bars; most armed robbers, however, operate with automatic and semiautomatic rifles and guns.

## Self-Protection Measures

Cook (1986: 7) argues that the behavior of criminals "influences the nature and amount of self-protective measures taken by potential victims, and changes in self-protection make criminal opportunities, more or less, attractive." Hindelang et al. (1978: 11) have classified self-protection activities as follows:

- Actions that make successful commission of a crime difficult, for example, storing valuables in safes and avoiding deserted places at night.
- Actions that increase the apparent risk that a criminal will be arrested and punished, such as installing alarms and closed circuit television, and using identification numbers and markers on personal property.
- Actions that minimize loss if victimization occurs, for example, keeping a minimum of cash or valuables on hand and keeping weapons available for self-defense against attack.

Most Nigerians have begun to take concrete steps to protect themselves and their families and property against victimization by robbers. New architectural designs and "mini-fortresses" have emerged, and many houses are now fitted with metal burglary-proof separate guards behind doors and windows, as well as brick walls and solid iron gates to deter or delay armed intruders. Many people also keep "security dogs" for guard duties, particularly at night.

In addition, many individuals now work either part-time or full-time as day- or night-guards. Professional security organizations and consultants have also become part of the lucrative security business by offering their services to the well-to-do in their homes and business premises. Many of the security guards employed are retired members of the armed forces and former policemen.

There has also been a proliferation of firearms, ostensibly for self-protection. Although it is a serious offense to own or possess a firearm without a valid license, many people keep these weapons illegally as protection. This is due to the prohibitive cost of the legal alternative, which only a few can afford and which often lasts several months. In contrast, locally manufactured pistols and shot-guns can be purchased easily and cheaply from local blacksmiths in remote rural and urban areas. This is a potentially dangerous development with far-reaching consequences for violent crimes generally.

### The Need for Policy Reviews

A number of policy changes can have far-reaching consequences for armed robbery in Nigeria. These include:

1. *Decapitalization.* Because of the extreme violence associated with armed robbery in Nigeria, it has been made the second "capital" offense (after murder) involving the death penalty. However, there is an urgent need to "decapital-

ise" it or to substitute imprisonment for the death penalty in order to safe-guard against needless loss of lives.

2. *Right to Appeal.* To deny convicted armed robbers of the right of appeal is an infringement of their fundamental human rights as guaranteed in Nigeria's constitution. Convicted offenders should be allowed to appeal their sentence, particularly when it carries the death penalty.

3. *Reduction of Inequality.* The large army of unemployed and frustrated youths who feel cheated, deprived, and marginalized constitute a potential source for recruitment of armed robbers. There is, therefore, a need for well-meaning policies and programs to reduce inequality and social injustice in Nigeria.

4. *Comprehensive Welfare Package.* Government should establish a comprehensive social welfare program, including unemployment benefits, family allowances, and child benefits to take care of the disadvantaged.

## CONCLUSION

Post–civil war Nigeria has experienced alarming and unprecedented cases of robbery with violence that, more often than not, leads to loss of lives and severe physical injuries to the victims. In armed robberies, physical violence appears to be the norm rather than the exception in Nigeria. With the death penalty and a long prison sentence hanging over their heads, armed robbers have become more desperate and violent in their bid to eliminate all traces of incriminating evidence against them, whether such evidence be with victims, witnesses, or law enforcement agents. As Aguda (1986: 11) has rightly observed, brutal punishments tend to escalate brutal crimes and brutal crimes tend to escalate brutal punishments, thus creating a never-ending spiral of brutalization of the whole society.

In a nutshell, since independence in 1960, Nigeria has had a checkered history of political thuggery, civil war, and proliferation of firearms and other dangerous weapons. The country has also witnessed recurring military coups and countercoups, public executions by military firing squad, and the visible presence of armed police and military personnel on the streets, with instructions to shoot-at-sight persons suspected of being dangerous criminals. These conditions have encouraged a subculture of violence which, in a situation of economic deprivation in a highly ostentatious society, can have serious consequences for violent crimes generally and armed robbery in particular.

A number of policy changes can have far-reaching effects on the incidence of armed robbery and associated violence in Nigeria, including

• Decapitalization of the offense and its substitution with imprisonment.
• Restoration of the right of appeal to convicted offenders.
• Reduction of inequality and social injustice.

• Institution of a comprehensive welfare package to ameliorate the harsh living conditions of the majority of the population.

If the experiences of Nigeria are any measure, other African countries must guard against repeating its mistakes. Sadly, however, many African countries appear to be following in Nigeria's footsteps, particularly with respect to military coups and countercoups, civil wars, and armed conflicts. These are ominous signs for violent crimes generally.

Military coups and military governments, undemocratic governments, and armed conflicts, tend to increase the level of violence in a society. These armed conflicts lead to a proliferation of firearms, which escalates violent crimes as a whole and armed robbery in particular. Given this scenario, we would expect a rise in violent crimes and armed robbery in those countries that have witnessed or are witnessing protracted armed conflicts. All these countries need a sensible social policy that will drastically reduce the number of firearms in circulation and at the same time make adequate provision for their demobilized soldiers and militia men as well as their disadvantaged populations. Above all, there is a need to work for democracy and human rights.

## REFERENCES

Achebe, C. (1958). *Things Fall Apart*. London: Heinemann Educational Books.
Aguda, T.A. (1986). *The Crisis of Justice*. Akure, Nigeria: Erasu Hill Publishers.
*Annual Report of the Nigeria Police Force*. (1993). Lagos: Force Headquarters.
Cook, P.J. (1986). "The Demand and Supply of Criminal Opportunities." In M. Tonry and N. Morris (eds.), *Crime and Justice: An Annual Review* (pp. 178–194). Chicago: University of Chicago Press.
*Daily Times*. (1984, October 24). Lagos.
*Daily Times*. (1986, May 31). Lagos.
Dansanda. (1985). *The Nigeria Police Journal* 7(1).
————. (1995). *The Nigeria Police Journal* 27(1).
Einstadter, W.I. (1969). "The Social Organisation of Armed Robbery." *Social Problems* 17(1): 173–182.
Ekpenyong, S. (1989). "Social Inequalities, Collusion, and Armed Robbery in Nigeria's Cities." *British Journal of Criminology* 29(1): 21–34.
Ekpu, R. (1986, December 22). "From the Editorial Suite." *Newswatch* 4(25).
Government of the Federal Republic of Nigeria. (1980). *Crime and the Quality of Life in Nigeria*. The Nigerian National Paper for the Sixth United Nations Congress on Crime Prevention and the Treatment of Offenders. Caracas, Venezuela.
*The Guardian*. (1985, April 14). Lagos.
Gunn, J. and Gristwood, J. (1976). "Twenty-Seven Robbers." *British Journal of Criminology* 16(1): 56–62.
Hentig, H.V. (1967). *The Criminal and His Victims*. Hamden, CT: Shoe String Press.
Hindelang, M., Gottfredson, M., and Garofallo, J. (1978). *Victims of Personal Crime:*

An Empirical Foundation for a Theory of Personal Victimization. Cambridge, MA: Ballinger.

Igbo, E.U.M. (1990). Armed Robbery in Nigeria: A Study of Offenders in Enugu Prison in Anambra State of Nigeria. Ph.D. Thesis, Sheffield University, England.

————. (1994, May/September). "Background to Nigeria's Armed Robbery Problems." Journal of Liberal Studies 4(1 and 2): 109–121.

Letkemann, P. (1973). Crime as Work. Englewood Cliffs, NJ: Prentice-Hall.

Mankoff, M. (1976). "Perspectives on the Crime Problem." In W.J. Chambliss and M. Mankoff (eds.), Whose Law/What Order? (pp. 87–192). New York: John Wiley.

Nkpa, N.K.U. (1976). "Armed Robbery in Post Civil War Nigeria: The Role of the Victim." Victimology 1(1): 71–83.

Normandeau, A. (1968). Trends and Patterns in Crimes of Robbery. Ph.D. Thesis, University of Pennsylvania.

Omotunde, S. and Oroh, A. (1987, January 26). "To Die by the Bullets." This Week 3(4).

Reckless, W.C. (1973). The Crime Problem. New York: Appleton.

Repetto, T.A. (1974). Residential Crime. Cambridge, MA: Ballinger.

Rossi, P.E., Bose C., and Berk R. (1974). "The Seriousness of Crime: Normative Structure and Individual Differences." American Sociological Review 39(2): 224–237.

Rotimi, A. (1984). "Perspectives on the Armed Robbery Offence in Nigeria." Indian Journal of Criminology 12(2): 122–135.

Sanwo, T. (1984, March 23). "The Return of Bar Beach Show." Lagos Weekend.

Schafer, S. (1968). The Victim and His Criminal: A Study of Functional Responsibility. New York: Random House.

Scott, J.E. and Al-Thakeb, F. (1980). "Perceptions of Deviance Cross Culturally." In G. Newman (ed.), Crime and Deviance: A Comparative Perspective (pp. 42–67). London: Sage Publications.

The Sunday Concord (1984, April 22).

Walsh, D. (1986). Heavy Business: Commercial Burglary and Robbery. London: Routledge and Kegan Paul.

West Africa. (1987, August 10). London.

Chapter 11

# Africa's Refugee Crisis

## Rodreck Mupedziswa

### INTRODUCTION

Refugees are commonly understood as persons who have fled their countries and crossed international borders. The United Nations High Commissioner for Refugees (UNHCR) defined the term in this way in the 1951 United Nations Convention relating to the status of refugees, and in the 1967 Protocol, both of which have to date been ratified by over 100 countries worldwide. In the context of Africa, the UNHCR definition of a refugee was adjudged inadequate. This was because Africa generated types of refugees, which according to the Organization of African Unity (OAU) categorization, placed asylum seekers in three clusters: political refugees, freedom fighters, and rural refugees.

Consequently, the African countries promulgated the 1969 OAU Convention to augment the provisions of the 1951 UNHCR Convention. The new Convention expanded its definition of the term *refugee* to include persons fleeing generalized violence in their countries. The expanded definition made it possible for states to grant asylum to groups of persons compelled to flee because of political conflict in their countries, without the need to impute persecution (Rogers and Copeland, 1993). While in the context of the traditional international conceptualization, protection was necessary only after a refugee had crossed a border, the new OAU definition made it possible to assist people even while within their borders.

The OAU Convention on refugees also gave prominence to a category of refugees that has often been overlooked: vulnerable refugee groups, notably unaccompanied children, people with disabilities, women, and the elderly. The situation of these groups was especially poignant because they were vulnerable in addition to being refugees. In other words, they were victims among victims (Mupedziswa, 1993).

The refugee problem in Africa is perhaps the greatest single challenge that will face the continent into the new millennium and beyond. Africa's refugee crisis is accelerating like an express train at high speed. The problem daily becomes increasingly intractable. While the state of the world's refugees is not always one of unbroken gloom, the situation in Africa is such that as some refugee situations end, fresh ones begin with amazing regularity (Mupedziswa, 1997a).

## DIMENSIONS OF THE REFUGEE PROBLEM

The statistics regarding refugees in the African continent make sad reading. In 1988 when the world's refugee population was still around 17 million, Mwase (1988) observed that one out of 66 Africans was in fact a refugee, while at the world level, one out of every three refugees was an African. The situation has only gotten worse. Out of an estimated 24 million refugees worldwide today, over one-third are believed to hail from Africa. By one account apart from over 6 million refugees being assisted by UNHCR in the African continent, another 12 million Africans are internally displaced (Norton-Staal, 1994). However, one report ("Various Dispatches," 1997) noted that Zambia alone had at one point hosted 6 million Zairean refugees. Concern was expressed that this situation weighed on the stability of a country undergoing strong political tensions. On the African continent, most refugees flee to neighboring countries; hence, the largest concentrations are found in the same regions as the refugee-generating countries.

For instance, in 1990, over half a million Liberians were living in exile, while in 1991, 1 million Somalis, constituting about one-tenth of the country's entire population, was in exile. The vast majority of these Somali refugees were in Kenya where over 400,000 refugees were reported to have escaped violence in Somalia, civil war in Sudan, and insecurity in Ethiopia (UNHCR, 1993: 31). In June 1993, 280,000 people fled from political repression in Togo to settle in Benin and Ghana.

Africa has the distinction of having on its soil some of the greatest concentrations of refugee populations. For instance, in the late 1980s during Mozambique's crisis, Malawi, a tiny poor country of 9 million people, was sheltering over 1 million Mozambican refugees, with one out of every nine people in that country being a refugee. In March 1992, Kenya was receiving around 3,000 refugees a day. In 1993, the Hartisheik camp in eastern Ethiopia had 250,000 inhabitants made up of returnees, internally displaced persons, drought-affected locals, and ex-soldiers. In more recent times, that record has been surpassed by Benaco camp in Tanzania, which, with a population of 250,000, was then the largest in the world (*The Herald*, June 13, 1996). The refugees in Africa are scattered all over the continent, with areas of major concentration shifting regularly.

Undoubtedly, perhaps one of the greatest explosions of all time on the African continent that triggered an unprecedented refugee movement occurred recently in the Great Lakes region. The countries affected include Rwanda, Burundi, the Democratic People's Republic of Congo (DRC), Congo (Brazzaville), Uganda, and Zambia. The wars that have raged in Angola and Sierra Leone have also generated serious refugee movements within as well as across the borders of these countries. Although the tensions that produced the mass exodus in the Great Lakes region date back many decades, the immediate cause was the genocide of up to 1 million people, mainly Tutsis, which occurred in 1994 in Rwanda. The tension in neighboring Burundi also resulted in many people fleeing the region. While thousands of Burundian refugees sought refuge in southwest Rwanda, many Rwandese fled into the DRC (then Zaire). Others fled to such countries as Tanzania and Kenya.

At one point, an estimated 1.2 million Hutu refugees from Rwanda and Burundi were in Zaire. Zaire itself did not long remain a safe haven as a war instigated by a rebel movement started in earnest in late 1996. By October 1996, over 300,000 refugees had fled west from camps on the Zaire border. In November 1996, thousands fled Zaire across Lake Tanganyika, mostly by boat. Tanzanian officials soon reported 4,000 arrivals per day in the Kigoma area, with hundreds dying on the way. As the fighting heated up, the situation became desperate. In late 1996, Tanzania was hosting more than 600,000 Hutu refugees ("Tanzania," 1996).

By May 1997, the rebel movement in Zaire had gained power in the country. No sooner had Laurent Kabila taken over as president and renamed the country the DRC than fighting broke out in neighboring Congo (Brazzaville), setting off yet another mass exodus. *The Herald* (June 28, 1997) reported that once the fighting started, over 17,000 people fled from the inner suburbs of Brazzaville into Kinshasa in neighboring DRC.

The war situation in the Great Lakes region has taken many twists and turns, creating untold security problems for the refugee populations there. In February 1997, UNHCR reported that more than 200,000 Rwandan refugees were unaccounted for in eastern Zaire since being uprooted by fighting between troops and rebels ("Various Dispatches," 1997). There were also reports that refugees in east Zaire had been caught up in the rebel advance in Kinshasa, with thousands being killed. At Biaro camp in Zaire, refugees were reportedly dying at the rate of 50 a day in early 1997.

The refugee camps in the Great Lakes region have not been safe havens for those fleeing the wars in the region. For example, in one instance, the rebel advance in eastern Zaire prompted 25,000 refugees at

Kalima to flee into the forest. Their fate could not be ascertained. Most of these were Rwandan Hutus who had been on the road since the 1994 Hutu-orchestrated slaughter of nearly a million Rwandan Tutsis and politically moderate Hutus alluded to earlier.

Although some of the wars have apparently stopped, the security situation in the Great Lakes region has remained volatile. In February 1997, hundreds of unarmed civilians, including children, were being killed in Rwanda in an ongoing upsurge of violence linked to the 1994 genocide ("Various Dispatches," 1997). The UNHCR has not found it easy to intervene on behalf of the refugees in the region. For example, on May 15, 1997, Zaire rebels reportedly blocked a senior UN official seeking access to Rwandan refugees south of Kinshasa. This happened amid reports of fresh killing of Rwandan refugees by Tutsi-dominated rebels. In the case of the DRC, these problems have continued even after the new government took power; UNHCR officials investigating alleged massacres of refugees have been blocked.

## CONTRIBUTORY FACTORS

The causes of refugee populations in Africa fall into basically three categories: political, economic, and environmental factors (Mupedziswa, 1997a). However, as Mazrui (1988) has correctly observed, in Africa it is often difficult to tell where political asylum ends and economic asylum begins. By the same token, at times it is equally difficult to identify political refugees from those fleeing from natural disasters. When Mozambicans fled their country in 1983, it was difficult to distinguish between those fleeing Renamo because of perpetrated atrocities and those fleeing because of the severe drought that ravaged that country.

Nonetheless, in African context, the political factor is probably the single most important causal factor, followed perhaps by environmental and economic factors in that order. Part of the explanation for politically instigated mass flights revolves around the continent's own history of plunder and suppression under deposed and current political systems, which are mostly a legacy of the colonial past (Mupedziswa, 1993). Indeed, armed conflict, insurgency, and militarism have caused many people to flee their countries. Conflicts over decolonization in the late 1950s and 1960s also generated large numbers of refugees. These included the conflicts in Algeria, Rwanda, and Zaire.

Some of the politically instigated conflicts on the continent have been a result of a lack of representative political institutions, acts of wanton aggression, and internal upheavals. Examples with regard to lack of representative institutions include Liberia and Somalia. The problems in the Horn of Africa today are partly a result of aggression. For instance, Somalia's ambition to incorporate the Ethiopian Ogaden region led to the war in 1977 (UNHCR, 1993). It also created a state of instability that persists today.

Conflicts between ethnic groups have proliferated in Africa, generating mass population movements, usually into exile. Examples include Ethiopia, the Sudan and the former apartheid regime in South Africa. In the Sudan, the imposition of laws (Sharia) that were unacceptable to the south ignited a secessionist struggle. Armed opposition groups, such as Renamo in Mozambique, have also caused mass exodus.

The political conflicts in Africa have sometimes been so confused that in some instances, refugee groups from neighboring states such as DRC and the Republic of Congo (Brazzaville) have met at the borders while fleeing to each other's country. This has also been true of Ethiopian and Sudanese refugees, who have fled in opposite directions into each other's country. In other situations, people who are already refugees have been uprooted a second time. For instance, in 1991, Sudanese refugees in Ethiopia were attacked, with 380,000 of them being forced to spill back across the border only to be attacked by Sudanese government forces. In a separate incident, over 500,000 Ethiopian refugees fled back from Somalia during 1991–1992.

In some instances, the refugee movements have involved refugees going home even before the situation has normalized. They have opted to return because in the final analysis, the dangers at home have become the lesser of the two evils. For example, in 1989 over 80,000 Ugandan refugees returned from southern Sudan after having been attacked by Sudanese rebel forces. Similarly in 1991–1992, Angolans in Zaire and Ethiopians in Somalia fled back to their country only to encounter more dangers, after the security situation in exile had become intolerable.

Africa's general state of poverty, coupled with its pervasive conflicts, have combined to produce a serious economic environment on the continent. Economic problems have caused many people to abandon their homes and sometimes to flee into neighboring countries. The economic problem has been characterized mainly by deprivation resulting in poverty. In some instances, flight into exile has been a consequence of disputes relating to distribution of meagre resources. The austerity measures introduced in the context of the economic reform programs established in many African countries have worsened the situation, particularly among the marginalized groups (Mupedziswa, 1997b).

Environmental factors have been a major element in the mass movements of Africans. Human-induced factors, such as environmental degradation, have resulted in thousands of people in Africa fleeing their homes. For example, people have fled areas subjected to deforestation and soil erosion. Persistent natural disasters such as droughts and floods have also been among important factors. In this regard, the UNHCR

(1993) observed that the dislocation of the natural resource base, coupled with demographic pressure among other concerns, has exacerbated tensions that have led to refugee movements. One natural disaster that has caused mass movements of people is that of the Sahel region, which is rapidly turning into a desert. In the Sahel, as well as in the Horn of Africa, the combination of population explosion, drought, and competition for land resulted in conflict. The flight of Mozambicans into neighbouring countries as a result of severe drought in both the early 1980s and 1992 is also a case in point. During the 1992 drought, over 100,000 Mozambicans crossed the border into Malawi.

The UNHCR (1993) reported that disputes over irrigable land in the Senegal River basin caused Senegalese and Mauritanians to cross their common border in both directions. In southern Ethiopia, on the other hand, incursions by certain clans into the traditional grazing land of other clans resulted in conflict that created refugee flows to Kenya. Thus, there are many reasons for the refugee situation in Africa.

## PROBLEMS FACED BY REFUGEES IN EXILE

Refugees experience many problems from the time of their flight into exile through to the period they remain in exile. The problems range from social, economic, and psychological through cultural and political. The South African Council of Churches (SACC, 1982) has lamented that no amount of theorizing can permit humanity to ignore the plight of the African refugees, noting further that the refugees have crossed parched deserts and tangled jungles in search of a secure life. The refugees are vulnerable not only to the ravages of disease and the vagaries of the weather but to human brutality as well.

Africa's refugees frequently flee their homes unceremoniously, leaving behind their personal belongings—even their personhood. This has been largely because the vast majority of Africa's refugees are illiterate or semiliterate, inarticulate, and unsophisticated. Economically, most African refugees are poor and extremely underprivileged even before their flight from home. Most come from rural backgrounds and leave particular areas in large numbers. SACC (1982) has observed that the refugees often live on the barest of means, lacking adequate food, water, clothing, or shelter. Shortage of food is often rampant, and this lack often results in malnourishment.

The flight into exile itself is often stressful and may involve numerous sleepless nights in transit to the country of asylum. There are often stories of fear, panic, flight, illness, and hunger ("New Roles," 1989: 70). The Mozambicans who fled to Zimbabwe, for instance, related harrowing stories of how some of them traveled two to three weeks on foot in hot dry land, with a limited supply of food and water. Stories abound of how men went on their knees, begging mothers with lactating babies to give them a few drops of breast milk or how others drank urine to quench their thirst (Makanya and Mupedziswa, 1988).

Numerous other problems are experienced during the flight into exile, including sniper fire, rape, or death from exhaustion. The dangers and difficulties experienced during the flight to safety are often beyond description. The refugees are exposed to many problems that put both their physical and mental health at risk. Psychologically, the dangers faced by refugees make them withdrawn. Psychosomatic problems often become commonplace because of the traumatic experiences they go through (Mupedziswa, 1993).

Perhaps the only positive aspect of this experience is that status for the African refugees is often determined en masse, sparing the refugees the pain of applying for status and anxiously waiting for lengthy periods for a determination. This progressive policy has earned Africa the reputation as perhaps the most hospitable continent in terms of refugee assistance. However, the policy is not being followed across the board (Rogers and Copeland, 1993). For instance, in 1990 Sierra Leone refused to accept Liberian refugees. Similar negative reactions were reported during 1990 and 1991 in Kenya and Djibouti, respectively. Liberia has also been a culprit in this respect.

Although Africa has a good record in respect to hospitality, some African refugees, particularly the urban based, have faced legal problems. Unfortunately, often the refugees are not absolutely certain of their rights, and even when they are they have little power to have these rights upheld. Consequently, widespread violations of human rights do occur in Africa. Many of these human rights violations go both unnoticed and undetected, for they are often not recognized, or are simply ignored by the mass media.

Detention without trial or without justifiable cause is rampant in the continent. In spite of the fundamental principle that refugees should not be forcibly sent back or expelled, incidents of this continue to occur unabated. In some African countries, refugees have been subjected to physical torture, detention under harsh conditions, and other harrowing experiences. In other instances, refugees have been forcibly recruited into the army, exacerbating their already difficult situation.

On arrival in the country of asylum, much needed respite is often not forthcoming. The refugees often find themselves in a new hostile environment, even though many refugee movements in Africa occur across borders. Even when their reception is warm, they are distraught and bitter. Uprooted from their traditional, spiritual, cultural, and economic base, they now face the emptiness and uncertainty of exile. The conditions African refugees encounter, whether within Africa or abroad, are often deplorable. In exile, their status is devalued and their self-authority lost, particularly in countries that have questionable human rights records.

Theoretically, refugees can settle in either urban or rural areas, but in Africa very few (about 15%) end up in urban areas. Rural refugees often have three options in terms of settlement. First, a large majority spontaneously settle. Second, a fair percentage ends up in refugee camps. Indeed, refugee camps are the only option for some African countries, especially Somalia and Sudan. Third, they may be placed in planned settlements where they can grow food. In the mid-1980s, 25 percent of Africa's refugees were in settlements (Rogers and Copeland, 1993). Encampment of refugees, though popular with some host governments, exacerbates the state of poverty of the African refugees, for it usually offers no space to grow food crops or graze animals.

For those who settle in rural areas, even the terrain may not be welcoming. The refugees sometimes fail to find such essentials as herbs. One refugee gave a moving description of the environment that confronted his group in exile. "Arriving in the area of resettlement, we were scared to death. Never had we seen such thick forests, inhabited only by wild animals, snakes and big biting flies. Homeland was full of gentle hills and peaceful grazing cattle. My dreams are still bound to my homeland" ("Voluntary Repatriation," 1987: 43). This observation was apparently made 15 years after flight, indicating how difficult it can be to adjust to a foreign environment.

In any refugee emergency, protection is a crucial concern, but in Africa, protection has been the first casualty. Various problems have been associated with protection, ranging from logistical through legal to practical. Despite Africa's purported hospitality, in recent times, there have been reports of refugees in exile on the continent encountering threats to their security and well-being. Thus, some countries have failed to adhere to both the letter and spirit of international conventions.

Refugee camps in particular have been highly visible targets of attack by either government or rebel forces. Prominent examples have included the highly publicized South African apartheid regime's raid on Chasing camp in Angola in 1978. Others were the then Rhodesian forces' raid on the refugee camps of Nyadzonya, Chimoio, and Tembwe based in Zimbabwe's neighboring countries of Mozambique and Zambia in the late 1970s. Somalian camps in Kenya, and Rwandese camps in Zaire have also drawn fire from hostile forces. In July 1996, it was reported that over 2,000 Sudanese refugees had disappeared from Acholpii camp in northern Ugandan district of Kitgum after at least 90 were killed by rebels (*The Herald*, July 17, 1996). It could not be established whether these refugees had been abducted, were hiding in the bush, or were on the move following the attack on the camp in question. These are just a few examples of the numerous problems refugees face in Africa.

## CHALLENGES FACING ASYLUM COUNTRIES

The presence of refugees poses numerous challenges in any country. In the context of Africa, these challenges have been presented primarily in the form of problems, which include the following: destruction of the environment, security concerns, land scarcity, illegal trade, promiscuity, and increased levels of crime.

Security can be a major concern for both the host country and the refugees themselves because hostile armed groups belonging to the "opposition" will sometimes attempt to get at the fleeing refugees. In other cases, the source of concern is the armed forces of the country from which the refugees are fleeing. Examples have included strikes by the then Rhodesian forces on refugees in neighboring Zambia and Mozambique. More recently, there has been the plight of Rwandese who fled into neighboring Zaire and Tanzania.

Countries that receive refugees often have to grapple with the problem of environmental degradation triggered by the sudden onset of large influxes of refugees. In many parts of the continent, refugees, in their struggle for survival, have depleted the environment surrounding their settlements of virtually all fauna and flora. The natural resources most affected have been the forests, from which they obtain fuel wood and building materials; the land, utilized both for accommodation and for grazing animals and growing food crops; and water, for human and animal consumption, and sanitation.

The mere presence of refugees in an area can have devastating environmental effects. Tsehai (1991) observed that the area of land clearance required for building shelter for 100,000 refugees is estimated at 333 hectares and that the same number of refugees consume 85,000 tons of wood annually. In general, large-scale movements and concentration of refugees result in extensive decimation of wildlife as well as wild fruit. The refugees' struggle for survival has often resulted in the destruction of fauna and flora in the rivers. Land degradation has also resulted in soil erosion, which in turn has produced siltation of rivers, even causing some of these rivers to dry up completely (Mupedziswa, 1993).

Land scarcity is yet another issue of grave concern for refugees. In many parts of Africa, land is generally considered a scarce resource largely because of the artificial shortage that is the colonial legacy. The colonial settlers appropriated for themselves large tracts of land for commercial and estate farming. In some areas, this state of affairs led to an artificial land shortage, which resulted in the indigenous population and even government being starved of land, while in other instances, as in Kenya, Zimbabwe, and South Africa, it precipitated wars of liberation.

Thus, colonization created an artificial shortage of land that is still felt in many parts of the continent today. It is in this kind of situation that many countries have received refugees in large numbers, often over-whelming the local populations. Malawi, for example, with a total land area of 128,000 square kilometers and a population of 9 million, was at the height of the refugee influx host to over 1 million mostly Mozam-bican refugees. This was about 10 percent of that country's popula-tion.

Other problems associated with the arrival of refugees in an African host country have included illegal trade, which may create untold ten-sions between locals and the refugees. In addition, criminal activity often increases whenever large influxes of refugees enter an area. The criminal activities do not necessarily involve the refugees themselves. Sometimes locals hide behind the refugees while committing criminal activities. Un-doubtedly the refugees, desperate for survival, have also resorted to crime.

In Southern Africa, for instance, in Zimbabwe, locals have claimed that refugees have stolen their livestock, slaughtered the beasts under cover of darkness, and then concealed the meat, which is subsequently smug-gled into the settlements in small quantities to avoid detection. Problems associated with land allocation and deforestation have also created ani-mosity between refugees and local people, with the locals concerned that the refugees were creating deserts in the vicinity of the settlements (Mu-pedziswa, 1993).

## INTERVENTION INITIATIVES: CURRENT AND POTENTIAL

Over the years, the international community has given much attention to the refugee crisis in Africa and has launched various initiatives. Through conferences, seminars, and workshops, they have generated material and other forms of assistance. The initiatives have included the Arusha Consultation on Refugees (1981), jointly sponsored by the All Africa Conference of Churches (AACC), the Lutheran World Federation (LWF), and the World Council of Churches (WCC), whose basic focus was to explore the possible role of the church in refugee assistance in Africa.

Although the churches have done their part to address the refugee problem, it still persists. Clearly, the political issues had not been fully appreciated, and so the search for effective intervention strategies con-tinues. Perhaps the international community's first serious effort to ad-dress the African refugee crisis was the first International Conference on Assistance to Refugees in Africa (ICARA-1) held in Geneva in April 1981. Attended by representatives of 99 governments, ICARA-1's chief objec-tives were to focus international public opinion on the plight of the refugees in Africa, to mobilize additional resources for them, and to aid host countries to bear the burden of large refugee influxes.

Although this effort had some impact, it was not complete. Consequently, a followup initiative, the second International Conference on Assistance to Refugees in Africa (ICARA-2), was held, again in Geneva, in July 1984. This joint effort involved the UNHCR, the OAU, and UNDP. Its objectives were to review the results of ICARA-1, to mobilize additional assistance, and to consider the impact of large population influxes on national economies. Like its predecessors, however, the effort had its limitations. The major problem was that the large influxes occurring on an almost daily basis had overwhelmed the continent (Mupedziswa, 1993).

In the late 1980s, refugee influxes were concentrated mainly in the central/southern Africa region, with the majority hailing from Mozambique. For instance, in Mozambique alone, well over 4 million persons were reportedly displaced within that country. A decision was therefore made to organize initiatives focusing directly on this region. As a result, the International Conference on Refugees, Returnees and Displaced Persons in Southern Africa (SARRED) was organized in Oslo in August 1988. The gathering brought together some 600 delegates from more than 100 UN member states. The conference basically sought greater participation by the international community in addressing the refugee crisis in Southern Africa. In many ways SARRED was a followup to ICARA-2, for it actually took the opportunity to review progress of ICARA-2.

Various organizations have been involved in the African refugee crisis in the context of all these initiatives. These have included the host governments, the UNHCR, and its associated agencies such as the WHO, FAO and UNDP. The UNHCR has particular responsibility for refugee affairs worldwide, including Africa. It works closely with the other agencies in the UN system. However, because of the nature of the refugee problem in Africa, the UNHCR has often found itself with an inadequate budget. For example, the cost of looking after the 1.7 million Rwandese refugees in DRC, Tanzania, and Burundi was U.S.$1 million per day (*The Herald*, June 13, 1960). When the cost of hosting refugees in other troublespots on the continent is added to this figure, it becomes easier to appreciate how expensive the African refugee crisis has been.

National governments are particularly important players in refugee assistance, for it is they who grant refugees permission to settle on their territory. In collaboration with UNHCR, they also coordinate the work of NGOs involved in work with refugees. Some have special units to deal with refugee matters, and a commissioner of refugees may head these units. Many national governments in Africa have been most accommodating, although there are now signs of fatigue and inertia setting in.

Nonetheless, many African countries still adhere to international conventions. Consequently, even in the midst of brutal fighting, some states have continued to acknowledge their international obligations, as the following examples illustrate.

In the Horn of Africa, in the midst of hostilities, countries in the region still managed to get together in April 1992 to sign a declaration of intent, among other things, to implement international conventions (Harrell-Bond, 1988). In some instances, cease-fires have been declared or other humanitarian measures taken to give respite or safe passage to refugees. For instance, a cease-fire that was negotiated in southern Sudan enabled UNICEF to carry out a massive immunization exercise. In other cases, corridors have been opened to allow overflights or other forms of transportation of relief supplies to refugees. For example, the Eritrean port of Massena was opened briefly in 1990 for such a purpose. Although some of these efforts have held together for a long time, others, being more fragile, have quickly broken down and hostilities have resumed (Mupedziswa, 1997a).

In addition to the national government efforts, various nongovernmental organizations, both local and international, have also played their part. The African continent is well known for its hospitality, and in this respect, the communities' role cannot be overstated. They are involved at various stages of the refugee plight. Various nongovernmental organizations work with refugees in their settlement areas, providing the refugees with emergency relief or the opportunity to start self-help projects.

Many of the long-term intervention efforts in relation to the African refugee crisis have been envisaged in the context of the UNHCR's "durable solutions," namely, voluntary repatriation, local integration, and resettlement in a third country. These approaches have had varied appeal in the context of Africa. The most popular durable solution in Africa has been voluntary repatriation. Examples of repatriation programs on the continent date back to the 1960s and have included Algerian refugees who were repatriated from Tunisia and Morocco in the 1960s. Refugees have also been repatriated to Guinea Bissau and Algeria. Similarly, Southern African refugees returned to Angola, Mozambique, Namibia, and Zimbabwe after independence. In the case of Mozambique, the repatriation of 1.3 million Mozambicans, one of the largest organized repatriations ever attempted in Africa, got under way in July 1993 and was quite successful by most accounts. Some successful exercises have been those involving the unorganized repatriation of spontaneously settled refugees, who have voluntarily and unofficially organized their return home, often crossing borders at unofficial points (Mupedziswa, 1993).

The international conventions declare that the voluntary repatriation option should be effected only when the situation in the home country has improved and when the refugees themselves have expressed a wish to return. Sometimes, however, this solution is forced on the refugees, who decide to return under duress. In some cases, the refugees have gone back to tenuous cease-fires. The examples cited have included Ethiopians and Eritreans from Djibouti, the Burundians from Tanzania, and Mozambicans from Malawi, Zambia, and Zimbabwe (Harrell-Bond, 1988). Crisp (1984) shows that in 1982, Djibouti, for example, forcibly repatriated refugees to Ethiopia against their will.

In other cases, refugees have gone back to areas devastated by war, making their reintegration rather difficult; this has been the case in Angola, Chad, Eritrea, Ethiopia, Mozambique, Rwanda, Somalia, and Western Sahara. Interestingly, sometimes home countries have refused returning refugees permission to reenter their countries. Examples have included the government of Rwanda, which initially refused to accept the return of some of its citizens who were living as refugees in Uganda, citing land shortage as the reason. In Ethiopia, the repatriation of Tigreyan refugees from the Sudan was similarly delayed for unclear reasons (Harrell-Bond, 1988).

Local integration, which refers basically to settling refugees within the host country, has not been a very popular option in the African context, although, there have been a few examples of application of this solution. Local integration was successfully executed in Tanzania, for example. By the 1970s, over 60,000 Mozambicans had been settled there. When some of these refugees were repatriated after Mozambique attained independence in 1975, some 20,000 opted for Tanzanian citizenship. Botswana, too, allowed some 2,500 of an initial figure of 4,000 Angolans and Mozambicans who opted to remain to settle permanently in that country (Kabera, 1988). In 1991, some 130 Zimbabwean refugees also became citizens of Botswana (Rogers and Copeland, 1993). Other countries, such as Kenya and Malawi, which have allowed local integration, have predictably been chafing under the burden of providing refuge to exiled groups.

Local integration has had a very limited impact in Africa (Mupedziswa, 1993), partly because of the negative attitudes of governments, the land shortage, and the security issue. Many host governments associate integration with assimilation and "permanence" (Makanya and Mupedziswa, 1988), and so they are likely to resist a policy that appears to promote the absorption of the refugee population into the host country. In the case of the problem of security, hit-squads are sometimes secretly sent on missions to disrupt the life of refugees in exile.

Africa's refugees have themselves often resisted local integration efforts. The connotations of permanence associated with local integration create resistance from the refugees and sometimes from their hosts as well. A study of Mozambicans who were in exile in Zimbabwe revealed that, in general, they did not relish the idea of being integrated into the

Zimbabwean society (Makanya and Mupedziswa, 1988). The hosts sometimes declined to accept the refugees for fear they might be caught up in the crossfire in the event of an attack. This fear is real. During the apartheid era, for instance, the South African regime in power would conduct raids into its neighboring countries on the pretext of flushing out freedom fighters. Many locals were killed in the resulting crossfire.

This strategy has also been unpopular because refugees often flee into neighboring countries only to settle a short distance away from the border, making it difficult for them to bury memories of home (Mupedziswa, 1993). Consequently, they constantly live with the hope of returning. Notwithstanding this argument, where local integration has been applied in Africa, it has presented tremendous potential for success because the colonial boundaries cut across ethnic boundaries, which means that people on different sides may share the same culture and speak the same language, facilitating easier integration. The most successful situations of local integration, however, have been those of spontaneously settled refugees.

The resettlement strategy in a third country focuses on refugees who are unable either to return safely to their home country or to stay indefinitely in the first country of asylum. It involves sending the refugees to a third country. Refugees who take this option often face numerous challenges, including that of communication. In addition, the refugees have to grapple with a host of other problems, including local customs, traditions, belief systems, norms, and values.

Very few African countries have adopted resettlement in a third country as an option. In Southern Africa, before South Africa attained majority rule, countries such as Botswana, Swaziland, and Lesotho would send some South African refugees, albeit reluctantly, to countries further north for fear that they would be attacked by the apartheid regime's commandos. Similarly, countries like Botswana and Zambia used to send Zimbabwean refugees (before the country attained independence) to the north for the same reasons.

In terms of settlement outside Africa, the number of refugees from the continent has been negligible. Few Africans have found their way to the United States, Canada, and other Western countries. While the United States, for instance, granted Africa a quota of refugees that could go to that country, African refugees have been reluctant to settle there for a variety of reasons, including cultural concerns. Consequently, the quota has at times not been fully subscribed.

Of the 87,500 refugees who settled in the United States in 1988, some 3,000 were from Africa (Mupedziswa, 1993). In 1985, France took in 8,961 Africans out of the total 171,790 refugees from all over the world seeking entry into that country. Switzerland accepted 74,335 refugees in 1985, and of that figure, some 2,000 were from Africa. Other countries, such as Italy, have discriminated against refugees from developing countries, including Africa. Generally, European countries are admitting fewer and fewer asylum seekers. For instance, in 1992, out of the 272,000 individual applicants (including those from Africa) considered for asylum in Western Europe, only 25,000 (or 9%) were granted refugee status, while an additional 29,000 were allowed to stay on humanitarian grounds (UNHCR, 1993: 308).

The OAU's policy on resettlement in a third country generally dictates that African refugees remain on the African continent (Kabera, 1988). This is partly because there are too many African refugees to find a place overseas and also apparently because the major refugee-receiving countries like the United States, Canada, and Australia see the African refugee problem as a local one requiring local solutions. Harrell-Bond (1986: 1) has observed that "the mood of industrialised countries towards many African refugees from the continent is highly restrictive," perhaps because resettlement of the inarticulate, unsophisticated, often illiterate or semiliterate, mostly rural African refugees, would, by and large, not be feasible (Mupedziswa, 1993). And, of course, the stance taken by some Western countries may have racial overtones.

## CONCLUSION

The refugee experience is painful, for it dehumanizes the individual. In Africa, the statistics on refugees are frightening. Certain groups of refugees, the vulnerable, have been neglected or even ignored on the continent. Undoubtedly, the international community's various initiatives to deal with the resulting hardship have had some positive impact within the purview of the durable solutions. Nevertheless, two issues stand out. First, the number of refugees in Africa continues to escalate daily as new tricky situations emerge and old ones take much longer to resolve. Second, the situation of the African refugees continues to get worse against a backdrop of diminishing resources, particularly in the wake of the SAP-triggered socioeconomic environment and donor fatigue. Future efforts must therefore address these aspects.

While they await a durable solution, refugees are left in a continuous state of "emergency" in which they have been forced to accept food handouts in perpetuity from various sources. Blame for this state of affairs can been laid on the UNHCR, some host countries, and some NGOs. NGOs have done too little in the area of advocacy: They need to focus attention on sensitizing the politicians as well as members of the mass media, among others, on pertinent refugee issues and to link the immediate and long-term needs of refugees. In other words, there is need for a developmental approach that goes beyond emergency relief (Mupedziswa, 1993).

According to Omari (1988), the developmental approach, seeks to provide skills and knowledge for the present and future, to make the refugees more self-reliant, and to educate the hosts about the refugee problem in an international context to facilitate solidarity. The approach encourages participation by refugees in matters that affect their lives. It helps them to face both their current situation and their future with determination and resilience and it enables them to lead a productive and dignified life (Mupedziswa, 1993). It may include such activities as literacy training, health and sanitation, production of food crops, introduction of skills training, and income-generating projects.

Among the obstacles to this approach is the refugees' view of themselves as people in transition (or host governments may regard them as such); hence, there may be lack of motivation and enthusiasm in this respect. Second, many aid workers are trained in emergency relief and therefore may not have the relevant skills to implement a developmental strategy (Omari, 1988). However, with will power and oneness of purpose, these obstacles can be overcome. Imaginative workers with the correct vision and motivation are therefore needed to deal with the situation.

Although these efforts may be effective for situations where refugees have already been generated, there is a need to go beyond this and to stop the refugee situation from occurring in the first instance. Consequently, with regard to countries that generate refugees in the African continent, more emphasis must be directed at preventing refugee-inducing situations from happening through peacemaking and peace-keeping. The focus point of prevention must be on defusing tensions from occurring, that is, on addressing the unresolved political, ethnic, religious or nationality disputes that may lead to human rights abuses (Mupedziswa, 1993; UNHCR, 1993).

This is indeed a tall order and one that is often easier said than done, but as the adage goes, "where there is a will there is a way." The UNHCR should assume this role more aggressively than is currently the case. It can do so in conjunction with various international peace agencies such as the Carter Center or with committed individuals such as the late Tanzanian President Julius Nyerere, all of whom have been most active in spearheading African peace efforts.

Regional organizations like the OAU and SADC should play a more positive and prominent role and should stop hiding behind the guise of noninterference in the affairs of sovereign states. These organizations should not shrink from responsibility. For example, the collective action taken by some Southern African countries (the Frontline States) to defuse a potentially explosive political stalemate in the recent past involving Swaziland is commendable. Similar action could be taken in other trouble spots in the continent. In pursuing this option, the strategy should be to address the causes of flight before it occurs, nipping it in the bud. Proactive rather than reactive action is called for in efforts to defuse potential refugee-generating situations in Africa.

## REFERENCES

Crisp, J. (1984). "Voluntary Repatriation Programs for African Refugees: A Critical Examination." *RSP Refugee Issues* 1(2): 6–8.

Gasarasi, C.P. (1984). "The Tripartite Approach to the Resettlement and Integration of Rural Refugees in Tanzania." *Sweden Refugee Report* No. 71. Uppsala: Scandinavian Institute of African Studies.

Harrell-Bond, B. (1986). *Imposing Aid: Emergency Assistance to Refugees.* Oxford: Oxford University Press.

———. (1988). *Breaking the Vicious Circle: Refugees and Other Displaced Persons in Africa.* Workshop on the African Situation, June 26–30, Oxford University, Oxford.

*The Herald.* (1996). "Benaco Camp Has 250,000 Refugees." June 13, p. 6.

———. (1997). "Thousands Flee Brazzaville." June 28, p. 7.

Kabera, J. (1988). *Potential for Naturalisation of Refugees in Africa: The Case of Uganda.* Paper presented at the ASAUK Conference, September 14–16, Cambridge University, Cambridge (Unpublished).

Makanya, S. and Mupedziswa, R. (1988). *Refugee Protection in Zimbabwe: Local Integration—a Permanent Solution to a Temporary Problem?* Paper presented at the ASAUK Conference, September 14–16, Cambridge University, Cambridge (Unpublished).

Mazrui, A., quoted in Mwase, N. (1988). *The Namibian Refugee Situation: Past, Present and Future.* Paper presented at the ASAUK Conference, September 14–16, Cambridge, Cambridge University (Unpublished).

Mupedziswa, R. (1993). *Uprooted: Refugees and Social Work in Africa.* Harare: JSDA Publications.

———. (1997a). "Social Work with Refugees: The Growing International Crisis." In M. C. Hookenstad and J. Midgley (eds.), *Issues in International Social Work* (pp. 110–124). Washington, DC: NASW Press.

———. (1997b). *Empowerment or Repression: ESAP and Children in Zimbabwe.* Gweru: Mambo Press.

Mwase, N. (1988). *The Namibian Refugee Situation: Past, Present and Future.* Paper Presented at the ASAUK Conference, September 14–16, Cambridge University, Cambridge (Unpublished).

"New Roles and Relationships: The Family in Exile." (1989). *Refugees* 70: 16.

Norton-Staal, S. (1994). "African Refugee Families." In *Refugees.* Geneva: UNHCR, pp. 29–30.

Omari, C.K. (1988). "Working with Refugees: Some Experiences from Tanzania." *Refugee Participation Network* 3: 23–25.

Rogers, R. and Copeland, E. (1993). *Forced Migration: Policy Issues in the Post Cold War World.* Medford, MA: Fletcher School of Law and Diplomacy.

SACC (1982). *Refugees: A Challenge to South African Churches.* Johannesburg: South African Council of Churches.

"Tanzania Hosts 600,000 Hutu Refugees." (1996). *Refugees Daily,* November 27.

Tsehai, F.M. (1991). "Refugees in Ethiopia: Some Reflections on the Ecological Impact." *IDOC Journal* 22(2) (April/June): 7–9.

United Nations High Commissioner for Refugees (UNHCR). (1993). *The State of the World's Refugees: The Challenges of Protection.* New York: Penguin Books.

"Various Dispatches on African Refugee Crisis." (1997). *Refugees Daily,* February 21.

"Voluntary Repatriation: The Hope of Thousands of African Refugees." (1987). *Refugees* 43: 13–14.

Chapter 12

# Social Change and Organized Crime in Southern Africa

## Daniel D. Ntanda Nsereko

## INTRODUCTION

Crime is conduct that is proscribed by the law under the threat of punishment. The conduct may be a forbidden act or the omission to perform a legally imposed duty. Lawgivers proscribe such conduct because they consider it harmful to society as a whole. Proscribed conduct generally falls under four categories. The first category includes acts or omissions that undermine state institutions. Examples include acts of treason, sedition, perjury, and official corruption. The second category includes acts of violence against individuals and their property, such as murder, manslaughter, assault, rape, theft, robbery, burglary, arson, and malicious injury to property. Though directed against individuals, conduct in this category is considered harmful to the public at large because of its potential to disturb societal harmony and public tranquillity. The third category encompasses immoral behavior or behavior of a depraved nature, such as sexual relations against the order of nature, bestiality, prostitution, gambling, and substance abuse. Such behavior is considered injurious to society's moral values and a threat to its very existence because of its tendency to weaken the physical and moral integrity of its members and to impair their potential for public service. The last category includes acts and omissions that endanger public safety and public health, or violate public standards. Such conduct encompasses the whole gamut of regulatory offences against codes of conduct that set standards of behavior in various spheres of human endeavor. Examples of such codes include traffic and building codes, food and drug laws, and environmental protection laws.

Crime falling within these categories is rampant throughout Southern Africa. Crime debases the quality of life in this area because it instills fear and insecurity in the minds of the general public and creates woe and suffering for its victims. Crime is costly both in terms of the direct damage it causes and the resources that have to be defrayed to combat it. In this respect, it is estimated that crime caused the Republic of South Africa damage totaling R11,500,000,000 during the first eight months of 1995 alone (South African Police Service, 1995). Thus, there can be no gainsaying crime's deleterious impact on the region's social and economic well-being.

It is axiomatic that where there is society there is also bound to be crime. This is so because of the intrinsically imperfect nature of man and of the inherent imbalances and inequities in any human society. The incidence of crime will, however, depend largely on the conditions existing in a given society. Change in these conditions will also invariably affect its incidence. Change may constitute either the cause or catalyst for the incidence of crime. It may also help reduce crime. What, then, is this change, and how does it relate to the incidence of crime in Southern Africa? The following discusses the relationship between social change, which has taken place within Southern Africa, and the incidence of crime. The focus, however, is on organized crime, especially drug trafficking.

## SOCIAL CHANGE AND CRIME

Social change is change in the composition, practices, and values of society. It is the product of changes in the physical environment, an increase or decrease in the population, the types of economic activities engaged in by the population, the political system in place, the nature and typology of the family, and the educational standards of the community. Social change may be evolutionary or revolutionary. It is evolutionary when it comes about gradually; it is revolutionary when it comes about suddenly, often as a result of political struggle, as in the case of Botswana, Malawi, Zambia, and Tanzania, or as a result of armed struggle as in the case of Angola, Mozambique, Namibia, South Africa, and Zimbabwe. Where the change comes about as a result of struggle, power devolves from the alien rulers to the indigenous people or from a minority group of people to the majority of the population. This devolution of power somehow affects the social, political, and economic relations in the country, and it has ripple effects throughout the country. It thus becomes a catalyst for change.

The change that has taken place in Southern Africa has tended to be more revolutionary than evolutionary, although the evolutionary element cannot be ruled out. The attainment of independence or majority

Table 12.1
Urban Population in Botswana, 1971–1991

| Urban Center | 1971 | 1981 | 1991 |
|---|---|---|---|
| Gaborone | 17,713 | 59,657 | 133,468 |
| Francistown | 18,613 | 31,065 | 65,244 |
| Lobatse | 11,936 | 19,034 | 26,052 |
| Selebi-Phikwe | 4,940 | 29,467 | 39,772 |
| Orapa | 1,209 | 5,229 | 8,827 |
| Jwaneng | * | 5,567 | 11,188 |
| Sowa Town | * | * | 2,228 |
| TOTAL | 54,411 | 150,019 | 286,779 |
| National Population | 574,094 | 941,027 | 1,326,796 |

*Source*: CSO, 1991a.

rule in the countries of the region has inexorably affected the demographic configurations of those countries. Their largely rural populations have been transformed into increasingly urban ones. People who have all along been confined to rural areas have flocked into towns either to take up government employment or to accompany their relatives who were catapulted into governmental positions. In particular, the abolition of apartheid and its attendant restrictions in South Africa has resulted in the unparalleled rural-urban migration of Africans in search of employment and happier lives. The establishment of industries, including mining, in many countries of the region has also spurred the ongoing rural-urban migration. Men and women have drifted and continue to drift to areas where the industries are concentrated in search of work. These areas are characterized by high-density populations which are steadily increasing everyday. For example, the population of the city of Gaborone in Botswana rose from 17,713 in 1971 to 59,657 in 1981 and to 133,468 in 1991. Indeed, according to Table 12.1, the total population of all the towns in Botswana rose—from 54,411 in 1971 to 150,019 in 1981 and to 286,779 in 1991. Thus, over this 20-year period the percentage of the population in the towns over the total population rose from 9.4 percent in 1971 to 15.9 percent in 1981 and to 21.6 percent in 1991 (Central Statistics Office [CSO], 1991a). These figures are limited to towns only. If we used the current Botswana definition of "urban settlement" as a locality of 5,000 or more people with 75 percent of the labor force in nonagricultural activities and any settlement with a municipal authority, the urban population would be much larger than that shown above. According to the 1991 census, it would come to 614,911 people, or approximately 40 percent of the total population. Botswana remains a largely rural society, but as these figures reveal, the urban population is steadily rising and by the year 2001 it will have risen to 51.4 percent of the total population (CSO, 1991a). Statistics from other countries of the region reveal a similar picture (United Nations, 1995).

Most of the rural-urban migrations in the region are unplanned. No employment awaits the new arrivals in the towns. There is no adequate housing to accommodate them; hence thousands of shacks have mushroomed in squatter camps such as those that belt cities like Cape Town in South Africa, Windhoek in Namibia, or Lusaka in Zambia. These camps are characterized by squalor and inhuman living conditions. Relatives and friends who arrived earlier sometimes accommodate lucky new arrivals. Those not so lucky pitch up cardboard shacks into which several families huddle, or they sleep on verandahs, abandoned buildings, or in gutters. In general, the places where these newcomers live are overcrowded and lack amenities and lighting. No wonder that they invariably degenerate into slums such as Katatura in Windhoek or Old Naledi in Gaborone, where unemployment, drug abuse, and alcoholism are the order of the day (Mazonde, 1995).

The incidence of crime is higher in urban and densely populated areas (especially slums) than in rural communities. Among the explanations for this phenomenon is the fact that the urban population is not as homogeneous as the rural population and urban dwellers are strangers to each other. Furthermore, the closely knit family element that characterizes the rural communities and helps to exert control on social and moral behavior is absent in cities, and the population is constantly shifting, resulting in lack of commitment to the moral reputation of the community. Additional problems that confront the urbanites are unemployment, lack of housing and social amenities, and the sheer need to survive. The end result of all these elements is the high incidence of crime.

Another facet of rural-urban migration in the region has been the presence of a large percentage of young people among the migrants. For example, of the total 119,559 people who migrated in 1991 from rural to urban centers in Botswana, 79,768 were under the age of 25 years (CSO, 1991a). They constituted 66.7 percent of the total number of migrants that year.

Children accompany their parents to urban centers; while some go there for better educational opportunities, others are among the thousands of early school dropouts who flock to urban centers in search of jobs and a better life (CSO, 1996). They get neither and thus serve to swell the numbers of the unemployed. Unemployed and often unemployable and improperly housed, these young people help swell the crime numbers. Many join such criminal gangs variously known in Botswana as the *Ma-Westerns, Ma-Easterners,* and the *Ma-spotis.*

Another change that has taken place in many Southern African societies has been the nature and typology of the family. Traditionally, the family, both the nucleus (the man, his wife, and their children) and the extended family, was the major agent for social control of behavior in many a community. This kind of family has largely disintegrated due to the migration by men to distant places in search of work; delayed marriages, especially by men; demographic imbalances; and changes in sexual morality. With respect to these change in sexual morality, it may be observed that most children in the region are no longer born within wedlock as in the past. This has been particularly so in Botswana where about 60 percent of all the children born in any given year are born out of wedlock. These children are raised by single parents—invariably the mother or grandmother. The result is that 45.2 percent of all the households in Botswana and 52 percent in the rural areas are headed by women (CSO, 1991a). Commenting on this phenomenon, Fako (1983: 10) says:

The father who is customarily the founder and legal head of his family and who must formally recognize his children as his own at the time of birth, by giving them a name and providing for the mother during her confinement . . . is, in many instances, permanently absent in a child's life. By being socialised in a fatherless context, the child is bound to come to accept fatherlessness and is likely to be engaged, as an adult, in behaviours, which will perpetuate some form of father absenteeism. Instead of learning that father is someone who protects his children, and who helps to keep order and maintain discipline over his children, father becomes a vaguely remembered or unknown "man" who sends little to no money; who may occasionally visit, or who is simply best known to mother and is of no immediate significance to children. The absence of a father is not only economically burdensome to a mother, but denies the family an important element without which the definition of family becomes problematic.

Often unemployed and poor, the mother or grandmother becomes overwhelmed by the burden of raising the children unassisted. For their part, the children, upon realizing that they cannot receive minimal support from home, decide to drift to towns to fend for themselves, hence the growing number of street children, the *bobashi.* Today, in the context of Botswana, they number in the thousands. One writer (Matebele, 1995: 15) describes their situation as follows:

As bitter winter wind whips through the streets of Gaborone, 14-year-old Moses, huddled in the car park area of Broadhurst mall, takes a sniff from his glue carton, hoping it will block out the cold. His face, once smooth-looking, is now roughened and aging. For Moses is an outcast from the society. His crime is having no home, no parents and no place to sleep. He is the child of the streets. There is an estimated more than 1,000 children like Moses in the streets of Botswana. They can be seen at many a car park, alone or in groups, begging, pilfering, pick-pocketing or shop lifting to survive. At night they sleep in gutters, dustbins, doorways, parks, scrap yards, deserted buildings or anywhere they can lay their heads on. Sometimes they build fires to guard against the cold and often dreadful burns result from dozing too close to the flames. Many suffer from bronchitis or venereal diseases, and show the mental effects of dagga, glue, petrol and any other substance they can get hold of to escape their constant misery.

A similar phenomenon has been reported for Zimbabwe (Marina, Jordan, and Kormie, 1995: 1–24). Thus, the overall effect of family disintegration is the loosening of parental control over children. This in turn means that societal values can no longer be transmitted to the younger members of the community. The end result is the youths' tendency toward crime. It is these youth who are later recruited into organized crime, particularly car thefts and drug trafficking, the most prevalent forms of organized crime in Southern Africa. They start off as apprentices of seasoned criminals and later blossom as full-time operatives.

## ORGANIZED CRIME

Organized crime is a form of criminality that is *organized*, being part of a system with a hierarchy sprawling from the village or town, major cities, provinces, the whole country and internationally. It operates through organizations, syndicates, networks, and agents planted at strategic places or in institutions within a country and beyond its borders (Fijnaut, 1990: 321–340). These agents may be members of a police department or other security organizations. They may be bank employees, customs and immigration officials, or members of public or private institutions. Sham companies and other financial outfits that facilitate fraudulent transactions and the transfer of funds are usually part of the network. The now defunct Bank of Credit and Commerce International, for example, was a haven for international financial crooks.

Organized crime often employs full-time operatives to direct its activities at any given level. These operatives are usually people with high professional skills in all fields of human endeavor. Employment of these professionals is necessitated by its elaborate networks and sophisticated modes of operation. Organized crime often relies for its protection on the services of highly placed and respectable public officials. It is in this sense that it is often referred to as "white collar crime" (Fijnaut, 1990: 321–340). Organized crime, like an octopus, spreads its venomous tentacles throughout all fabrics of society, national and international. It employs and corrupts plebeian and mighty alike. It churns out colossal sums of money—hence the involvement of so many people.

Organized crime is not limited to the Mafia families with Italian origins operating in the United States or the Russian Mafia operating in Europe. It is a worldwide phenomenon. It is present and active throughout Southern Africa.

Organized crime is not a separate category of crime. Rather, it covers a wide spectrum of criminal activity that involves the commission of a variety of crimes on the criminal calendar. The commission of one type of crime may sometimes be essential for the consummation of another type. For example, for a drug trafficking operation to be successful, other offenses such as bribery, forgery, fraud, robbery and murder may have to be and are often committed. Generally, however, the typical offenses that fall under the rubric of organized crime and are commonly committed in Southern Africa are illegal immigration, smuggling of weapons, smuggling of precious stones and endangered species (Ellis, 1994: 53–69), motor vehicle thefts, and drug trafficking. These crimes are interrelated, and one syndicate may be involved in the commission of more than one of them.

Illegal immigration involves entry into a country without permission or with improper or forged documents. In Southern Africa, the long, porous borders that are a common feature of the region facilitate this activity. The ethnic and cultural affinity of the peoples of the region also makes it possible for people to slip through border controls unnoticed. The countries that are the most seriously affected are Botswana where 2,918 immigrants were tried for illegal entry or stay in 1995 (*Botswana Police Report*, 1995); and South Africa where 1,052 illegal immigrants were arrested by the Illegal Immigration Unit of the South African Police in 1995 (South African Police Service, 1995). The majority of these immigrants were economic refugees seeking job opportunities in these relatively prosperous countries. Others were transnational criminals traveling on forged or stolen documents procured for them by criminal syndicates in these countries. Illegal immigrants often clash with the local populations for invading their job market (which is already inadequate for the citizens); imposing on the already meagre social services; and for their tendency to crime for sheer survival. In addition, illegal immigrants constitute a burden on the criminal justice system and on the national economies because they often have to be repatriated back to their countries of origin at great cost. For example, in 1995 alone, the South African government had to repatriate 157,084 illegal immigrants.

Weapons smuggling is most common in the strife-torn countries of the region. It has occurred in South Africa where weapons have been smuggled into the country from Mozambique (via Swaziland) and Angola (via Namibia or Botswana). Here, again, some specialized syndicates are at work. Smuggled weapons often get into the hands of criminals who use them to commit violent crimes and thus to terrorize innocent and law-abiding citizens.

Motor vehicle theft, mostly from the Republic of South Africa, is also very common in the region. According to the South African police, about 112 crime syndicates specialize in motor vehicle theft and facilitate the movement of the vehicles from the Republic to markets in Botswana, Malawi, Zambia, Zimbabwe, Zaire, and Tanzania. The high incidence of motor vehicle thefts in South Africa bears testimony to that country being the capital of this crime in the region. For example, the number of motor vehicle theft cases that was reported to the South African police rose from 68,254 in 1990 to 97,947 in 1995 (South African Police Service, 1995). Thieves manage to cross borders with their loot by using forged registration cards, falsifying identification marks on the vehicles, or bribing border guards and customs officials. The vehicles are often bartered for narcotic drugs, which, as we shall see presently, are in high demand in South Africa.

Drug trafficking is the single largest *organized* criminal activity in the region, and for this reason it constitutes the bulk of this chapter. South Africa, again, seems to be the leader in this activity. As of 1995, there were 136 known drug syndicates operating in and out of that country. Again the South African police reported that in 1993 and 1994 they confiscated or destroyed illicit drugs worth R1,000 (U.S.$27 million) and R7,500 (U.S.$202.5 million), respectively. They estimate that this constituted only about 10–15 percent of the total estimated value of the illicit drug trade in South Africa for that period (South African Police Service, 1995). In neighboring Botswana the police seized and destroyed illicit drugs worth P9 million (U.S.$3 million) (*Botswana Police Report*, 1995). This is big sum for a country the size of Botswana. More and more people in the region are getting involved in the trade because of the huge and quick profits they derive from it. Thus, hundreds of nationals of Southern African countries languish in foreign jails on account of drug trafficking. In 1994 alone, 8 Malawians, 10 Mozambicans, 31 South Africans, 8 Swazis, 32 Tanzanians, and 10 Zimbabweans were arrested as couriers in Europe, the United States, Canada, Thailand, and other Asian countries by the World Customs Organization (INTERPOL, 1994).

Drugs find their way in and out of the region because of its strategic location on the world's major sea and air routes to Asia, Europe, and North America. The traffickers regularly use seaports such as Mombasa, Dar es Salaam, Maputo, and Durban. Because of the weak controls at these ports as well as at other entry points, huge consignments of various drugs slip through undetected.

Drugs such as cocaine, heroine, morphine, cannabis, and methaqualone are common in the region, but cannabis and methaqualone are the most popular with the traffickers. Cannabis, variously known as marijuana, dagga, or motokwane, has been traditionally grown and used by the indigenous populations of the region in the same way that tobacco is grown and used elsewhere. Cannabis grows well even in infertile soil. In some areas it is the only cash crop that can be grown. With the ever-increasing demand for it in Europe and North America and with the encouragement of international drug syndicates that provide ready cash for it, rural people continue to grow the crop in large quantities. Large plantations of cannabis reportedly exist in Botswana, Malawi, Mozambique, South Africa, and Zambia. It is reported that in 1993 South Africa alone had about 82,734 hectares of land under cannabis cultivation, making it the world's largest cannabis producer, second only to Mexico. The South African police estimate that the total street value of cannabis produced in South Africa, together with that from neighboring Botswana, Lesotho, and Swaziland in 1994, amounted to about R54 billion (U.S.$15 billion) (INTERPOL, 1995). Small wonder that the plant has become so difficult to eradicate.

Methaqualone originates from India where it was first synthesized in 1955. It is transshipped to such countries as Kenya, Uganda, Zambia, Zimbabwe, Mozambique, Botswana, and Namibia, which are used as distribution points. The ultimate destination of the bulk of the drug is South Africa, which, according to INTERPOL, is "the world's biggest methaqualone market" (INTERPOL, 1995). According to INTERPOL, a network of organizations, syndicates, and agents in India and in Eastern and Southern Africa ensures that the drug reaches its destination. The agents include African students in India and Indian expatriates in the region. However, with vigilance and stricter controls imposed by the Indian authorities, the Indian sources have of late dwindled. Undaunted, the traffickers have responded by manufacturing the drug in the region. This is borne out by the discovery and closing of laboratories in Kenya, Tanzania, Zambia, and South Africa.

The quantities of methaqualone seized in the various countries of the region indicates the total volume of the trade and benefits derived from it by the traffickers. In 1993 alone, the following quantities of the drug were seized and destroyed in the following countries: Botswana, 5,475 tablets; Namibia, 2,033 tablets; South Africa, 3,533,567 tablets; Swaziland, 105,318 tablets; Tanzania, 240,224 tablets; Zambia, 319,792 tablets; and Zimbabwe, 1,413 tablets. The value of the drug per tablet ranged from U.S.$2 in Zimbabwe to U.S.$5 in South Africa and U.S.$15 in Namibia (INTERPOL, 1995). This explains why so many people are attracted to drug trafficking and are readily willing to risk the consequences of involvement. Occasionally involved in the trafficking are cabinet ministers, their spouses and children, as well as diplomats. These people often get away with it because of their diplomatic status.

Although countries such as Botswana, Malawi, Zambia, and Zimbabwe are principally transit routes for methaqualone, they too sooner or later become consumers. The consumers of this reputedly "love drug" are generally to be found in urban centers. They often include young adults, the unemployed, and secondary school and university students. Paradoxically, children of well-to-do members of the community are also well represented in this last group.

People often resort to narcotic or psychoactive substances to escape from reality or to seek solace and sensational pleasure. They do so for many and varied reasons, including impulsiveness and sensation seeking; childhood stress and trauma; lack of self-esteem; antisocial behavior during early adolescence; and failure or lack of interest in school. Other reasons involve economic and social deprivation; peer pressure; lack of recreational facilities, particularly for the youth; promotion of use by traffickers; availability of drugs; and cultural or religious factors.

Persistent abuse of narcotic drugs leads to addiction or to permanent dependency. Addiction is harmful to the abuser's physical and mental health and even to that of his or her offspring (Nurco et al., 1985: 94–102). In this respect, it has been reported that addiction (of cannabis) accounts for about 17 percent of all admissions to mental institutions in Malawi (Macdonald, 1996: 127–144). Addiction to drugs is also harmful to society as a whole in that when addicts are "high," they often lose self-control, become violent, and, if they operate a motor vehicle while under the influence, may cause accidents. Drugs also often turn addicts into bums, social misfits incapable of productive work and unable to support themselves or their dependents. This has serious social and economic repercussions for the addict's family, the community, and the nation at large. It is debatable whether addiction per se turns persons who, prior to initiation into the drug habit, were not already so into criminals (Greenberg and Adler, 1974: 221–270; Helmer, 1977: 405–418; McBride and McCoy, 1982: 52; Silverman, 1982: 167–183; Otero-Lopez et al., 1994: 459–478). However, it has been empirically established that addiction emboldens and settles persons who, prior to initiation into the habit, were already inclining toward criminal ways. It is also generally acknowledged that addicts often commit crimes of an acquisitive nature to acquire funds to finance their habit (Nurco et al., 1985: 94–102; Jarvis and Parker, 1989: 175–185; Asuni, 1992: 179–190). Addiction to drugs is particularly harmful to young people, especially adolescents and teenagers. Not only does it impair their physical and mental health, but also it adversely affects their learning capacities. This impairment, in turn, has undesirable and long-term consequences for them: It prevents them from reaching their full intellectual potential and thus ruins their future career prospects. No society, and especially not a developing one, can afford to see its youth, its most precious asset, wasted in this way.

## THE RESPONSE OF THE LAW TO ORGANIZED CRIME

There is, then, a need to protect the individual, particularly the young and unwary, and the public at large from the effects of drug addiction. The criminal law should be used to accomplish this goal because after all criminal law is designed to protect society from harmful conduct or from tendencies that weaken or imperil its very existence, as well as to educate society as to that harm or tendencies and the need to eliminate or minimize it. Criminal law has been used in Southern Africa to combat the narcotic drug menace using a four-pronged approach:

• Prohibiting the unauthorized possession and use of habit-forming drugs.

• Providing for the compulsory treatment of the addicts.

• Controlling dealing in drugs by outlawing their unauthorized production, sale, import, and export.

• Rendering illicit dealing unprofitable by depriving the dealers of the fruit of their dealing by forfeiture and confiscation orders.

### Prohibition

Prohibiting the possession or use of narcotic drugs has been justified on three major grounds. First, it represents society's most formal stamp of disapproval of substance use, especially synthetic drugs which it considers to be new agents that threaten accepted values and norms. According to Western European norms, which influence the drug policies in Southern Africa, "chemical happiness is something to be avoided at all price, unless obtained by the drug that has been used in Europe since times immemorial: alcohol" (Fromberg, 1993: 127–136). Use of psychoactive substances other than those already approved by society is considered an alien practice that must be resisted by, among other means, the law. Second, prohibition reduces the availability of harmful drugs by making them inconvenient, expensive, and risky to obtain. This strategy can be used to discourage people from experimenting with the drugs. Those who are already using them on an experimental basis will be discouraged from advancing to habitual users, and those who are habitual users may hopefully also be motivated to voluntarily reduce their levels of use or seek treatment (Moore, 1979). Third, prohibition, with the accompanying punishment, serves as an educational tool for violators and others, showing the harm that abuse of narcotic drugs engenders.

For all these reasons, the Drugs and Related Substances Act of Botswana prohibits the unauthorized possession or use of "any habit-forming drug or any plant from which an habit-forming drug can be manufactured." It empowers the minister to declare any drug, plant, preparation, or substance or mixture of substances to be a habit-forming drug. The Act defines possession as "including keeping, storing or having in custody or under control or supervision of the said substances." Merely having in one's custody or control does not per se amount to an offense. To constitute an offense, such custody or control must be accompanied by an *animus possessendi*, knowledge—actual or constructive—of custody or that the thing in custody is a forbidden substance.

For possession or use of habit-forming drugs, including cannabis, the Act prescribes a minimum sentence of imprisonment for a term of not less than one but not more than five years, *and* a fine of not less than P1,500 but not exceeding P5,000, or in default of payment imprisonment for a further term of not less than one year or more than five years. However, where the drug in question is cannabis and the amount involved is less than 60 grams, the punishment is only a fine of P1,000 and imprisonment for three years. The imprisonment is discretionary and not mandatory (Interpretation Acts, 38(2)). The law's lenient stance on cannabis is based on historical factors and social realities. This drug was traditionally and widely grown and used in Botswana. Its use is therefore culturally sanctioned. To punish severely a practice that is socially acceptable would appear unduly harsh. It must nevertheless be pointed out that the apparently lenient sentence attendant to the use of cannabis is not that lenient to the offenders. Many of them are usually unemployed young adults who cannot afford to pay the fines. They therefore often end up in prison. A judicial officer told this writer that since there are as yet no treatment or rehabilitation facilities in Botswana to which drug abusers can be sent, a term in prison for say two years helps those abusers to reduce the demand for drugs. There is, however, no empirical evidence to show that this is true. What is certain is that imprisonment has a harmful effect on them and tends to turn them into hardened criminals.

Some writers have criticized prohibition as criminogenic and as ineffective in combating drug abuse (Helmer, 1977: 405–418; Conrad, 1993). It has a multiplier effect. It creates scarcity of the drugs; scarcity in turn results in making the drugs too costly for the ordinary abuser; this may, in turn, lead the abuser to commit acquisitive crimes in order to procure the costly drugs to satisfy his or her addiction. These arguments cannot be easily gainsaid. Moreover, prohibition cannot altogether eliminate drug abuse. The U.S. failure to prohibit the use of liquor supports this assertion. To be efficacious, therefore, prohibition must be accomplished by vigorous public education campaigns against drug abuse, together with measures that aim at addressing those societal conditions, such as unemployment and stress, which lead to the abuse.

## Treatment and Rehabilitation

Treatment and rehabilitation should be available sentencing options to a court dealing with a convict who appears to be an abuser. Centers to which such convicts could be compulsorily committed for treatment and rehabilitation need to be established in all countries of the region. Through total abstinence and treatment of withdrawal symptoms as well as counseling, treatment and rehabilitation will help reduce the addict's demand for drugs. Gradual withdrawal or substitution of the hard drugs, as practiced in developed countries, is impracticable in the African context. As Asuni (1992: 179) argued: "It is inconceivable for a poor African country to provide drug addicts with their drugs or drug-substitute, when they have not been able to provide free milk to young school children, or free prophylactic anti-malarial drugs for children. It is understandable that the object of the treatment of drug abusers is total abstinence."

Be that as it may, treatment and rehabilitation is an essential component in the strategy for fighting drug-related crime. Their usefulness in this respect is borne out by the studies elsewhere, demonstrating their effectiveness in reducing levels of addiction and, consequently, criminality on the part of the addict (Nurco et al., 1985). It is unfortunate that in the Southern African region only South Africa has treatment and rehabilitation facilities. Elsewhere abusers are often sent to psychiatric hospitals for treatment. Unless it is the court that has committed them to a psychiatric hospital for treatment, however, abusers will be loath to go there voluntarily. In the meantime, their condition may deteriorate, to the prejudice of their families and the community at large.

## Dealing in Drugs

Dealing in narcotic drugs must be forbidden as a means of making the drugs unavailable to the abusers. The Drugs and Related Substances Act of Botswana may again be used as an example in this respect. The Act makes it an offense for anybody to deal in habit-forming drugs. It defines "deal in" as including "any act in connection with collection, importation, supply, transshipment, administration, exportation, cultivation, manufacture, transmission or prescription" of any habit-forming drug or any plant from which such a drug can be manufactured. The punishment for dealing in the drugs, other than cannabis, is imprisonment without the option of a fine and without the suspension of any part of it, for a term of not less than 10 or more than 15 years, *and* a fine of not less than P15,000 or in default of payment an additional term of imprisonment of not less than three or more than five years. The punishment for dealing in cannabis is imprisonment without the option of a fine and without suspension of any part of it for a term of not less than five years or more than ten years. The offender must also pay a fine of not less than P7,000, or in default of payment an additional term of imprisonment of not less than one or more than two years. Dealing in drugs is punished more severely than mere possession or use because it is committed for gainful purposes. Only by dealing with it in this way can dealers be deterred from it. The reasons for the relatively low sentences for dealing in cannabis are the same as for possession and use.

### Depriving Dealers of Profits of the Business

Dealing in drugs is big business, usually involving huge sums of money. Dealers often use part of the money to buy their way out of the criminal justice process by bribing and corrupting law enforcement agents, court personnel, and other government officials. Dealers are hard to catch. This explains why even countries with the best intelligence services and the best equipped and most efficient police services are still bedeviled by the drug pandemic, with no end in sight in the nearby future. Dealers are apparently above the law or beyond the reach of the law. However, one way of discouraging them from the business is to take money, the oxygen of crime, out of it, thereby rendering it unprofitable. This goal can be accomplished by creating the offenses of "unexplained lifestyle" and "money laundering." Botswana's legislation will once again be used to elaborate these techniques.

Regarding the unexplained lifestyle, the Corruption and Economic Crime Act of 1994 empowers the Directorate on Corruption and Economic Crime to investigate any *person* whom they have reasonable grounds to suspect (1) is maintaining a standard of living above that which is commensurate with his current or past known sources of income or assets; or (2) is in control or possession of pecuniary resources or property disproportionate to his present or past known sources of income or assets (Section 34). That person's failure to furnish the Directorate with a satisfactory explanation of how he was able to maintain such a standard of living or how he came by such pecuniary resources or property renders him guilty of the offense of corruption.

Not only may he be punished for the offense, but he may also have the suspect's assets forfeited to the state. *Ex facie*, this provision is draconian: By casting the burden of proof on the suspect, it does violence to the basic principle of the law that he who alleges must prove; it interferes with the individual's constitutional right to property which may be forfeited or confiscated without any proof by his accusers that it is property acquired as a result of a crime of which he has been convicted. It also infringes on his right to his secrets and business confidences by forcing him to disclose them or risk loss of his liberty or property without any proof of any wrongdoing on his part. The provision may, however, be justified because of the need to fight organized crime. The culprits are usually powerful individuals who easily bribe or intimidate witnesses to silence and destroy all incriminating evidence against them. On top of this they live ostentatious and lavish lifestyles disproportionate to their known sources of income, while the general population around them wallows in abject poverty. If such lifestyles are supported by honestly acquired means, let them prove it. After all, the standard of proof by which they discharge this burden is not high. It is only on a balance of probabilities and is not beyond reasonable doubt. Nevertheless, because of its harshness and doubtful constitutional rectitude, excising the penal sanctions from it, leaving only the confiscation orders, could tone down the provision. However, to ensure that such orders are effective and enforceable even beyond the country's borders, there is need for cooperation with as many countries as possible. This cooperation can be secured by the states concerned concluding treaties on mutual assistance in criminal matters.

Concerning money laundering, the Proceeds of Serious Crime Act, 1990 provides that

a person shall be deemed to engage in money laundering if he engages, directly or indirectly, in a transaction that involves money, or other property, that is the proceeds of a serious offence, whether committed in Botswana or elsewhere, or if he receives, possesses, conceals, disposes of, or brings into Botswana, any money, or other property that is the proceeds of a serious offence, whether committed in Botswana or elsewhere, and the person knows or, or ought reasonably to know, that such money or other property is derived or realised, directly or indirectly, from some sort of unlawful activity. (Section 14)

It would thus be an offense to sell a house or any other property to a person convicted of "a serious offense" (an offense punishable by death or by imprisonment for not less than two years) and receiving payment in the form of tainted money. It would also be an offense to receive fees from tainted sources for professional services rendered. It would likewise be an offense for a bank to accept deposits of tainted money, to refine it, to accept it for custody in its safe, or to facilitate its transfer to foreign bank accounts. A person convicted of money laundering is liable to a prison term. The assets, which were the subject of the charge, may also be forfeited to the state.

Four points are worth noting here.

1. For the offense of money laundering to be proved, the money or property in question must be shown to be proceeds of a "serious offense."
2. Someone, not necessarily the accused, must have been convicted of that crime. For obvious reasons such a conviction may prove impossible in the case of powerful drug traffickers or arms dealers.

3. In most money laundering schemes there would be no identifiable victim. Consequently, there would be no report or complaint to the police. As a result, money laundering would be difficult to detect (Chaikin, 1991: 467–510). One way that might facilitate detection is through cooperation of financial institutions by way of reporting suspicious transactions to the police. However, such reporting would violate customer-bank confidentiality, which the banking industry holds sacrosanct. It might expose the financial institutions to both civil and criminal liability, particularly when their suspicions turn out to be unfounded and the transactions innocuous.

4. Criminals may render confiscation/forfeiture orders ineffectual by transferring the proceeds subject to such orders to other countries. Those countries may prove to be havens for the criminals if they do not have legislation criminalizing money laundering and/or establishing a machinery for assisting other countries by enforcing their forfeiture orders and by immobilizing the criminals' assets (Snider, 1995: 377–389).

At the time of this writing, South Africa did not have such legislation on its books. Consequently, the police in that country regretted the absence of the legislation, stating that "South Africa lags behind other countries in this regard and has . . . become a haven for money laundering activities" (South African Police Service, 1995).

## CONCLUSION

One significant aspect of social change in Southern Africa has been rural-urban migration. The attainment of independence or majority rule, the transfer of power to Africans, the abolition of apartheid and travel restrictions in South Africa, as well as changes in the mode of production have resulted in people shifting from rural to urban areas. Modern education has also contributed to rural-urban migration. It has awakened the African youth to the inadequacy, drudgery, and monotony of rural life and the rural economy—mostly farming or cattle rearing—and has created in them expectations of the good life in the electrified towns with cinema halls, discos, and recreational facilities. So, they flock to the urban centers. Unfortunately, many of them are dropouts from the region's pyramidal education systems and lack the skills needed for lawful and dignified economic survival in the towns—hence, the phenomena of homelessness, slum dwelling, and criminal gangs.

Rural life with closely knit communities and long-cherished social values and behavior control mechanisms is rapidly being replaced by impersonal living in uncaring and alienating conglomerations of strangers in towns. The traditional family, headed and maintained by a father able to instill discipline in the children, has disappeared and has been replaced by the family headed by struggling mothers or destitute grandmothers. A number of children who grow up under such conditions end up on the streets of the towns.

Frustration arising from unemployment, lack of opportunities for further education, and sheer alienation has led many people, particularly the young, to resort to drunkenness, drug abuse and dealing as couriers, and ultimately to crime.

To prevent these undesirable effects of social change, planners overseeing national development need to factor the crime phenomenon into their development strategies. To stem the tide of unplanned rural-urban migration and the ills that accompany it, planners must devise ways and means of making rural life attractive and rewarding. Education planners must always remember that for the time being the majority of the youth will not go on to tertiary institutions; they must therefore be prepared for an independent productive existence, preferably in their rural communities. Whatever remains of the traditional family must be preserved and strengthened because the family remains the best social agent for behavior control.

Organized crime, particularly illicit drug trafficking, respects no borders; it is truly transnational. Illicit drugs, weapons, and motor vehicles are smuggled across borders without hindrance. Criminals, sometimes with forged or no travel documents, bring their contraband across the borders with relative ease. Organized crime is a menace to all countries. To combat it effectively all countries, starting with those that have common borders, must cooperate with each other. They must suppress the production and export to other countries of narcotic drugs. By means of incentives and education, they must encourage rural people who grow cannabis for sheer economic survival to grow other types of cash crops suitable for the climate. They must share information and intelligence on the movement of known or suspected criminals. They must also enter into mutual assistance arrangements under which they can assist each other in detecting, investigating, and prosecuting crime, freezing, or confiscating proceeds of crime regardless of their country of origin, and surrendering suspected criminals for prosecution and punishment. They must harmonize their laws so that the criminals can use none of their territories as a safe haven. Those with common borders must put in place machinery for monitoring the movement of persons and goods to prevent illegal immigration and the illicit movement of contraband, particularly narcotic drugs, motor vehicles, precious stones, and endangered species.

The Southern African Regional Police Chiefs Co-operation Committee (SARPCCO) was set up to facilitate police cooperation in these areas and has borne fruit. A sizable amount and variety of contraband (particularly motor vehicles and weapons) has been intercepted at border crossings. Efforts to concretize this cooperation in the form of a binding treaty, the

Draft Protocol on the Movement of Persons and Goods in the Southern African Development Community, has, to date, not materialized. Countries with relatively thriving economies such as Botswana and South Africa have expressed misgivings about the treaty (Matsila, 1996). Already burdened with thousands of illegal immigrants, these countries fear that free migration within the region will result in an uncontrollable influx of nationals of their poorer neighbors into their territories. They fear that these foreign nationals would threaten their already shrinking job market. They have also expressed fears that the foreign nationals will also bring with them new techniques of crime, as well as make the control of epidemic diseases difficult. Because of these fears, the treaty remains shelved. In the meantime, it is urged that tireless efforts be expended to address the imbalances in the levels of development in the various countries of the region. This will serve to check the osmotic conditions that result in the one-way movement of persons that Botswana and South Africa are complaining about.

With regard to drug abuse, prohibition alone is not enough. Measures aimed at reducing the demand for narcotic drugs must be stepped up. Treatment and rehabilitation facilities must be set up in all the countries of the region. School and college campuses must not be allowed to turn into bazaars for peddling drugs but must be used more and more as demand-reduction education centers. Religious institutions as well as youth organizations also have an important role to play, especially in countering misdirected peer pressures. The states within the region and beyond should cooperate among themselves so as to cut off the free and easy flow of narcotic drugs. In this regard, the Southern African States conclusion in 1996 of the Protocol on Illicit Drug Trafficking in the Southern African Community marked a significant milestone in the regional struggle against organized crime. When in force, it will facilitate cooperation among the parties by providing them with the necessary legal framework that has hitherto been lacking.

## REFERENCES

Abucar, M.H. (1995). *Family or Families, Inequality and Social Change in Botswana: A National Study*. Unpublished paper presented at the 18th SAUSSC Annual Meeting, University of Swaziland.

Adeyemi, A.A. (1992). "Corruption in Africa: A Case Study of Nigeria." In T.M. Mushanga (ed.), *Criminology in Africa* (pp. 83–103). Rome: United Nations Interregional Crime and Justice Research Institute.

Asuni, T. (1992). "Drug Trafficking and Drug Abuse in Africa." In T.M. Mushanga (ed.), *Criminology in Africa* (pp. 179–190). Rome: United Nations Interregional Crime and Justice Research Institute.

*Botswana Police Report*. (1995). Gaborone: Department of Printing and Publishing Services.

Central Statistics Office (CSO). (1991a). *Population and Housing Census.* Gaborone: Department of Printing and Publishing Services.

———. (1991b). *Statistical Bulletin.* Gaborone: Department of Printing and Publishing Services.

———. (1996). *Education Statistics.* Gaborone: Department of Printing and Publishing Services.

Chaikin, D.A. (1991). "Money Laundering: An Investigatory Perspective." *Criminal Law Forum* 2: 467–510.

Clarke, M. (1983). *Corruption: Causes, Consequences, and Control.* London: Frances Printer Publishers Ltd.

Coldham, S. (1995). "Legal Responses to State Corruption in Commonwealth Africa." *Journal of African Law* 39(2): 115–126.

Conrad, C. (1993). *Hemp: Lifeline to the Future.* Los Angeles: Creative Expressions Publications.

Directorate on Corruption and Economic Crime. Annual reports. Gaborone: Department of Printing and Publishing Services.

Dorn, N. and South, N. (1990). "Drug Markets and Law Enforcement." *British Journal of Criminology* 30: 171–188.

Ellis, S. (1994). "Of Elephants and Men: Politics and Nature Conservation in South Africa." *Journal of Southern African Studies* 20: 53–69.

Fako, T. (1983). "The Family and National Development in Botswana: A Plea for Research." *Botswana Notes and Records* 15: 9–14.

Fijnaut, C. (1990). "Organized Crime: A Comparison between the United States of America and Western Europe." *British Journal of Criminology* 30: 321–340.

Fromberg, E. (1993). "Prohibition as a Necessary Stage in the Acculturation of Foreign Drugs." In N. Heather, A. Wodak, E.A. Nadelmann, and P. O'hare (eds.), *Psychoactive Drugs and Harm Reduction: From Faith to Science.* London: Whurr Publishers.

Good, K. (1994). "Corruption and Mismanagement in Botswana: A Best-Case Example?" *Journal of Modern African Studies* 32: 499–521.

Greenberg, S.W. and Adler, F. (1974). "Crime and Addiction: An Empirical Analysis of the Literature, 1920–1973." *Contemporary Drug Problem* 31: 221–270.

Harsch, E. (1993). "Accumulators and Democrats: Challenging State Corruption in Africa." *Journal of Modern African Studies* 31: 31–48.

Helmer, J. (1977). "The Connection Between Narcotics and Crime." *Journal of Drug Issues* 7: 405–418.

International Criminal Police Organization (INTERPOL). (1994). *Evolution of the Illicit Methaqualone Traffic Phenomenon.* A paper prepared for the Second Interregional Meeting on the Illicit Traffic in Methaqualone between the Indian Sub-Continent and the Eastern/Southern Region of Africa, Sun City, South Africa, August 22–24.

Jarvis, G. and Parker, H. (1989). "Young Heroin Users and Crime: How Do the 'New Users' Finance Their Habit?" *British Journal of Criminology* 29: 175–185.

Leroy, B. (1992). "The European Community of Twelve and Drug Demand: Excerpt of a Comparative Study of Legislation and Judicial Practice." *Drug and Alcohol Dependence* 29: 269–281.

Macdonald, D. (1995). *Corruption and Economic Crime as Barriers to Reconstruction and Development in Southern Africa.* Paper presented at the 18th Southern African Universities Social Science Conference (SAUSSC), University of Swaziland, December 4–7.

———. (1996). "Drugs in Southern Africa: An Overview." *Drugs: Education and Policy* 3: 127–144.

Marina, R. Jordan, J. and Kormie, K. (1995). "Conversations with Street Children in Harare." *Zambezi* 22: 1–24.

Matebele, M. (1995). "The Plight of Street Children." *The Botswana Guardian,* July 28, p. 15.

Matsila, H. (1996). "Government Urged not to Sign Treaty." *Daily News,* August 16, p. 1.

Mazonde, I.N. (1995). *Old Naledi and Poverty in the City.* Gaborone: National Institute of Development Research and Documentation.

McBride, D.C. and McCoy, C.B. (1982). "Crime and Drugs: The Issues and Literature." *Journal of Drug Issues* 12: 137–152.

Moore, M.H. (1979). "Limiting Supplies of Drugs to Illicit Markets." *Journal of Drug Issues* 22: 291–308.

Nilsson, H.G. (1991). "The Council of Europe Laundering Convention: A Recent Example of a Developing International Criminal Law." *Criminal Law Forum* 2: 419–441.

Nurco, D.N., Ball, J.C., Shaffer, J.W. and Hanlon, T.E. (1985). "The Criminality of Narcotic Addicts." *Journal of Nervous and Mental Disease* 173(2): 94–102.

Otero-Lopez, J., Luengo-Martin, A., Miron-Redondo, R., Carrillo-De-La-Pena, M.T., and Romero-Trinanes, E. (1994). "An Empirical Study of the Relationship between Drug Abuse and Delinquency among Adolescents." *British Journal of Criminology* 34: 459–478.

Otlhogile, B. (1991). "Drugs Control and the Law in Botswana." *Comparative and International Law Journal of Southern Africa* 24: 248.

Quansah, E.K. (1994). "The Corruption and Economic Crime Act, 1994 of Botswana." *Journal of African Law* 38(2): 191–196.

Silverman, I.J. (1982). "Women, Crime and Drugs." *Journal of Drug Issues* 12: 167–183.

Snider, W.J. (1995)."International Cooperation in the Forfeiture of Illegal Drug Proceeds." *Criminal Law Forum* 6: 377–389.

South African Police Service. (1995). *Illicit Cross-Border Drug Trafficking as a National and International Threat.* A paper presented by Major General C.J.D. Venter at the Joint Southern African Development Community (SADC)/ European Union (EU) Regional Conference, Mmabatho, North West Province, South Africa, October 30–November 2.

Tesfaye, A. "Rural-Urban Migration and Problems of Crime and Delinquency." In T.M. Mushanga (ed.), *Criminology in Africa* (pp. 179–190). Rome: United Nations Interregional Crime and Justice Research Institute.

United Nations. (1995). *1993 Demographic Yearbook.* New York: United Nations.

Wilson, R.J. (1991). "Human Rights and Money Laundering: The Prospect of International Seizure of Defense Attorney Fees." *Criminal Law Forum* 3: 85–103.

# Index

# About the Editor and Contributors

DAUDA ABUBAKAR, a Nigerian, is Senior Lecturer and Head, Department of Political Science and Administration, at the University of Maiduguri. Dr. Abubakar has been teaching political science since the early 1980s at both the undergraduate and graduate levels. He has published many articles in scholarly journals and contributed chapters to books, including those edited by Africanist scholars in the social sciences.

ANTHONIA ADINDU, a Nigerian, is Senior Lecturer in Health Planning and Management at the University of Maiduguri, where she has served as Coordinator of Departmental Programs. Dr. Adindu also works for Pathfinder International, Nigeria, where she is responsible for reproductive health and community development. She has published several articles in such areas as health systems administration, health systems development, and primary health care management.

OLUDELE A. AKINBOADE is Senior Lecturer in Economics at the University of South Africa, Pretoria. Previously Dr. Akinboade taught economics at Oxford University and at the University of Botswana. His international experience includes work with the United Nations Development Program (Gambia) and the Commonwealth Agricultural Bureau, Oxford, United Kingdom. He has also undertaken consultancies for the UNDO (Nairobi) and the PTA/COMESA (Nairobi). He has published numerous articles in such journals as the *Canadian Journal of Development Studies*, *Oxford Agrarian Studies*, *African Development Review*, *Agrekon*, *African Review of Money*, and *Development Southern Africa* on economic development issues relating to agriculture, labor, and poverty alleviation.

EMMANUEL U.M. IGBO, a citizen of Nigeria, is Senior Lecturer in the Department of Sociology and Anthropology at the University of Nigeria, Nsukka. His teaching and research interests lie in the areas of criminology, sociology of development, and social change and social problems. Dr. Igbo's published work includes book chapters and many articles in a wide range of local and international journals.

KYAMA K. KABADAKI, born in Uganda, is Assistant Professor in Social Work at Ball State University. Dr. Kabadaki was formerly a lecturer at Makerere University, Kampala. Her research interests include social development, women in development, international social work, and child welfare services. She has written and practiced extensively in these areas.

EUPHRASE KEZILAHABI, a Tanzanian, is Associate Professor of African Literature at the University of Botswana, where he has taught since 1995. For 24 years Professor Kezilahabi taught at the University of Dar-es-Salaam, and he was Head of the Department of Kiswahili from 1987 to 1991. He is a well-known writer who has published six novels, two books of poetry, four short stories, and one play. In 1990 he received the Edoardo Sanguineti Memoria Prize in Italy for his poetry, and in 1994 he was awarded the Shaaban Robert Memorial Prize for his contribution to Swahili literature. He currently teaches creative writing, African literature, and studies in African thought.

DAVID MACDONALD, a citizen of Scotland, is a Senior Lecturer and Head of the Department of Sociology at the University of Botswana. Prior to this appointment he was co-director of the Scottish National Drug Training Project, located in the Department of Sociology and Social Policy at the University of Stirling. He has also taught courses in social problems for universities in Italy, Korea, Japan, and the United Kingdom and has published work on AIDS, drug problems, economic crime and corruption, and stress management. In 1991, with V. Patterson, he co-authored the book *Drug Training: Learning about Drugs and Working with Drug Users*, and he has contributed articles to such journals as *Social Science and Medicine*, *Journal of Comprehensive Health*, and *Drugs: Education, Prevention and Policy*. He is the Southern African regional editor for the journal *Drugs: Education, Prevention and Policy* and is engaged in action research on alcohol misuse among Bushmen/San communities in the Kalahari.

RODRECK MUPEDZISWA, a Zimbabwean, is Professor and Deputy Principal of the School of Social Work, an Associate College of the University of Zimbabwe, where for more than two decades he has taught in undergraduate and graduate programs. Dr. Mupedziswa's research focuses on vulnerable and disadvantaged groups, including refugees. He has authored a number of books and many professional articles. He has served as an executive member of the International Association of Schools of Social Work (IASSW), the International Research and Advisory Panel (IRAP) based at the University of Oxford, and the Southern Africa Universities Social Sciences Conference (SAUSSC).

TIBAMANYA MWENE MUSHANGA is a distinguished Ugandan criminologist and diplomat. Since the mid-1980s Dr. Mushanga has served as Uganda's ambassador to Southern Africa, Canada, and Germany, respectively. Prior to entering the diplomatic service, he taught sociology, criminology, and psychology at Makerere University and the University of Nairobi. He is an internationally recognized expert in criminology. He is the author of several books, including *Criminology in Africa*, *Deviance and Crime*, and *Criminal Homicide in Uganda*. His articles have appeared in various international journals. He has served as a consultant to many organizations, especially the United Nations, on crime prevention and treatment of offenders.

DANIEL D. NTANDA NSEREKO is Professor and former chair of the Department of Law at the University of Botswana. Professor Nsereko has taught at Makerere University in Uganda, where he also practiced law. His teaching interests have spanned public international law, criminal procedure and evidence, and constitutional law and human rights. He has served as the Walter S. Owen Visiting Professor of Law at the University of British Columbia, Canada, and Senior Associate of the International Centre for Criminal Law Reform and Criminal Justice Policy, an affiliate of the United Nations Crime Prevention and Criminal Justice Program. He has been visiting scholar at the Max Planck Institute for Foreign and International Criminal Law in Germany and consultant to several United Nations Congresses on the Prevention of Crime and Treatment of Offenders. He has published extensively in the areas of international law, criminal justice, and human rights. He serves on the editorial boards of several reputable international journals, such as the *Journal of Church and State* and *Criminal Law Forum*.

FELIX E. ONAH, a Nigerian, is Senior Lecturer in Economics at the University of Nigeria, Nsukka, where he teaches undergraduate and graduate students. Dr. Onah's teaching and research interests lie, *inter alia*, within the fields of international economics and micro- and macroeconomic theories. He has published widely in these areas, and he has won prizes for his outstanding academic performance from his alma mater.

NORMA ROMM, a South African citizen, is currently a Senior Researcher in Systems Studies at the University of Hull, United Kingdom. From 1991 to 1993 Dr. Romm was Associate Professor of Sociology and also Dean of the Faculty of Social Sciences at the University of Swaziland. Previously she was Associate Professor of Sociology at the University of South Africa. Her main research interests revolve around the meaning and relevance of research in society and what is involved in developing accountability in social research. She has published several books, including the *Methodologies of Positivism and Marxism* (1991) and *Critical Systems Thinking* (with R.L. Flood, 1996). She has also published more than 50 journal articles and chapters in books on a wide range of topics.

APOLLO RWOMIRE is Associate Professor of Social Work at the University of Botswana, where he has taught social work and psychology since 1993. Prior to his current appointment, Professor Rwomire, a regionally known educator, taught sociology at several other universities including the University of Nairobi, Kenya, the University of Jos, Nigeria, and the University of Swaziland. His research and publications encompass social policy, social science methodology, education and development, and social problems such as poverty, labor stratification, unplanned parenthood, domestic violence, and crime. He is the author or co-author of many books, book chapters, and articles in leading journals. He has served as a consultant to FAO and UNICEF.